GW00694607

Derek Ezra: Leadership in Energy

A Collective Memoir on the Life and Work
of Lord Ezra

Chairman of the National Coal Board:

1971-1982

Published by the Worshipful Company of Fuellers

on the occasion of the 10th Anniversary
of the first Fuellers' Energy Lecture,

Drapers' Hall, London, September 11th 2014

Editor: Roderick Braithwaite FRHistS

LIST OF SUBSCRIBERS

George Alberts
Colin Ambler
Chloë Andrews-Jones
Geoff Ashmore
Prof William Ashworth
Richard Austin A.O.
Jane Ayre

Andrew Bainbridge
John Bainbridge
Jean Claude Banon
James Aloysius Bellew,
(Proprietor, Athenaeum, Liverpool)
Norman Biddle
John A.Boddy
Jean Bonnefont
Michael Borkett
Clare Braithwaite
Isobel Braithwaite
Nick Braithwaite
Phoebe Braithwaite
Colin Brinkman
Mrs A.J.Bryer Ash
Michael Bryer Ash
Dr Michael Bryer Ash
Richard Bryer Ash
Mrs Rosemary Bryer Ash
Tim Burton
Nigel P.Byrne

Ernest Cantle
Sarah Pauline Carr
Rod Castle
John Clarke
The Coal Authority
Jill Clements
Ralph Cohen
F.Colley
John D.Cowcill
Martin Cruttenden
Paul Cutill OBE

Lord Davies
John Demont
Alan Dowdell
Diane Dowdell
Hal Dunstan

Malcolm Edwards CBE
Energy Institute

Viscount Falkland
Bernard Forterre

Dr Paul Glover
T.P. Glover
A.H. Goodman
David Green

Haberdashers' Company
John Hallam
Lady Harris
Brian, Janet & Peter Harrison
Brian Heap
Andrew Horsler

James Hoskins
House of Lords Library
Mrs Pat Howard
Mrs Margaret Hunter

Peter Jones
John Jordan
T.J. Josling
Dr Bill Kee
Simon Kermode

Keith Leigh
Liberal Democrat Library
Tim Lines
Elizabeth Lockley
LSE Library

Prof Averil Macdonald
Magdalene College, Cambridge
Monmouth School Library

National Mining Museum Scotland

Michael Parker
Dr Mark Pegg
Christopher Pennell
Bob Perrin
Debbie Phipps (née Horne)
David & Lynn Port
Ron Price
Lord Prior

Ronald Reay
Reform Club Library
Repton School Library
Rex Rose
Bernard St. André
Mrs Lisa Salisbury
Tony Shillingford
Lord Shutt
Snibston Discovery Museum, Coalville
John Spence
Peter M. Stafford
Lord Steel
Edmund J. Stephenson Clarke
Richard L. Stephenson Clarke
Thérèse Stephenson Clarke

Lady Thomas
Kathy & Christopher Turrall

University of Southampton Business School

Bertram Eric Walley
Allan Watson
Edward Wilkinson CBE
Edgar Wille OBE
Lady Williams
Vaughan Williams
D.R. Wilson OBE
Kelly Wilson
Kevin Wilson
Dennis & Suzan Woods

Georg Yeomans
Gerry Yockney

Derek Ezra: Leadership in Energy
A Collective Memoir
on the Life and Work of Lord Ezra

Chairman of the National Coal Board: 1971-1982

The Rt. Hon. Lord Ezra, of Horsham

MBE (Military: 1945) Hon Ll.D. (Leeds: 1982)
D.Sc. (Cranfield: 1979) MA (Cantab.: 1939)

Grand Officer, Order of Merit
of the Italian Republic (1979)

Officer of the Légion d'Honneur (1981)

Commander of the Order of Merit
of Luxembourg (1981)

Fig.1: Derek Ezra: appointment as Chairman, National Coal Board, 1971.
Portrait by Baron, of Knightsbridge

THE FUELLERS' ENERGY LECTURES 2005-2014

2005 The Lord Ezra, of Horsham

2006 John Harris CBE DL
(former Chairman, The Coal Authority)

2007 Sir Bernard Ingham

2008 The Lord Browne of Madingley
(former Chief Executive BP plc)

2009 Fuellers' Past Master Richard Budge

2010 Charles Hendry MP
(former Energy Minister)

2011 John Cridland, CBE
(Director General, Confederation of British Industry)

2012 David Mackay FRS
(Chief Scientific Adviser, The Department of Energy
and Climate Change)

2013 Bob Dudley, Group Chief Executive, BP plc

2014 David Gray, Chairman, OFGEM

Acknowledgements
Firstly to Derek Ezra himself, for the example, courage and vision which have been the mainspring for this Memoir; also to all those identified in the Contributors section (p107) who have offered their witness, not least of all to Paul Glover and the Fuellers' Working Party. The Editor's abiding thanks go also to computer trainer Katrina Wheatley, to Christopher and Kathy Turrall at Ravenscourt Design, and to Clare Braithwaite for her copy-editing inputs.

2014
Published by the Worshipful Company of Fuellers, London
Designed and typeset by Ravenscourt Design Partnership, Farnham, Surrey
Printed and bound in the UK by Blackmoor Printers
All rights reserved. Copyright, The Worshipful Company of Fuellers, 2014
The right of Roderick Braithwaite to be identified as editor of this work has been asserted
in accordance with Section 77 of the Copyright, Designs and Patents Act 1988.
A CIP record for this book is available from the British Library
The views expressed in this Memoir are those of the Contributors, and should not be attributed
to the Publishers. Every attempt has been made to secure approvals for quotations, but if inadvertently
there have been any omissions, the Editor apologises and asks for forgiveness.

ISBN: 978-0-9929210-0-2

CONTENTS

ILLUSTRATIONS

INTRODUCTION

Evolution of the Project – "the eye of the storm"

The idea of compiling a due tribute to Derek Ezra's life and work had been in many people's minds for some time. His National Coal Board predecessor, Lord Robens, had reviewed his own management philosophy in **Human Engineering** and his years as Chairman in **Ten Year Stint**; one of his successors, Chairman of British Coal (as the NCB became in 1985), had also given his account. Insight into Derek's business thinking was in fact already there, for those who chose to look, in **Advice from the Top: Business Strategies of Britain's Corporate Leaders**, which he edited in 1989.

Although many views had been advanced on nationalisation, and the politically fraught 1970s, the era of the Ezra chairmanship - carried out "in the eye of the storm" (1971-1982) – a long and indeed controversial gap, which the coal industry's formal History could not have covered, still needed to be filled. This included several new 'covert' factors, underlying the more 'overt' issues, above all what have emerged as 'the Thatcher Legacy' and 'the Scargill challenge'.

In 2005, former Fueller John Josling, an advertising consultant to the NCB, who later became the Ezras' close friend, was the first to help Derek record some reminiscences, with this idea in mind. This eventuated as a form of autobiography, to which Derek had given the interesting provisional title, "Below the Surface". (It now forms part of The Fuellers' Archive; although never published, some of its insights have been incorporated in this Memoir: it is included in the Bibliography). Having been John's predecessor as MD of Interlink, the company appointed by the Board in the 1960s to assist its marketing drive, I was able to take up the theme again; this followed my research for **The Fueller's Tale**, the history of The Fuellers' Livery Company. They had been deeply indebted to Derek Ezra in their early years and he had encouraged senior members of the NCB to join the emerging Company, hosting receptions at the House of Lords for potential Fuellers from the expanding field of the energy industries. In 2005, having given a donation to the company, enabling the establishment of an annual Fuellers' Lecture, he was asked to inaugurate the series.

In 2011, a Fueller Past Master, Brig. Edward Wilkinson, offered a sympathetic ear to the concept of an Ezra Memoir. He had had long experience of working with Derek in various roles, including Associated Heat Services Ltd, and as Chairman of the Coal Industry Society. With Michael Bryer Ash, also a Past Master of the Company, an informal working party was formed, to which I and Dr Paul Glover, as another Past Master of The Fuellers, and former Director General of Staff at the Board, were added. There had been some communications between Edward, and Derek's Assistant at the House of Lords, Mrs Jill Clements. As an outcome of this process, on 22 September 2011, Paul Glover was able, with Michael Bryer Ash, to secure Lord Ezra's agreement to their working with myself as the Memoir's Editor. We were also already in touch with Dr Mark Pegg, the joint author with Professor William Ashworth of what may in due course become the penultimate volume of the coal industry's History – the Vol.5 already published in 1986. (Mark is now CE of The Leadership Foundation for Higher Education, and formerly a Director of Ashridge Business School. and he had served under several Coal Board Chairmen). The project was formally blessed and financed by the Coal Meters Committee and by The Fuellers early in 2012; PMs David Port and John Bainbridge joined the group.

A discussion with Derek in September 2011 provided a background, although the Memoir's value to management thinking was yet to emerge. Its gist can, however, be briefly summarised. Derek won a scholarship from his Prep School to Monmouth School, where he debated, authored, played in the 2nd Rugby XV, and took leading thespian roles including Shakespeare's Anthony, and where he is still remembered as a distinguished 'O.M.'. From the outset, he had benefitted from a liberal upbringing. This was enhanced by his State Scholarship, and a Senior Scholarship at Magdalene College, Cambridge; there he once more demonstrated his penchant for mastering an audience – and memorising his lines – by acting in more Shakespeare for "The Mummers", as well as an uncharacteristic early *non*-speaking walk-on part of the butler in the ADC's new play, "Rope"! (His birthday co-incided serendipitously with that of another famous College *alumnus,* Samuel Pepys). He also rowed, spoke at and was a Committee Member of the Union Debating Society, found time to take a double First in History, and also manifested the first signs of his deep Liberalism, evidenced in his espousal of the Liberal "New Radical". This was later to find expression in his membership of the Lords, and of wider liberal activities, such as becoming a Patron of the John Stuart Mill Institute. Although not conscious of it then, he had indeed been linked from early on to Britain's mining culture, as epitomised in the South Wales coalfields: "I got to know a part of the world that I previously didn't know; in that period I went down my first pit, so I saw something of industrial life as a schoolboy".

He would be thereafter unalterably shaped by the events of 1939-45; his generation was conscious that "things needed to be better after the war". He also shared the then popular belief that public enterprise was one way to achieve this end – a concept whose long-term value to the national good some feel has yet to be fully assessed. (Of course, as any balanced account must reveal, many currently rebut that view, as did – ominously for Derek – Margaret Thatcher).

Derek saw how the traditional insular British distinction between 'officers and men' had changed: this was not by reason of any political dogma, but because it seemed in those testing days that the best way, indeed the only apparently lasting way, to get results in any workforce, military or industrial, was to get people to work *together.*

That fundamental conditioning of Derek and men like him turned out to be one of his great strengths. It also later transpired, as will be related in excerpts from various Ministerial diaries of that era, to be an area of some vulnerability in the vastly different ideological climate of the late 1970s-early 1980s. The monetarist school of politicians and economists of that time neither understood – nor had any commitment to – what Derek believed in; the idealistic had been subsumed in the theoretical, and a different world seemed to be dawning. The ironical rediscovery of the value of the State's pragmatic participation in exceptional situations, evident today not only in Europe and again in Britain, but even in the US, came too late for Derek's industrial career, although not too late for his involvement in the nation's debates in the Upper House. A third formative aspect of his earlier experience had been a widening European horizon, gained at school as a fluent French speaker, and at university. His army service had sharpened that view as a result of early assignment to the top secret planning for the invasion of France and the final post-Ardennes breakthrough into Germany: (his brilliant war record is detailed later in this Introduction).

When he was demobbed, he joined the newly formed NCB, initially occupying a scullery in an apartment block in Lansdowne House, Berkeley Square! All his earlier influences seemed to come together in his appointment in 1952 to the UK delegation at the emerging European Coal and Steel Community. It appeared to Derek at the time as a welcome contribution to his focus within the Coal Board. That focus manifested itself in 'the marketing revolution' of the 1950s, moving on from the era of coal 'allocation' and the industry's historical production-orientation. His career thereafter came to exemplify a theme that is today as central a topic for debate on management, as it has become for this Memoir: that of *leadership*. A recent article pinpointed the paradox that although today "Leadership has never been less fashionable" – yet "it is when things fall apart that leadership comes into its own".[1]

The particular Ezra brand of leadership, following on the lead of Lord Robens, illustrated one of the *leitmotivs* in this Memoir. The need for a united workforce and its unions to *combine* with management in the ultimate aim: to sell the Coal Board's – and the nation's – products: all this in 22 increasingly competitive all-energy markets overseas, as well as at home, and having to be carried out under the new threat of 'four-fuel' economic thinking (electricity, gas, nuclear power, and oil – with coal's role diminishing). It was to prove a Herculean task: managing what would turn out to be part of the apparent gradual decline of many of Britain's native industries during the last quarter of the 20th century. Coal would lie on the same beleaguered path. It, too, had to adapt to the differential pressures of external geo-political events and internal, historically-based forces – political, social and industrial. These marked the sad post-war evolution of the UK's one-time greatness as a world power; miners' leader Arthur Scargill was one aspect of those forces. That mammoth challenge was Derek Ezra's destiny.

The Memoir also reveals, for the first time, some unique first-hand evidence about another political phenomenon that has dominated the headlines over the past year and decade – what has been called "The Thatcher Legacy". It will illuminate as well, through the writings of the Permanent Under-Secretary at the Department of Energy, Sir Jack Rampton, how the Ezra years at the helm of the NCB co-incided belatedly with a more interventionist, 'post-Herbert Morrison' approach by Government towards the nationalised industries in general.

These concepts are crucial to the historical record. The distinguished contributors to this Memoir have therefore been encouraged to comment on what can now be discerned, from discussions with him and those who worked with him, as Derek Ezra's instinctive 'philosophy' for the leadership role. This had evolved from his earliest years – very much, in a phrase from that early autobiographical sketch, the 'outsider' joining the newly-nationalised industry; it also derived from the way he developed his strong, very individual management process. He himself suggested in discussion, with some diffidence, that his two main weapons in this task might well have been "an ability to think clearly, and to communicate that thinking". These attributes, combined with what appeared to some as an almost "Morse"-like singlemindedness and determination, emerge prominently in the background chapter on leadership, Chapter 1, and in the central complementary Chapters 2, 3, 4 and 5.

Derek has accepted the opportunity to add his own personal – and typically modest – Postscript to the Memoir, which is included in appropriate conjunction with the Contributors' page, p.107.

This very special collection of recollections is published in the tenth anniversary year of the Fuellers' Energy Lecture – a year which, while witnessing a nostalgic, backward-looking TV documentary on **"When Coal Was King"**, also brought onto the headlines the forward-looking issues of the Energy Gap and a re-focus on fossil fuels, highlighted in the new Californian oil-fields, and the possible development of fracking, and mine subsidies, in the UK.

Roderick Braithwaite

ACROSS THE TECTONIC PLATES

"Coal"? – "The Miners"? – "Nationalisation"? – the 'Hidden Theme'?

Before this Introduction re-focuses on Derek Ezra, it is salutary to briefly recognize the transience of the public's awareness about deeper industrial matters, in contrast to the external events intruding an industry into the national consciousness. Stories of the war-conscripted 'Bevin Boys', or the tip disaster at Aberfan in "Alf" Robens' era, (and consequently one of the lowest ebbs in Derek Ezra's own life) still come all-too easily to mind. This sober reflection may help to clarify this Memoir's purpose.

If today's 'man on the Clapham omnibus' were asked what the words "Coal", or "The Miners", let alone "Nationalisation", conjured up, the response would be fairly vague, if not prejudiced: perhaps on the lines of "who uses it now?" – "noble manual workers in an environmentally unfriendly industry from a bygone age" – "a political system of dyed-in-the-wool Trade Unionism". If the question were limited to the format for that industry in the nation's economy – the National Coal Board – the reaction would probably be even vaguer.

To any further query about figures from the industry's past, no doubt only one would emerge from the headlines: the man whom Andy Beckett dubbed the 'upstart with a loudhailer', militant NUM President of the 1980s, Arthur Scargill. At a popular level, this process might perhaps be aided by theatrical revivals such as Alan Plater's classic **"Close the Coalhouse Door"**, with its understandable nostalgia for the now abandoned North-east coalfields, or by the evocative 'Miners' sketches of sculptor Henry Moore.[2] The names of others who ran the unions a great deal better, such as Joe Gormley, let alone Roy Link, or of those NCB Chairmen who actually managed the entire industry including its workforce, on behalf of the nation, such as Lord Robens, or Lord Ezra himself, would probably tax the memory.

There would also be an understandable ignorance of an historic 'hidden theme': the vital link between the two leaders – of management and Union – who worked out an unprecedented and practical *modus vivendi* for their industry in the 1970s – Derek Ezra, and his almost exact contemporary in the workforce branch of the coal industry tree, Joe Gormley, their careers at the top running practically in parallel from start to finish.

Yet such a limited, populist perspective would demean a key feature of one of the most riven, crucial periods of Britain's post-war economic and political history. For the British electorates of the 1970s, those names and these concepts were in the forefront of their everyday lives,

Fig.2: Sketch, "Pit Boys at Pit-Head", by Henry Moore, OM: one of a series privately commissioned in 1942, at the colliery in his home town of Castleford, Yks; these were in the same genre as the more famous "Shelter Drawings" of people sleeping on the platforms of the London Underground to escape the German night bombers' "Blitz" overhead, of 1941. In the 1970s, Henry Moore, son and grandson of miners, lent a selection of his sketches to the NCB, at Derek Ezra's invitation, for display at the Hobart House HQ, (see Ch.5 and back jacket). [Reproduced by permission of the Henry Moore Foundation; also, courtesy R.Berthoud, **"The Life of Henry Moore"**, Faber & Faber]

demanding headline news billing – divisive, central, dominant. The coal industry had played a pivotal role in Britain's post-war industrial recovery. With the advent of Ted Heath's government of 1970 to 1974, this role had become the touchstone for both political parties, and of the anti-inflationary imperatives of successive regimes, both within the industry and over the whole spectrum of the public sector, its inevitably long capital investment timescale at odds with the short electoral cycle.

The leaders of this essential publicly-owned industry were placed in the unenviable position of reluctant middlemen between government and unions. Chapter 2 outlines the events of the mid -1970s – "the eye of the storm" – whereby a short coalminers' strike and the "three-day week" led to the fall of the Conservative administration. This ushered in a pragmatic inflationary settlement of the NUM wage claim by the incoming minority government of Harold Wilson, himself the former wartime Whitehall architect of coal nationalisation. Although "Seventies' Britain" has been decried by such writers as Andy Beckett as nationally "the worst of times" – the era **When the Lights Went Out** – yet paradoxically it also facilitated a decade of revival for the coal industry under Sir Derek Ezra's then reinvigorated leadership.

This Memoir did not set out to be a comparative study of 'leadership' nor an insight into the concept of public ownership. Yet it has in fact evolved to become the unique story of one man's visionary, and at times controversial, leadership – of one publicly-owned industry, Coal, at an extraordinarily challenging period – to be explored below as the overlap of the two 'tectonic plates' of British post-war political thinking. This metaphor's significance will become clear as the story unfolds.

Although Lord Ezra was better known in this management role, it is in his equally long 'second life', as international industrial advisor and Member of the House of Lords, that his political colleagues rate him just as highly. As Chapter 9 will reveal, it is in the debates in that House, often unnoticed in the country at large, that his true stature as a public figure fully emerges: his energies applied not merely to Energy itself but across the whole spectrum of topical industrial issues.

Yet Derek Ezra is also a quintessential man of his time. That time, which has conditioned him, has seen six-years of world war, followed by a Cold War (he will be seen to have played a part in both), in an insular, impoverished but slowly recovering Britain, beside a re-energized, idealistic Europe. His long working life, as both industrial manager and respected guru on energy policy, mirrors the revolution, technically and conceptually, in the global economy of the last half of the 20th century, and on into this second decade of the 21st.

As this Introduction records, four of his early working years with the NCB, at one time Western Europe's largest employer of manpower, brought involvement with the burgeoning post-war European institutions. These were predicated on the social-democratic focus around the supposed "commanding heights of the economy"- above all, coal, and steel. Responding to the need to manage their initially only-too apparent shortages paved the way for the UK's Labour policy of nationalisation – in Derek's words, "a change of form rather than of substance" - and later to the European Coal and Steel Community. Although this is neither an economic nor a political appraisal, these issues will need to be addressed here.

From the late 1950s onwards, however, attention began to re-engage with the growing predominance of the oil and automotive industries as the 'drivers' of the global economy. At the same time, the West began to recognize that national security decisions had to reckon with rocket-power from the skies rather than steel-based forces on the ground, as the real threat from the East. However until the 1973 oil crisis, most public thinking assumed an energy surplus. That rosy view was not shared by all energy experts and writers, notably including – as this volume will underline – Derek Ezra himself. Although climate change is today's buzz-word, there is still concern with "the Energy Gap", and the vital need to re-think its sourcing. That shortage presupposes a key relationship – and the title of one of Derek Ezra's most future-provocative books – **Coal and Energy** – reproduced in part as Chapter 12.[3]

Within that wider context, Derek Ezra's working life embraces two distinct, and distinctive, phases, with both ups and downs: at one of those downs, "following the fall of the Heath Government, for my efforts – a heart attack and a knighthood".

At 95, he is still as thoughtful and articulate an observer of the public life of the country as ever. His acute intellect has illuminated many House of Lords debates on Energy issues – the strategic topic which continues to underlie future thinking about what his NCB predecessor, Lord Robens, nicely called 'GB Ltd'.

The three opening chapters offer a background to the recollections in subsequent chapters, compiled by contemporaries inside and outside the fuel industry. They reveal a complex, reserved, even, in his own account, "rather introverted" man, with a self-deprecating sense of humour, who has yet been described as "The Man of Energy". Necessarily, they concentrate on the first of his two career phases, his service with Coal from 1948, to his final time as Chairman of that historic industry from 1971 to 1982. 'How' Derek actually did his job, through the eyes of those working closest to him, forms the subject of Chapters 4 and 5. The 'Time-Lines' chronology at the end of this Introduction balances the picture. As it succinctly details, he has spent as long again bringing his wide experience to serve other parts of the public and private sectors of the economy: they are covered in Chapters 9 and 10, followed by extracts from his output of lectures, books, and letters to *The Times*.

Inevitably, new energy vistas have opened up in the intervening years, for example shale exploration and the fracking process, and the possibility of coal subsidies as an insurance against the looming 'Energy Gap'. Nevertheless, the lines of approach to this field were all laid down clearly in the public speeches, writings and actions of Derek Ezra, both while at the NCB, and thereafter in the Lords and in the public prints. As the Memoir's Conclusion will suggest, 'the works of Ezra' remain highly relevant to today's world.

FORMATIVE YEARS: EDUCATION, SECRET ARMY SERVICE, D-DAY, "THE BATTLE OF THE BULGE"

Before this narrative resumes the industrial thread already outlined, and before it reaches too far into Derek's post-war career, there is some value in having a sense of the eight-year experience which preceded that thread of continuity. By contrast, for all those who were drawn into World War Two, that time would appear at first glance like a wholly destructive discontinuity. As recounted in Famous Firsts, a symposium devised by his friend Elizabeth Sieff, and edited by John Mills,[4] he had been grounded in a good classical education (a disciplined quotation-rich paper on 'The Age of Pompey' helped win him his Cambridge degree!). Derek was called up for army service at the outbreak of hostilities, just down from Magdalene, crowned with academic distinction, and indeed vaguely thinking that academe might be a future path. As he said, it is clear that "time I spent there before being swallowed up in the War will never be forgotten, and did much to shape my subsequent life."[5] That time is now briefly described.

TRAINS WITHOUT JANES

Handy Hints on Air-Ground Recognition of
ENEMY TROOP TRAINS

If we can speedily and accurately discover Jerry troop movements, we can not only anticipate important shifts in his order of battle, but attack where it will do most good. Inside Germany you'll see two kinds of trains. First, the ordinary freight train, which accounts for perhaps 80% of all present-day German railroad traffic. Second, standard military trains of which there are four distinct types:—(a) Infantry Troop Train; (b) Mechanized Troop Train; (c) Medium Tank Train; (d) Heavy Tank Train. When you know what to look for, it's as easy to distinguish one type from another as to tell Babe Ruth from Gypsy Rose Lee. Remember . . the more often you're right in reporting enemy troop train movements, the swifter and more decisive will be our own counter moves.

HEAVY TANK TRAINS—Long, extra-wide flat cars are required to move the heavy Mark V Panther tanks, Mark VI Tiger Tanks, and heavy self-propelled artillery. Very orderly in design, the Ps train (Panzerschwerzug) is very short, because of the great weight per car; very few box cars.

RECOGNITION FEATURE—10 Long extra-wide SSY flat cars, with heavy tanks mounted centrally. These are divided into two rakes of 5, on each side of 4 box cars and an AA car. Sometimes these heavy tank flats are spaced out evenly throughout length of train, with other wagons between.

FREIGHT TRAINS

HEAVY TANK TRAINS

INFANTRY TRAINS

ACHTUNG

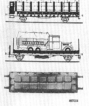

R-CARS (FLAT CARS WITH REMOVABLE SIDE STAVES)
These long flat cars are used for carrying ammunition, artillery, trucks, food and all kinds of supplies. Will carry loads up to 15 tons. Try to notice how many of these cars there are, and whether they're in front or back. In the following pages, you'll see why.

FMM CARS FOR MEDIUM TANKS
About 11% longer than the average box car and 30% longer than the ordinary F flat car for carrying lorries, these FMM cars are used to carry loads up to 25 tons, mostly medium tanks—Mark III's, IV's, or artillery pieces. Generally used only in the medium tank train.

Fig.3: Somewhat cryptically entitled "Trains Without Janes, Handy Hints on Air-Ground Recognition of ENEMY TROOP TRAINS" was a restricted "user-friendly" US Air Force Guide for pilots and navigators, using famous WW2 cartoonist "Giles" as illustrator. It facilitated pin-point bomber attacks on German military trains on the railways in France Belgium and Germany, 1944. The Introduction to this Memoir details how clandestine Intelligence gathered by the G-2 Unit, under Maj Ezra, enabled this prelude and follow-up to the D-Day landings to interdict crucial German reinforcements to Normandy and later fronts. Derek Ezra's experience in military management was to serve as a good platform for his subsequent industrial management career

Partly fulfilling the remit of that book's title, Derek wrote that "the first pay I received was the King's shilling on 15 September 1939, when I joined the Army as a gunner ... I was posted to Larkhill on Salisbury Plain, near Stonehenge ...Thereafter the pay was two shillings a day ... In due course I was promoted to the exalted rank of Acting Unpaid Supernumerary Lance-Bombardier, the longest title I ever had" – and one which neither he nor the Army ever understood! He added: "I had been earmarked for the Royal Artillery on the simple but irrelevant basis that I had read History at Cambridge. Selected as 'officer material', as they called it, my OCTU training at Aldershot was probably the most demanding of my service career". He was commissioned in 1940, and posted to 51st Medium Regiment RA, in Bedford.

Fig.4: First phase of the WW2 army career:2/Lt D.J.Ezra, RA; 1940

With the benefit of 20:20 hindsight, those *discontinuities* take on a more connecting flavour: there was one incident in the young officer's experience at that time which portended things to come – recounted with that lighter touch of his which only a select few have come across. One of the gunners under his command had gone out at night on the town, had had too much to drink, and failing to find a convenient convenience, had relieved his over-full bladder at the side of the street. Apprehended by the law, he was duly brought before the civil magistrates; Derek was asked to represent him in court, but spoke with such vigour on behalf of his man, of whom he thought highly, that the gunner got off with a caution. Back in the Unit this example of loyalty made Derek something of a hero in everyone's eyes: he had looked after his own – and yet another early lesson in good management was being demonstrated.

Derek followed his Commanding Officer on the latter's promotion to Northern Command at York. Some months later, two officers came round asking innocuously who in the Unit spoke French. Despite Derek's bi-lingual skills, the inbuilt army scepticism about volunteering for anything at all weighed somewhat heavily on him but he gave in to curiosity, and found himself drafted down to London, for another of what he called the *'non sequiturs'* which determined the nature of his career. This new job, after the start of SOE in 1941, was to join the top secret British Intelligence team serving COSSAC, at Norfolk House, St James' Square (policy unit for the 1944 invasion, and also the codename for the CiC, General Morgan himself), and, in due course, part of SHAEF. His crucial role was to receive, de-code and analyse the numerous rail movements communicated through clandestine channels from French and Belgian railway officials, and relate these to likely German troop movements into or out of the West, from the Russian front. Rarely, these courageous officials were flown over secretly to London for a personal de-briefing. "I only met two or three of them; they were here for a few hours, then off they went back": (echoes of the heroic work of French railwaymen depicted in the famous Burt Lancaster/ Jeanne Moreau film, *Le Train*). Teamwork, confidentiality, patience, imagination, and meticulous problem-solving were thus called for, qualities that would figure in much of his later career.

As Derek's own research in the War Office now discovered, the German 'straight-line' military mind, unlike the more 'lateral' British mentality, had from the First World War onwards decided that, for four specific transport purposes, optimal, unvarying 'configurations' of wagons were necessary. Thus to transport a Panzer train-load (armoured train), there evolved a fixed '*Panzer-Zug*' configuration, another for an *Infanterie-Zug* (infantry-train); there were also specific Teutonic formulae for a Medium Tank train, and a Heavy Tank train. This information derived from spies at key rail points, noting what rolling-stock was passing and whither. The Allies brought this to a fine art: "if a single empty wagon of a special train configuration was seen going through a French or Belgian frontier station, we could deduce where, and why, that train was going to next". Amazingly, "we managed to anticipate every single German troop movement". Photographic intelligence (PI) could then corroborate the train's movement, guiding bombers to pinpoint the right targets. This formed a fundamental part of the plan to support the Normandy bridgeheads in June 1944. Its effectiveness could be illustrated by the example of a troop train from Belgium having to be diverted via Alsace to Normandy, causing massive delay. At a de-brief, the responsible General from the German High Command expressed admiration for the "wonderful espionage system" which must have led to these results. These results had actually been achieved very simply, under their very noses.

Inspiration in Paris

Lord "Solly" Zuckerman – the scientist, whom Derek experienced as outstanding and full of ideas "somewhat like our [NCB's] own Dr Bronowski" – became Scientific Adviser to the Government. He wrote extensively in his autobiography, **From Apes to Warlords**, about Derek's subsequent part in applying this technique and experience in late 1944, prior to the German counter-offensive in the Ardennes.[6] After D-Day, Derek's Intelligence Unit was moved to Normandy, then to Versailles, where he had access to the

Fig.5: Maj., later Lt.Col.D.J.Ezra, MBE, G-2, SHAEF, with US colleagues in Versailles, France, summer 1944

French Railways plans and maps. There were endless rivalries between the Allied top brass about bombing strategy; whether to go for 'attrition' bombing, or go for specific targets, such as rail centres, bridges, and oil or munitions installations. "Bomber" Harris, for example, resisted the idea of diverting his planes from bombing city centres such as Hamburg or later Dresden, with the aim of demoralising the enemy. What was needed was hard evidence as to which strategy to follow. An inspired discovery by Derek was the key, as "Solly" Zuckerman wrote about the BBSU, the unit set up in 1945 to assess the effects of bombing strategy;[7] 'It was not long after this [1944] that the situation changed dramatically. One morning I received a phone call from Major Derek Ezra. He was then a member of G-2 SHAEF … Ezra had found some German documents, which he thought might interest me. His Unit was quartered in the *Ecuries* of the Main Palace at Versailles, and here he handed me what appeared to be two rolls of wallpaper, which, when spread out, proved to be graph-paper charts showing the daily flow of all rail traffic in the German-controlled railway region … the record started in 1940, on the day that the Germans had occupied France and the Low Countries, and ended in the last week of May 1944. One glance showed that the enemy had themselves provided us with the evidence that was going to carry conviction … French railway records had already revealed that a precipitous fall in traffic had begun about the middle of March that year … well advanced before the destruction of the Seine bridges in the last week of May. Analysis of the French records … made it perfectly plain that the disorganisation caused by the attacks had made it impossible for the railways of any region to deal with much of even the highest priority traffic … Two or three months of bombing had paralysed the economic life of France … All the main communications between French cities, and between French industries, were crippled.

'By the time Ezra gave me the German charts [they] left no doubt … Their value lay in the fact that they constituted evidence that could not be regarded as having been coloured by any preconceived ideas … with the overall result that industry in the region had more less come to standstill before the Normandy landings … the railway paralysis was in the main due to the destruction of the centres which regulated traffic … on 26 October [1944], within a few days of my showing him the charts, [Marshall of the RAF] Tedder, [and until January 1945, the Allied Deputy CiC] reconvened a meeting at Versailles of all the bomber chiefs … At the time of this meeting we were less than two months away from the German counter-attack in the Ardennes [the "Battle of the Bulge"]… Germany was already tottering on the verge of transportation collapse; a slight push, even a modest intensification of bomber attacks on rail centres, might have prevented her build-up for the Ardennes offensive … this was not to be'.

[Zuckerman's diary goes on to the December time prior to that offensive]. '*Tuesday December 19*: Ezra, in G-2, told me that that he himself had been aware of the extent of German rail movement, and that he also knew the names of the detraining stations …

'I asked whether he did not think that the Strategic Air Forces should have been called in to stop the build-up, and received the correct reply that that was not his business … *Wednesday December 20*: 'I saw Tedder again in the morning before he went off to join [General] Eisenhower [SACEUR] in a talk with [General] Bradley. I spent the rest of the day assembling exact figures for the attacks which had been made on the rail centres, and in encouraging Ezra to prepare a more extensive list of rail targets for the Combined Strategic Targets Committee in London … I was also able to tell Tedder that G-2 – in the person of Ezra – was now fully co-operating in 'thickening up' the rail centre belt [for potential attack].'

Many years later, Derek was attending a lunch at Buckingham Palace, sitting next to Lord Mountbatten, former Head of Combined Operations; Solly Zuckermann was also present: "He turned to me and said 'Ah, I remember your name because there was a famous occasion when Solly was arguing … against the saturation policy, and, in order to prove his point, he pulled out of his pocket a great length of paper, like lavatory paper, and threw it down on the floor in a great dramatic gesture. We all got down on our hands and knees to look at this damned thing – a report of a photo recce of German troop movements, and he said: <There you are, that is the sort of information that leads to special targets, as opposed to wasting your bombs on great marshalling yards and cities>. Mountbatten said to me: 'Your name was mentioned as having got this information together".

It can be seen that Major Derek Ezra, the personification of the secret G-2 unit, was able at this pivotal moment in the course of the war, to provide critically important advice for the supreme war command. Not surprisingly, Derek, by now with a SHAEF shoulder-flash on his uniform, was awarded a Military MBE for this work, and also the American Bronze Star. The two citations speak volumes for Ezra characteristics which would later enhance his career:

"[SHAEF] Action for which commended: REWARD: M.B.E.

"Major Ezra has controlled a subsection dealing with enemy transportation and movements. Before the commencement of OVERLORD this officer built up virtually on his own, a most efficient system whereby the movements of enemy divisions and their entraining and detraining areas could be accurately assessed. As a result of this work, G-2 were able by air reconnaissance to spot the entrainment and subsequent movement of practically every division which was directed towards the front from all parts of France. As operations progressed, movement from Germany and other parts of Europe was also spotted. The knowledge which this officer possessed of the rail system over which the enemy moved enabled immediate recommendations to be made to the Air Forces. The results achieved were absolutely outstanding; this, on numerous occasions, has been testified by prisoners of war.

Almost all the credit for this most important operational work rests with Major Ezra, who, during the whole period of operations, has never spared himself in order to produce the intelligence required. Further, by his tireless enquiries of railway officials in countries overrun, he has produced the most valuable data by which even greater efficiency was attained for the operations now in their final stages. Throughout the whole of the operations this officer has shown the greatest devotion to duty and ability far above the average." [*signed- H.M.Gale, Lieutenant-General, Chief Administrative Officer*]

"Citation for Bronze Star Medal"

"Major D.J.Ezra, British Army, for meritorious services in connection with military operations from 1 November 1943 to 15 April 1945. As head of the Enemy Communications Section, G-2 Division, [SHAEF] Major Ezra was responsible for the citation, evaluation and dissemination of all intelligence on German organisation and use of roads, railroads and inland waterways. His professional ability, resourcefulness and deep grasp of the enemy's employment and organisation of his lines of communication led to the production of intelligence which was the basis of estimates on the enemy's intentions and capabilities, and by means of which sensitive points in his lines of communication were selected for attack both from the ground and the air. He has, through exemplary performance of this duty, contributed materially to the success of Allied operations against Germany."

[*Official – sealed, Supreme H.Q., Allied Expeditionary Force*]

The spoils of war: vital German technological reparations

After the war, in January 1946 Derek's skills turned to a new use, becoming Secretary of the British Intelligence Objectives Sub-Committee back in London. Modestly, he merely says: "I co-ordinated a vast investigating team of military and civil members, bringing back details of German technology over the whole area of industry; many thousands of Reports were produced. This was regarded as a form of reparations, for the benefit of companies such as ICI. Some of it was no doubt useful".

This 'BIOS' data helped the ongoing war with Nazi ally, Japan, but was also an early hint of the Cold War, denying the Russians Nazi technology and scientists.[8] However, German industry was soon to be transformed by Marshall Aid, and so able to re-invest in new state-of-the-art equipment from the USA.

Though not what the Allies first intended, it too had an indirect value for the post-war Europe that was already a gleam in some visionary politicians' eyes - though not yet for the British. Derek was retained in service until 1947, with the rank of Lieut-Colonel, when, (in an event to be related later in the context of the Energy Lecture, Chapter 11), he joined the embryonic NCB. (Derek's personal BIOS papers are now with the Imperial War Museum in London).

"JULIE"

Turning the clock back briefly to the army period, with old 6" howitzers to play with, and prior to Derek's commitment to his hush-hush job in London, (when frivolities, and resplendent uniforms were no longer much in evidence) he recalled a moment that would transform his life, and indeed make possible all that succeeded it. At this juncture in the war, he had had time to relax a little, and, as an instance, he recalled one such relaxation when he was at a dance one evening, kitted out in his best navy blue No 1 kit – his "Blues" – which happened to be endowed with metal shoulder epaulettes. At the close of one dance number, he suddenly found that another lady dancer's long hair had wafted over and become entangled with one of his epaulettes, to the amusement of the assembled company of officers!

Such incidents were as nothing compared with one unforgettable evening, when, as Derek fondly remembered, he first met his "Julie". Although this is no all-embracing biography, no account of Derek's work has meaning without her. "I was dining with two friends at the Overseas League in St James's (like other London Clubs, open to service personnel). I was recovering from an accident on a huge motor bike, which we had had to learn to ride for some obscure Army reason. The dining room was practically empty. Across the room at another table I noticed this attractive young WAAF corporal, sitting on her own. I decided on an impulse to ask her to join us." (He speculated, with a wry smile, that to some onlookers, possibly even to Julie, the evidence of his 'civilian' disablement might have looked like the admirable outcome of a war wound!). 'She replied "Yes, but only if you join *me* on my table!"' Derek enjoyed retelling this first glimpse of Julie's independent spirit. They married some years later, after Derek had joined the NCB.

Fig.6: The future Lady Ezra, enthusiastic and popular "First Lady" of Britain's mining world, WAAF Corporal Julie Wilkins

Fig.7: The Wedding of Derek and Julie Ezra, in London 1950

COAL, STEEL, AND EUROPE

The first years with NCB had been spent as much abroad as at home. The European Coal and Steel Community was not yet fully operational by the time Derek was seconded in 1952, with the Foreign Office status of 'Counsellor', as NCB representative on the UK delegation in Luxembourg from 1952 to 1956. However, from 1948 he had already been accompanying Val Duncan, who represented the Board on the Economic Commission to Europe at the *Palais des Nations* at Geneva: "This was the beginning of my association with coal as an international commodity". The thinking that helped to form the ECSC was close to his heart. Although only one short, opening stage in his long career, that vivid experience deserves mention in this Introduction. Britain would not accede to the European Community until 1973.

It is not easy to look back at that entity with detachment across a 50-year gap, given the events that have intervened. These have entailed the unfolding and ultimately the ending of the Cold War; a diminished priority for the old basic industries of coal and steel; and the emergence of the Pacific Rim economies as major fuel and metal producers. Yet in its time, the new entity was an exciting, if fragile, leap into the dark, or, as its proponents saw it, into a bright future. The small community onto whose terrain the NCB delegation entered was star-studded: "the level of intelligence is extraordinary … an elite has foregathered" was one comment at the time.[9] The remit for the UK team coupled both national and industrial aims. They were three-fold: firstly, to see generally what the Europeans were up to; secondly, to watch out for any developments that might impinge on the commercial interests of the British coal industry, in imports or exports; but overall to maintain a British presence at the table as a vehicle for closer cooperation. A later judgment was that the newly formed High Authority devoted too much time to 'the chimera of British association'. In the tight Secretariat that formed around the inspirational but feet-on-the-ground first President whom Derek knew well, Jean Monnet, there were in fact already two Englishmen, Richard Mayne and François Duchêne, thus the ground was not entirely non-British. Interestingly, Derek has commented: "by virtue of the fact that the British were only there in an informal capacity, they actually had closer access to Monnet than did the coal and steel industries from the other Member-states". The NCB representative would touch base with the various officials who were staffing the Luxembourg *nomenclatura*. Indeed one of the accusations against the ECSC was that 'it was an unrealistic attempt of bureaucrats to impose uniformity upon a natural diversity of conditions'.[10] The abiding view today is that the Community was "the success of a failure": the failure was to be unable to meet Monnet's high ambition for the ECSC as a "sovereign power", answerable only to the European Assembly. The success was the simple truth that here was a profound step towards the economies of scale which the Americans, and many Europeans, perceived as essential for Europe's future as a global player. Only belatedly, with no thanks to President de Gaulle, but in Derek's time as Chairman of the NCB, did Britain at last get a place round this strategic table.

The post-war years witnessed a notable but grimly logical volte-face on the part of the Allied Powers vis-à-vis Germany. This veered from the 1945 era of a would-be punitive dismantling of the cartelized German Ruhr coal/ steel complex; (the policy of the U.S. Senator, Henry Morgenthau, and the aim of many Frenchmen), through and beyond the injection from 1948 onwards of regenerative capital under the properly termed 'European Recovery Program' – the Marshall Plan. A recent writer has encapsulated the nub of the problem as this: 'Economically, Europeans needed German revival; politically, they feared it'.[11] There evolved the stark realisation that a sound, reformed German economy was essential to a strong anti-communist Western Europe – as well as to American prosperity. One commentator expressed this about-turn as 'From the Morgenthau Plan to the Schuman Plan': the aim – to "Europeanise the Ruhr". It was eventually the French idealist, Robert Schuman, who would be credited with the phenomenon which bore his name; it crowned a process of both moral reconciliation and geo-political self-interest.[12] For the young Derek Ezra, "this was a wonderful time".

The hardening of the Cold War had begun to dawn on western politicians – even while the military war was in full progress, with Soviet Russia still the ally. The resulting Berlin Air-Lift of 1948 showed the erstwhile ally as the new enemy. Finally came the outbreak of the Korean War with the Chinese and North Koreans in 1950, the three major communist powers now seen as the real world opponents. These critical events accelerated the need to bring Germany into the comity of the West. As Anne Deighton succinctly encapsulates in 'The Remaking of Europe', (**The Oxford History of the Twentieth Century**): 'The struggle to defeat Germany quickly became the new struggle *for* Germany'. The great European spirits of this era - many of whom Derek knew personally – Pleven and Schuman for France, Spaak for Belgium, Chancellor Adenauer and his Finance Minister Erhardt for West Germany, but above all both General Marshall and Dean Acheson for the US, had all played their parts.

Although the British were absent from the vanguard, with what today would be termed "Eurosceptic" British governments watching from the wings, this did not stop those with a European vision from giving their support to what was emerging from the ashes of war. Derek Ezra had been brought up in a cosmopolitan environment; with an innately European perspective, he was proud to be numbered among these pioneers. He recalled a surprising factor of that time: "Britain was actually in a very powerful position, compared with the war-torn industries on the continent, and we were respected for that".

Two aspects were to prove formative for his subsequent career at the head of the British coal industry: firstly, the importance of long-term economic planning; and some form of co-determination in the workplace – or, to use the seminal German word for it, a concept familiar to and deeply endorsed by Derek – *Mitbestimmung*. Despite the fact that Britain had set her traditional face against any outright 100% "socialisation" of their basic industries, both these European-rooted ideas were to characterize many aspects of Derek's later impact on the NCB. At the monthly meetings in Luxembourg, and earlier for other reasons in Paris too, he met with delegates from France, Germany, the Benelux countries, and Italy. He could almost be seen as an individual embodiment of what emerged as the title of one of the main economists' studies of that pivotal decade, **Coal, Steel, and the Rebirth of Europe**.[13]

As a final wry comment, viewing coal from what at that moment seemed to be a natural British perspective, Labour Minister of Power and architect of the 1946 Nationalisation Act, Emanuel Shinwell, throws an ironical retrospective light in his memoirs on events as they impacted on his cherished political dream. That dream was rooted in the complacent view once epitomised by Nye Bevan's description of Britain as a "lump of coal, surrounded by fish". When faced with the possible integration of key parts of Britain's post-war industry within the new ECSC, either he (or Hugh Dalton - reports vary) is reported as saying with some fervour: "We had just nationalised the coal and steel industries of Britain, and we were certainly not now going to have them inter-nationalised!"

THE POLITICS OF COAL AND THE 'FAULTLINE'

Returning to the UK economy, and for those who may now only dimly recall the headline events of the latter part of the 20th century, Derek Ezra's destiny might be portrayed as having had to preside over the 'faultline' between two eras. As already suggested in this Introduction, they could be seen as the colliding 'tectonic plates' of post-war British political and economic history.

Extending on the one side was that deeply cherished idealistic dogma which had still, in the words of a famous ex-miner, and despite equivocal memories of the miners' strikes during WW2, "acquired a status akin to that of the Holy Grail" – common public ownership of the means of production and distribution.[14] This opened with the coal industry in 1946 (in what was, historically, a re-nationalisation). On the other side of the faultline evolved its emerging antithesis – the roll-back-the-state philosophy of successive UK political regimes from the late-1970s onwards. (The 'faultline' concept recurs in the title of a recent history of the 1984-85 'Great Strike', with the NUM's Arthur Scargill pitted against Ian MacGregor at the NCB).[15]

It would be no surprise to a 21st-century eye to discover that the NCB, even in its heyday, still occupied a mere 11 lines, not even a descriptive paragraph, in that time-honoured précis of the nation's life, **Whitaker's Almanack**. Symbolically, the coal industry's official history speaks of the steady 'downgrading of the affairs of the nationalised industries'.[16] It may be arguable as to when that heyday occurred, but despite – or possibly because of – the two hard years of national coal strikes from 1972 to1974, a good case could be made for it having been during the ensuing 1970s, the decade of the Ezra 'Plan for Coal'. Fortunately for one of the 'commanding heights', that decade, dubbed in Britain in the Seventies, as that of 'When the Lights Went Out', was dominated by a nationalisation-minded 'Old Labour' government, wary of the NUM's power. A commentary records the briefing note of a civil servant to Sir Derek Ezra on 18 January 1972: 'The union are winning a lot of public sympathy. That has its roots in history. We are not going to be able to change that'.[17] By contrast, the Department of Energy, to whose Secretary of State the coal industry at that time was responsible – together with the public corporations managing the other key sources of power – took up two full columns of **Whitaker's** 2000 pages, listing no less than 90 of those cautious civil servants. They also purported to cover electricity and nuclear energy, gas, oil, and a still nascent 'offshore technology' industry.

The edition welcoming the next decade, 1981, still showed as NCB Chairman, Sir Derek Ezra MBE - his political 'master' and opposite number again a Conservative, the Rt. Hon. David Howell MP. The salaries of the three politicians heading the Department come to nearly as much as the public servant reporting to them; each power industry had its neatly separate overseeing division, reporting to an Under-Secretary – 'oversight' might well be seen as a word with some double-meaning. There is a suggestion of a balance of power in this glimpse of the 'Politics of Energy' in the last quarter of the 20th century.[18] Although Energy was already gaining what is now once more its current pole position in the political agenda, its Ministerial role was not seen then as a path for a high-flyer. Indeed Howell was 'pushed off the sledge', in the words of one commentator, after what has been later described as the first "body swerve" by Margaret Thatcher – the inveterate late-1960s' shadow Minister of Power and critic of the nationalised industries – with the new Leader of the NUM, Arthur Scargill.[19]

On the face of it, all seemed to be a set of well-oiled cogs in a well-ordered machine. The reality was vastly different – turbulent, strident, 'in the headlines'. It was that grim reality of the "eye of the storm" which this fifth and longest-serving NCB Chairman – and the first to be recruited from within the industry – faced throughout his 15 years in office, initially as Deputy Chairman (1967 to1971) and then finally in the hot seat until he retired as Chairman in 1982, after one stint of five years and two of three years.

The 'X'-factor was widely seen to be industrial relations. The focus became, not the central long-term struggle for coal's markets, a cause which Derek, as a committed marketing man, fervently espoused, but the year-to-year battle over the wage-claim of 'The Miners'. The miner had become a figure within an industry which, in the wake of films, novels and nationally-experienced pit disasters, was now, to borrow Anthony Sampson's telling phrase, 'part of the nation's geology'.[20] As another writer has put it, for the (Old) Labour movement itself, 'coal had never lost its symbolic, almost romantic place'.[21] Arthur Scargill's subsequent campaign to determine that place, without regard to the economics of the industry, defined the 'faultline'. Derek's 'watch', and the later miners' strike, spelt an end to the remnant of what has been dubbed 'Attlee's Britain', with what commentators have called its 'Morrisonian structures' – the UK's convergent politics of the post-war era.[22]

This Memoir is neither an apologia for public ownership nor an addendum to the industry's official history; it simply marks a timely opportunity to flag up the 10th anniversary of the first Fuellers' 'Energy Lecture'. This opportunity records some aspects of the life and work of its original sponsor, one of that rare but now almost extinct breed – the chairmen of the nationalised industries – who managed swathes of the country's GDP during the last half of the 20th century. This selection of personal reminiscences about Lord Ezra has been brought together with his acquiescence – approval is too strong a word for an essentially modest man, who consciously decided not to proceed with an earlier planned 'autobiography'. Its aim is to try do justice to the leadership role that an outstanding public servant has performed in a long working lifetime, serving a controversial public office, in the crucial period leading up to the event that took over the news, the 'Great Strike' of 1984.

Also included are some of his published words. They highlight a common thread: his cogently argued and well-documented crusade, in the face of an endemic short-sighted scepticism, for a long-term national Energy Policy. Nationalisation, the original vehicle for such a policy, was at its inception a given factor, based initially at least, in a widespread public consensus. Born in a haste that laboured under a number of anomalies in its scope, it seemed for many decades the only solution to the problems of a uniquely basic industry.[23]

Derek's time at the helm even touched on the Constitution. Coal became – for some, almost unforgivably – the trigger for a government's fall from power, after the three-day week of 1973 under Prime Minister Ted Heath: a hark-back to the days of the mid-1920s, when the miners had first tried to exercise their power to throttle the national economy. NUM's Arthur Scargill would hubristically liken that historic trial of strength to mere "cricket on the village green, like they did in 1926". It also brought NCB, in the recollection of one commentator, to the extreme of having to conceal, until beyond the 11th hour, even fully-negotiated uneconomic pit closures in marginal Tory seats, for fear of last-minute political intervention, a tactic which, according to the memory of close observers, infuriated "No. 10".

(The editor had the opportunity to first work for Lord Ezra in connection with the marketing of solid fuel for the domestic market, the chief thrust of Derek's NCB career from early on, after his initial stint as the Board's representative at the ECSC. Later, authorship of **The Fueller's Tale**, the history of Lord Ezra's City Livery Company, 'The Fuellers', further enhanced this link).[24]

This Memoir's title underlines a fundamental point: the lodestar of Derek Ezra's leadership has never been simply to produce coal *per se*, nor to promote the ideals of public versus private ownership. These were accusations levelled unjustly at the man who – as the Ezra autobiographical essay of 1982 now reveals – blessed Derek's succession to him, Lord Robens. It is rather to convince a carbon-emissions conscious 'Green Lobby' that the revitalized non-carbon utilisation of clean coal, our native resource, could arguably one day reclaim its necessary, economically defensible place in any future 'energy mix'.

This legacy was certainly passed on to Derek's successor but two, the former Deputy Chairman of ICI, "Bob" Haslam, who declared, from his even wider view of industry: 'There is no doubt in my mind that we should plan for the resurgence of our coal industry, linked with investment in clean coal technology'… He was then paying tribute in his autobiography to Derek Ezra's time in the same hot seat, with many echoes of his predecessor's problems: 'He had served as a distinguished deputy chairman in the marketing field. In 1974 he negotiated the far-sighted "**Plan for Coal**" with the government … This necessary though costly blueprint to build a 'new' coal industry obviously had the full support of the unions, hence it proceeded as a tripartite commitment ... but the increased productivity did not come through in the 1970s as quickly as might have been expected, in view of the vast capital investment. In 1981 Scargill succeeded Gormley as President [of the NUM] and Ezra realized that he had to accelerate the closure of uneconomic pits. However,' [surely the crucial point in any fair reappraisal of Derek

Ezra's often controversial stewardship] 'the Government sadly did not feel able to support his immediate closure programme'.[25]

Notwithstanding those constraints, Derek Ezra, in the context of the 'macro' energy issues - like both that successor in office and his predecessor, Lord Robens - can certainly be seen in the first rank of public service "communicators", one of the main current criteria of leadership. Through the public media – frequent interviews on Radio Four's "Today" programme, books, articles and speeches – he has already achieved much towards this goal. He has proclaimed for the UK what the US writer, Chauncey Starr, has asserted globally: that 'energy' is no longer 'a mere parameter of our national health and welfare that could be treated in an *ad hoc* fashion.'[26]

It needs perhaps to be re-stated at the outset of this Memoir that – apart perhaps from Malcolm Edwards' personal overview in Chapter 2 – it does not set out as a whole to offer any overall economic analysis of the industry, and it hopefully avoids the trap of chairmen's biographies – "platitudes from the top of the pyramid". Nor does it detail the evolution of policies for energy under the Ezra leadership, a task properly performed by many other writers,[27] not least a former Director of Economics for British Coal, Mike Parker, in his work for the Oxford Institute for Energy;[28] brief extracts from this work will be made later in the narrative. Prioritizing here the underlying issue of Energy Policy, in the UK and worldwide, Derek Ezra knows better than anyone how much remains to be done, for this and future generations.

The Man in Context

It would be inappropriate in a short, unavoidably selective Memoir to offer anything other than the briefest of portraits of Derek Ezra the private individual. However, and always in inevitable relation to his working life, a few personal pen-portraits by friends and colleagues are set out in Chapter 8, 'Many Facets – the Ezras and Coal.'

Private individual he certainly is, as anyone visiting him at his home in SW London would confirm. The house is in a discreet Georgian terrace, a convenient stone's throw from the former offices of the NCB in Grosvenor Place. In the library in his second floor study it might be the tightly shelved collection of classical and modern literature and history, as well as much coal and energy reading matter, which would perhaps be the first thing to catch the eye of any visitor, suggesting an inward, reflective, academic man rarely glimpsed behind the public persona. The acceptance in 1977 of an Honorary Fellowship at his former Cambridge College, Magdalene, was one of the very few concessions that Derek appeared to make to what one ex-colleague imagined as an alternative career for a man (compared with his extrovert predecessor, he saw himself as "introverted") who could have headed some highly intellectual European '*Plan*'.

An unexpectedly light-hearted counterpoint to the precision of his normal approach to things is the large bowl of gaily-coloured commemorative match-box covers, which lies on the coffee table in the sitting room: informal mementoes of a lifetime of countless formal public occasions attended in his various official capacities. The Ezras had to have a home in London because of Derek's work, but they regarded Brook House near Horsham, with its large wooded garden, as their principal residence, acquired 50 years ago, and intended to retire there. For many years they went there frequently – every week-end when available and all holidays. Derek participated actively in local affairs and selected Horsham as part of his title. Unfortunately in more recent years their visits were curtailed due to Julie's ailments, which needed treatment in London. (Derek kept many of his coal memorabilia there; he has donated some to the Coal Mining Museum and earmarked others for The Fuellers).

Friends would always be struck by Derek's devotion to his "Julie" – a devotion that evolved into total responsibility for her as her only carer. She had partnered him throughout the ups and downs of his busy life, and her bubbly personality had enlivened the many challenging moments he had had to deal with. He looked after her unstintingly until her death a few short months after her one-hundredth birthday, in 2010. Receipt of the customary congratulatory telegram on that occasion from Buckingham Palace, orchestrated not by him but by a group of his former coal industry colleagues, was only marred for Derek by the realisation that her state of health was gradually deteriorating. Derek's grief at her death was profound; they were very much a couple unto themselves, with no children, only a brother and a sister, their wide circle of loyal and invariably influential friends steadily reduced over the years. He felt that her death might well have been hastened by her shock at his fall and broken hip earlier that year, necessitating his three weeks away in hospital.

Although hailed in a French paper as *"une haute personnalité britannique"*, French colleagues have also called Derek *un homme sérieux*. Yet no epithet can really sum up his very complex character. Given what to some was a rather austere presence, his success in stepping seamlessly into the shoes of his ebullient predecessor, "Alf" Robens – a "politico", a man of the people, with a reassuring track record in the Trade Union movement – is all the more remarkable. That was one measure of the man, as exemplified in Chapter 8. Against initial doubts within the mining fraternity, Derek became a trusted friend of the mass of miners: even, as asserted in **The Changing Anatomy of Britain**, the *'confidant'* of one above all – "Joe" (and later, fellow-Baron) Gormley, the NUM President.

The subtle calibre of this Union leader who faced Derek across the industrial divide can be gleaned from the extracts, headed "My Fighting Life", in the *"Daily Mail"* of March 15 1982, from Gormley's autobiography, **Battered Cherub**: 'I am a Socialist. I was born a Socialist and I shall die a Socialist ... but in my attitude towards achieving Socialism, I believe in negotiation and I believe in compromise ... there are those who want to change everything overnight. They try to jump from the ground over the top of the wall. I believe in putting a ladder to the wall, and climbing it step by step. I believe that progress should be made gradually, rather than by revolution'.

Insensitive to the astonishing achievement of their working relationship, for 'Whitehall and Westminster' the coal industry became known as the "Derek and Joe Show"; or at least that was how it was regarded by the Secretary of State for Energy in 1981-2, Nigel Lawson.[29] However, the goalposts were changing, as an academic study has commented. Under' the heading "Finding the Right "Chaps", 'Lawson, like Thatcher, put particular emphasis on choosing ... managers who were "one of us". Gone were the days when neutral, uncontentious figures would be chosen, to represent the wider public interest along "Morrisonian" lines. Lawson wanted partisan people ... At the NCB, Ezra had been first appointed by Heath in 1971, and re-appointed by Benn in 1977.'[30]

As subsequent chapters will reveal, this volatile political arena did not come naturally to Derek, yet he coped with it in his own disciplined way. Within the constraints of running a public business in the 1970s, coal's most politically charged period – and duly answerable to the taxpayer – Derek Ezra had brought himself for good reasons to be identified with the miners, a very special breed of men and women, with an honourable but troubled history in the face of adversity and danger. Their deep sense of community would be sadly witnessed once more in the Gleision and Kellingley pit accidents of 2011. Perhaps understandably, at one point Derek would define his strategic approach in these terms: "All I did deliberately was to seek to maximise the area of agreement. That applied both within the industry and the unions". The significance of that reference to 'the industry', with its implication of what was called "the mining mafia" – mining engineers – will become apparent later.

It needs to be recalled that in the nation at large, up to the era of the so-called "Battle of Orgreave" in 1984 under the next NCB Chairman but one, Ian MacGregor, this section of the nation's workforce commanded an attitude comparable to that held towards the armed forces. To the marketplace world of the 21st century, that reverence would be almost incomprehensible. The path now to be trodden by Derek lay between a familiar rock, as the leader of "his" people, and a new, "bottom-line" hard place.

Bound by the remits imposed on the NCB by all successive governments, Derek had nevertheless done all he could to improve the working lives of the miners; their safety and operating conditions were paramount to him. He had at the same time committed himself to a far more difficult task – to reach a political *modus vivendi* with them, anathema to a new cohort of revolutionising Conservative Prime Ministers. Even before "The Iron Lady", Margaret Thatcher, took office in 1979, he had come to be seen on high as the miners' champion almost as much as the industry's boss.

Since this delicate political balancing act may well be the reason why Lord Ezra's industrial achievements have not yet been fully recognized, and given that as with today's Network Rail, the nationalisation shibboleth is no longer as black and white as in the 1980s, a short reference to that theme may now be in order; its impact on Derek will be developed later.

Hugo Young, in his account of the Thatcher years, related the comment by her Chancellor, Nigel Lawson – highlighting the political maelstrom that Derek and his Board were now plunging into – that 'no industry should remain under state management *unless* [sic] there was a positive and overwhelming case for it'.[31]

Young wrote, in words whose harsh inner meaning will become more apparent in Chapter 2: 'Thatcher … might be stuck, for the moment, with the industries, but she was determined not to be stuck with all the industrial leaders whom she had inherited from an earlier age … She was soon dissatisfied with the men through whom she was supposed to carry out her task … some, like Sir Peter Parker, the chairman of British Rail, were seen as the embodiment of the old consensus … Others, like Sir Derek Ezra, chairman of the National Coal Board, had long since been marked down as a disposable asset … she said that when she got into power, he wouldn't get away with what he was doing in the Coal Board with the miners, she'd see to that'.[32] Another comment was that 'Thatcher thought that Ezra was too "conciliatory"'.[33] This savage if prophetic recollection of the "The Iron Lady" at her most swingeing, by Sir Monty Finniston, then Chairman of British Steel, at an informal meeting prior to the General Election of 1979, spelt trouble – and much distress – for Derek and those nationalised industry chiefs like him, who had genuinely tried to reach reasonable understandings with the Union leaders of the day; many of them - but not all - were equally reasonable men. Sometimes those understandings were achieved in subtle and unpublicized ways. Derek recalled to one ex-colleague how he and miners' leader, "Joe" Gormley, would do their final bargaining *à deux* behind closed doors, before any final public statement of agreement.

Indeed, this relationship with the "Battered Cherub" certainly served the long-term cause of industrial stability, even if some observers thought that in the short term the miners always came out too well from such a process. (That at least appeared to be the case up to the arrival of Gormley's confrontational successor, Arthur Scargill, with a new, starkly politicised agenda). Both these traditional but mutually respectful protagonists saw that advent as "the beginning of the end" for their industry. Subsequent events might well be said to have proved them right – at least with such perspective as the year 2014 can offer.

At the British Steel Corporation there had now surfaced by the early 1980s a Chairman whom the Bishop of Durham, David Jenkins, once described as "an elderly imported American", the Scottish-born Ian MacGregor.[34]

Events took what seemed at the time to most outsiders to be their inevitable course. 'At the NCB, instead of the later, tough, US-trained MacGregor, the Chairman was a moderate figure with no love for redundancies, Sir Derek Ezra. At the Ministry, Howell's objective was to force Ezra's hand by cutting the cost limits within which the NCB had to operate. This left Sir Derek with no option but to propose closures'.[35] (Chapter 1 will come back to this theme of the ultimate power that government and Treasury always retained to steer the nationalised industries along the desired politically-acceptable path).

It was known that Derek had no wish to extend his contract after his third – and the NCB's longest term. The second phase of his long public career was thereby given its opportunity, to the benefit of a vast array of enterprises – political, international, industrial, educational and charitable. The 'Time-Lines' section lists these appointments impressively: they cannot all be explored within these pages. However, Chapter 10 helps to illustrate the contribution that Derek's judgment and reputation were now able to bring to Board Tables and management groups both in the UK and further afield in his beloved Europe.

MAINTAINING THE BALANCE

This short Memoir attempts to get behind the vast official and statistical literature that has surrounded, sometimes obscured – and arguably occupied too much of the scarce management time – of coal, and its sister nationalised industries: all the Annual Reports; the Reports of Select Committees; the efficiency and wages investigations by Fleck and Wilberforce; the avalanche of papers to and from associated Ministers and their minions, from Treasury to Employment; the public speeches; the editorials.

Another fundamentally important aspect of the background to Derek Ezra's occupancy of the uncomfortable space "across the tectonic plates", which has to be omitted from this account, is that of the industrial relations and legislative context within which all parties had to work. Classic commentaries, such as the Kessler/ Bayliss text of 1992, **Contemporary British Industrial Relations**, underline just how central the coal industry story was for the evolution of both UK civil and criminal law in the 1980s, and how the Boards of the nationalised industries, particularly coal, had to tread a fine line between what they could do legally, and what it was politic for them to do from the government's point of view.[36] Thus for example, whilst it became, in due course, theoretically possible for an employer to take legal action against secondary picketing, in practice the Coal Board's hands were tied by the advice that such action would exacerbate the whole national industrial relations climate: double-guessing had to become second nature for the Board.

Something of the tightrope that Derek Ezra had to negotiate has already been outlined; a leading politician of the time will record his view that it was "an impossible task".[37] **Harold Macmillan said: "There are three things no sensible man directly challenges: the Catholic Church, the Brigade of Guards, and the National Union of Mineworkers".**[38]

This Memoir cannot do justice to all the events that commanded the time, skill, and particularly the presence of the NCB's Chairman – such as the new – but eventually doomed –

Selby mine in Yorkshire. It has also had to marginalise the many figures who played their comparably crucial parts in the industry's history, paving or guiding the way, for good or ill, for Derek's own incumbency: Hugh Gaitskell, Emanuel Shinwell, James Bowman, Will Paynter, Arthur Horner, Sir Hubert Houldsworth, "*Alf* " Robens, Harold Wilson, James Callaghan, Jim Prior *et al*.[39] As a final omission, these pages cannot do homage to the men at 'pit bottom' who were always close to Derek Ezra's heart, in 'the country's hardest and most dangerous industry': (this was the judgment of the chronicler of the Bevin Boys, who finally left Coal at the time of Derek's entry to its world).[40]

Each writer of the commentaries on the pages that now follow has set down his or her particular perspective of Derek Ezra in his many facets, the man who found himself at the centre of the penultimate phase of the coal industry in its nationalised state.

They also try to reflect the global economic insight into Energy – above and beyond the short-term political level – which Derek Ezra has striven to present in his writings: the idea – to quote one of the major American authorities on this issue – that 'energy may require a special analysis, and must not be treated … as just another economic variable'.[41] (This variability was most recently underlined by the 'electricity black-out' fears of mid-2013, but had also been highlighted by a Department of Energy and Climate Change report, released with ironical timing as these recollections were being written, under the headline: 'Old king coal is choice of today's generation – for now, at least'.[42] Although it merely reflected, at a level of over 33%, the 14-year high point in coal's use relative to other fuels by the UK's power stations, due to currently high gas prices - thus possibly constituting, by the same yardstick, 'coal's last hurrah'– it nevertheless illustrated the fact that in energy matters, no trends are invariable or permanent, and that no prophets on the possibility of change should go unheeded).

Even if some of the furore of past years has abated, public ownership still generates extreme views, witness the contemporary comment by a historian of the Falklands War: 'now barely a hillock in the economic landscape, for decades the nationalised industries cast a heavily subsidized and rancorous shadow over the whole of Society'.[43]

Despite Derek Ezra's unavoidable role at the centre of that continuing public debate, the views of the contributors to this Memoir may yet be thought to offer a more balanced picture of a man who many are now coming to see as one of the country's unsung industrial heroes; a man who both front-of-stage and behind the scenes performed a major leadership role in the national well-being, during a critical time in Britain's late 20th-century political and economic history.

Derek Ezra – a salute across the years

Time-Lines: 1 Life and Work: Key Dates – *Industry Highlights* – Political Calendar

1919	Derek born, in Tasmania, family of three, to David & Lillie Ezra, February 23	*Lloyd George [Lib/C]*
1920	*Sankey report recommends Labour Party to nationalise Coal*	
1925	*Pledge by TUC to back miners in dispute with private mine-owners*	*Baldwin [C]*
1926	*May: 9-day General Strike against Govment, led by TUC in support of miners*	
	Early education: France, then England	
1931	Scholarship to Monmouth School, foundation funded by Haberdashers Livery Company	
1936	Scholarships to Magdalene College, Cambridge, to read History: takes double First; CU Liberal Club (Meetings Secretary)	
1939	Called up for army, WWII; served in France & Germany; and in BBSU (Operational Intelligence) pre- D Day landings, and in BIOS; awarded Military MBE; demobilised 1947, rank of Lt Col.	
1945	*Formation of National Union of Mineworkers (NUM)*	*Attlee [L]*
1945	*Labour Govt manifesto for nationalisation of the 'heights of the economy', on model of government control of vital services during both World Wars; also of BBC, & Central Electricity Board*	
1945	*Alfred Robens, Trade Union official, elected Labour MP for Wansbeck*	
1946	*Coal industry nationalised, (after Bank of England)*	
1947	*Robens appointed Parliamentary Secretary to Minister of Fuel & Power, Shinwell*	
1947	Joined NCB Marketing Dept, Lansdowne House, on demob	
1948-52	Represented NCB on international coal committees in Paris, Geneva	
1950	Marries Julia Elizabeth Wilkins, of Portsmouth	
1952-6	'Counsellor', NCB Delegation to ECSC, Luxembourg	*Churchill [C]*
1956-8	Deputy Regional Sales Manager, London	*Eden/Macmillan [C]*
1958-60	Regional Sales Manager, London & Southern Region	
1960-65	NCB Director General of Marketing	*Macmillan/Douglas-Home [C]*
1961	*Conservatives appoint Robens as Chairman, NCB, 1961-71*	
1962-82	Member, West European Coal Producers' Association	
1965-67	Youngest NCB Board Member (for Marketing)	*Wilson [L]*
1966-90	Chairman, Associated Heat Services Ltd (AHS)	
1966-82	Non-Executive Director [NED], British Fuel Co.	
1967-71	Deputy Chairman to Lord Robens, NCB	
1971-82	Longest-serving Chairman, NCB	*Heath [C]*
1972/1980-81	Chairman, NICG (Nationalised Industries' Chairmen's Group)	
1973-82	Member, ECSC Consultative Committee	
1974	Kt: Sir Derek Ezra; heart attack	*Wilson/Callaghan [L]*
1975+	Positive Purchasing Initiative	
1975+	Member, Editorial Advisory Board, Henley Management College	
1977-82	Deputy Chairman, J.H.Sankey & Sons Ltd	
1978	Authorship: **Coal and Energy** published	
1978	Authorship: **European Community Coal Policy** published	
1979	Fuellers: with two leaders of coal trade, Jack Charrington, Ch. of Charringtons & Charles Stephenson Clarke, Ch. of Stephenson Clarke, helps found, and name, Worshipful Company of Fuellers, City of London Livery Company	
	(initially composed mainly of former coal trade personalities).	*Margaret Thatcher [C]*
1981-86	President, Coal Industry Society (Chairman 1961)	
1982	Retires as Chairman, NCB	
1983	Created Life Peer as Lord Ezra, of Horsham, in the County of West Sussex, Liberal-Democrat spokesman for Energy, later wider brief for all Industry	
1983	Authorship: **The Energy Debate** published	
1985-88	Chairman, House of Lords EU Sub-Committee on Energy	
1998-99	Member, Select Committee on Monetary Policy, Bank of England	

Time-Lines: 2 The Public Career beyond NCB

1945	MBE (Military)
1945	Bronze Star (USA)
1979	Grand Officer, Italian Order of Merit
1981	Commander, Luxembourg Order of Merit
1981	*Officier, Légion d'Honneur*

1979	Hon. Fellow, Magdalene College, Cambridge
1979	Hon. DSc, Cranfield University
1982	Hon. LLD, Leeds University

1971-82	Court of Governors, Administrative Staff College, Henley
1972-82	Chairman, Europe Committee, CBI
1972-82	Member, British Overseas Trade Board (Chairman, European Trade Committee)
1972-87	President, Combustion Engineering Association
1973-82	Governor, London Business School
1974-79	Member, Advisory Council for Energy Conservation
1976-78	Chairman, BIM; Vice-President 1978 *[now Chartered Management Institute]*
1977-79	Member, Energy Commission
1979	President, National Materials Handling Centre
1979-90	NED, Solvay & *Cie* (Belgium)
1982-85	Chairman, Petrolex Ltd
1982-89	NED, Redland PLC
1982-85	Director, Supervisory Board, Royal Boskalis Westminster NV (Holland)
1982-87	Industrial Adviser, Morgan Grenfell & Co. Ltd
1982-92	President, Institute of Trading Standards
1983-90	Member, International Advisory Board, Petrofina (Belgium)
1982-90	International Advisory Board, *Creditanstalt Bankverein* (Austria)
1983-86	Chairman, British Iron & Steel Consumers' Council
1983-86	Chairman, British Standards Institution
1984-94	Member, International Advisory Board, *Banca Nazionale del Lavoro* (Italy)
1984-91	Chairman, Throgmorton Trust PLC
1985-99	NED, *Compagnie Générale de Chauffe* (France)
1985-2000	Chairman, Sheffield Heat & Power Ltd
1985-2000	NED, Economic Research Council
1985-89	President, Keep Britain Tidy Group (Chairman, 1979-85)
1985-90	NED, Arran Energy (Ireland)
1986-2004	President, National Home Improvement Council (Hon. Vice-President 2004+)
1987-95	Chairman, Associated Gas Supplies Ltd
1989	Authorship: co-edited **Advice from the Top: Business Strategies of Britain's Corporate Leaders**
1990-99	Chairman, Energy & Technical Services Ltd
2000-05	Chairman, Micropower Ltd
2005-	Patron, Manpower Council

2010	*Julie Ezra dies, aet. 100*

1982-	Honorary Liveryman, Haberdashers' Company
1987-	Liveryman, Fuellers' Company

[Basis: 2012 Who's Who & DJE; Warner, Martin & Muir]

Time-Lines: 3 Ministerial Responsibility for Coal/ Energy 1965-1983

Some measure of the discontinuity that Derek Ezra, like other nationalised industry Chairmen, had to to cope with, may be inferred from the array of different titular departments served. No less than 13 different Ministers/ Secretaries of State occupied the appointing seats of Power, Energy or Technology over this period. There were three electorally-caused changes, and five different job-titles. Behind the Minister was the PM of the day (*see* page xxviii) and his or her Chancellor of the Exchequer, controlling the ultimate philosophy, and the financial reins, of the nationalised sector as part of the much maligned 'PSBR'. Reading the runes of each incoming Minister became a task for each nationalised Chairman. The evolution of the 'NICG' was very necessary for this embattled cohort. It would not have been surprising if a degree of cynical weariness might have overwhelmed those involved from time to time.

Years	Departments & Titles	Ministers	PM/Party
1964	Minister of Power	Fred Lee	Wilson/*Lab.*
1966		Richard Marsh	
1968		Ray Gunter	
1968-69		Roy Mason	
1966-70	Minister of Technology	Tony Benn	Wilson/*Lab.*
1970	Minster of Technology	Geoffrey Rippon	Heath/*Con.*
1970-72	Sec. of State for Trade & Industry	John Davies	
1972-74	Sec. of State for Trade & Industry	Peter Walker	
1974	Sec. of State for Energy	Lord Carrington	
1974-75	Sec. of State for Energy & Pres., Bd of Trade	Eric Varley	Wilson/*Lab.*
1975-79	Sec. of State for Energy (*)	Tony Benn	Callaghan/*Lab.*
1979-81	[Bd. of Trade again separate]	David Howell	Thatcher/*Con.*
1981-83	Sec. of State for Energy	Nigel Lawson	

[*Source: **History of British Coal Industry**, v.5, p.688*]

(* The cavalier, short-term way in which Energy was viewed politically in the 1970s is well illustrated by writers such as Andy Beckett in **When the Lights Went Out** [pp.174, 189, 200]: 'Harold Wilson demoted Benn to secretary of state for Energy .... the position may have been.... seen widely as a political dead-end' – notwithstanding Wilson's facetious and equally cavalier optimism that 'by 1985, the Labour [!] Secretary of State for Energy will be chairman of OPEC').

Time-Lines: 4 Main events for NCB and Energy 1971-1982

For ease of presentation, a dozen key factors can be baldly summarised as follows:-

   (i)   1972: first national coal strike, settled by Wilberforce Report.

  (ii)   Oct 1973: OPEC oil crisis resulting from Arab/Israeli Yom Kippur war.

 (iii)   'The Economic Case for Coal', leads to first '**Plan for Coal**', autumn 1973.

 (iv)   July 1973: demand by NUM ('praetorian guard of the Labour movement') for 31% wage increase leads to national strike, February 1974; and fall of Heath government; 'polarisation' becomes endemic; (*for full 1974 account, see Ch.5*).

  (v)   April 1974: tripartite' Coal Industry Examination'- Eric Varley: 'circumspect drafting' introduces ambivalence over key question of 'economic closures'.

 (vi)   1979: return of Thatcher government: followed by 1980s recession: second OPEC crisis; demand for primary energy falls 25m. m.t.c.e. tonnes in one year.

 (vii)   Coal Industry Act 1980: limits financial support to coal (abandoned by 1981).

(viii)   Jan 1981: Derek Ezra submits pit closures plan to Margaret Thatcher.

 (ix)   'Defining moment', 18 Feb 1981: tactical government concession ('capitulation') to NUM wage demand; strategic coal stockpiling begins.

  (x)   July 1981: NCB Development Plan to 1990, submitted to Secretary of State.

 (xi)   March 1982: referral to MMC: Report on Efficiency & Costs; published in 1983.

 (xii)   March 1982: Scargill elected President of NUM. adopts 'impossibilist' stance; 'The phase of coal industry history which comes down to the early [1980s] has to have, as its closing symbol, a large question mark'.

[*Ashworth/ Pegg: **History of British Coal Industry**, v.5.*]

CHAPTER 1: THE LEADERSHIP THEME

Successive chapters in this Memoir cover different aspects of Lord Ezra's life in public service, seen through the eyes of others. As they unfold, a vital, constant theme starts to emerge: that of leadership. Although unspoken or even conscious, there certainly has been a leadership 'philosophy' underlying his long career. The definition offered by Derek's friend, Henry Kissinger, was: 'the art of taking people where they would not have gone by themselves.' However defined, from the outset Derek Ezra clearly demonstrated leadership skills, and these took him to the highest levels of command.

At the risk of treading too far into the field of management theory, these skills require some brief analysis, and will reward the interest of all those with industrial experience, if at last there is to be gained a true measure of where Derek Ezra stands today in relation to the leaders of his era. This is all the more difficult because the templates by which they may be judged are often seen as subjective, albeit observable in action. The Memoir has benefitted here from the guidance of two contributors, Dr Paul Glover, and Dr Mark Pegg, each with healthy pedigrees in the study of management.[44] They have suggested that one new approach would be to look at leadership in the context of the organisation as a whole. An article in the Quarterly Review of global management consultants McKinsey, offers a starting point.[45] It argued that every organisation is a unique blend of seven identifiable but variable factors – the 'seven Ss': so-called Superordinate Goals – Strategy; Systems; Structure; Skills; Staff; and Style. Lord Ezra's very individual brand of leadership can only be fully understood when related over the years to these yardsticks, in the various contexts in which he worked. Paul Glover's commentary follows.

'*Superordinate Goals:* The McKinsey article defined such Goals as being 'of a higher order – guiding concepts, sets of values, and aspirations – that go beyond formal statements of corporate objectives'. For NCB, these were set out mainly in the Act of Nationalisation. How they were translated into strategy and plans by the Board, and the interface with Government, was largely in the hands of the Chairman – appointed by the Government. As outlined in the Introduction, Derek Ezra was first put in office by a Conservative and renewed in post by both Labour and Conservative administrations. He managed that interface for 11 long years - a test of leadership in itself. From the first days after nationalisation, the relationship between the industry management and the sponsoring Government department was a delicate balance. In the case of coal, the Act of Nationalisation ostensibly precluded the Government from directly influencing day-to-day matters - wages and prices. However, as Derek Ezra himself reflected, "the temptation to intervene was too great. Ministers and their Prime Ministers were in possession of so large a part of the public purse that they could not afford to keep their hands off it". That intervention often operated in 'mysterious ways', in telephone calls or off-the-record remarks, never in writing. Politics were ever-present.

'In Derek's early days Governments were advised in advance of likely closures. It became evident, however, as already touched on in the Introduction, that if any such pit were in a marginal constituency or if a bye-election was imminent, the word would be passed down that the closure was not to go ahead – at least, not yet. In the later phase of his chairmanship Derek therefore boldly decided that Government would in future only be informed after the decision had been conveyed to the Unions. This was risky territory. Government ultimately had – and would assert that they had both the right and the duty to have – the whip hand.

'Policy decisions on price control, wage levels and capital investment were subject to political necessity, even though this was contrary to what had been laid down as the NCB's role in the Nationalisation Act, leaving these matters ostensibly for the Board to decide. The reality applied equally to all nationalised industries, without exception. Or did it?

'In a memorable informal 'sound-bite' with Margaret Thatcher, after some joint meeting, Derek offered her a lift back to Downing Street in his car. In the car, she leaned forward in her earnest, emphatic, low-key way, and said to him: "You and the Coal Industry are trying to take us back into the 19th century". Since that aim was the last thing in Derek's mind, this remark stuck with him. It seemed to imply that the Government of the day, instead of prizing Coal as a natural resource, were looking at it almost with embarrassment, an overhang from a dirty, Dickensian past – it couldn't be a modern fuel – "bad for the image" – regardless of all that Derek foresaw for its modernisation. Forget the rational, future-piercing energy policy arguments: a value judgment was at work behind the scenes, influencing Government attitudes and therefore decisions.

'Derek had an even less subtle example under Ted Heath's short-lived regime, from 1973 onwards, of how Prime Ministers' predelictions, and limitations, could influence the Board's business. At a crucial time in the then wage-round, Ted Heath had effectively taken over the negotiations directly with the NUM.[46] In that one-to-one exchange Ted Heath had demonstrated a strange naivety in letting Joe Gormley and the NUM know what the fall-back figure was for settlement, something no industrial negotiator would ever have let slip – "never show your hand". In consequence the NUM were then able to go back to the Board, for the supposed final round, and tell them; "We know what the limit is", and inevitably this would therefore become the only politically acceptable level at which a settlement could be made. This unknown factor did not save the Board from being castigated publicly for giving in to the Unions and settling at too high a figure for the deemed national good.

Fig.8: The vital and symbolic – and much misunderstood – "Derek and Joe" show: NCB Chairman Derek Ezra with [*l.*] NUM President, Joe Gormley, at a Conference, 1970s. The iconic Miner's Lamp highlights the commitment of both leaders to the welfare of their workforce

'**Strategy:** in the period following nationalisation, the NCB developed its first strategic '**Plan for Coal**', published in 1950, and largely the work of Humphrey Browne – later to become the Deputy Chairman of the Board. The final 1974 '**Plan for Coal**' was developed in the closing years of Derek Ezra's chairmanship, primarily for capital investment, to make up for static productivity as the oil shock made coal more competitive. Although these Plans were not comprehensive, insofar as they did not deal with a number of important aspects of strategy, including prices and wages, the decision to develop separate 'value–in–use' price structures for industrial and 'carbonisation' coals in 1951 had had a profound effect on the competitive relationship of electricity and gas, before the discovery of natural gas. They could well be seen retrospectively as a strategic aspect of Derek Ezra's leadership. The similar decision in 1954 to go for national day-wage structures and rates, together with the price-loading of coals from high–cost areas, had determined the state of inter-coalfield competition for years to come. The National Power-Loading Agreement was also a way of recognising the reality of mechanisation, and the need to move to reward that fact acknowledged the investment in new coal-face equipment: perhaps another example of good strategic leadership. Yet year by year, as the organisation developed, the freedom of action of later managements was thereby constrained.

'The close relationship of goals and strategy, and the identification of both, raises the interesting question as to whether Derek was chosen to be the leader of a public enterprise because of a superior ability to grasp the strategic issues needed to develop the organisation, and meet the nation's energy and chemical feedstock requirements; that need was heightened by the far-reaching instability in global oil production, set in the wider UK context of economic planning. This had to be combined with the public scrutiny and accountability demanded of a leader in a public corporation.

'An instinctive capacity for leadership must have been a strong reason in Derek's appointment as Chairman. Commentators have observed that he had the knack of managing sensitive political relations at the intimate Ministerial level, and with Parliament – particularly for MPs with mining constituencies, and other stakeholders – the main industrial consumers. He was able to work comfortably in the complex world of public services, possessing a strategic view of performance improvement, willing to support investment in scientific progress and achievement: the purpose – to use the UK's coal reserves more efficiently, more cleanly, for lower cost, as an essential 'base-load' to complement a nuclear-, oil-, and gas-powered economy. His strategic vision for coal extended beyond the UK's own energy, industrial, and economic development. As a convinced European, he saw the '**Plan for Coal**' in the context of the European Community, as part of a wider collaboration, for the export and import of coal, as well as for the use of coal in electricity and steelmaking.[47] When his turn came to be President of the ECSC's Consultative Committee (composed of representatives of the participating coal producer countries) in the late 1970s, Derek was also able to help develop a truly European strategy for coal.

'*Structure:* The leadership structure of the coal industry in the years after nationalisation was production-orientated. The reorganisation of Marketing in 1966, and the elimination of Divisions the next year, established a structure which was to survive into the 1980s. However, under Derek Ezra's leadership, there was no fundamental re-think of the structure. Some consolidation of the subsidiary 'Areas' in the declining coalfields of Scotland, the North-East, and South Wales was effected, and 'Coal Products', Opencast Mining, and some other ancillary operations were reorganised, underlining Derek's interest in the European context.

A new International Department was established, and this and a Special Projects Branch reported directly to the Chairman. The Board's increasing interest in the domestic market, and in new coal products, was served by joint investments with partners in the appropriate trades. It acquired major shareholdings – for example, in Sankeys (a leading heating and builders' merchant) – to promote coal-burning installations in factories and homes.

As will be clear in Chapter 3, Derek Ezra only believed in and accepted evolutionary change. He was not tempted to divert from his primary goals and strategies by venturing into any major restructuring minefield. He has commented: "although we did of course carry out minor restructuring where necessary, for example in merging some Coal Areas, I preferred trying to improve the existing structure. I considered that wholesale re-organisation from the top took people's eyes off the ball: instead of thinking about the job – the NCB's overall 'job' – they would inevitably be diverted to thinking about their own individual jobs in any new set-up".

'*Systems:* in the context of organisation, "Systems" meant 'all the procedures, formal and informal, that make the organisation go, day to day and year by year: capital budgeting systems, training systems, cost-accounting systems', etc: the ways in which things were made to actually work. The definition can be widened, however, and can include the methods of production, coal utilisation, and in particular the improvement generally of safe practice, health and safety, and occupational medicine. In each of the fields of activity thus exposed, there were notable advances in the Ezra years, and help to define his leadership role: the evidence is there from which judgments can be made.

'Although not a scientist, Derek's sense of good leadership, coupled with his critical intellect, led him to take a personal interest in developing the NCB to become one of the front-runners in coal science, with some world-leading break-throughs in the design and application of a range of industrial services and processes'. Mark Pegg has observed that these included:

"**Mining research** – working with manufacturers to develop sophisticated mechanised techniques for longwall mining, to improve quality and productivity. These were exemplified by the Selby coalfield, with the latest advances in seismology, shaft sinking, horizon mining, full-shield tunnelling and high-output, heavy-duty coalface technology and coal clearance;

"**Coal Science research** – better coal preparation using flocculation [*see* Glossary], dense-medium technology and cyclone washeries; the use of coal for thermal efficiency and lower emissions, embracing fluidised bed combustion for alternative uses of coal, including coal liquefaction; and the manufacture and use of coal products – for example, the production from coal of caprolactam (used in nylon manufacture);

"**Management Science and Education** – mechanised coal mining being a continuous process, the NCB Operational Research Executive (derived from the WW2 Field Investigation Group) was one of the leaders in using scientific analysis to understand the vital systems required to improve coal flows from the underground to the surface. The NCB also ran its own 'corporate university' – a staff college, a ladder plan for people to study, develop skills and receive qualifications, in order to rise from the most junior levels of employee to the most senior;

"**Computer Science** – through its Compower subsidiary, NCB was one of the UK's – indeed the world's – leaders in industrial computer power. It used some of the most sophisticated mainframe computers of their time to run the management systems and payroll, and also to provide analytic power for systems analysis of coal flows from the coal face to the surface. It was one of the first employers to adopt word-processing and paper-free technologies for internal record-keeping and communications."

Fig.9:
NCB Board Lunch, 1960s.
Includes (*std, LH, l. to rt.*):
C.G.Shepherd, Board Member
for Industrial Relations;
Chairman, Lord Robens;
(*RH, Front to back*):
John Brass; Wilfred Miron;
Dep.Chairman, Derek Ezra;
John Marsh; Leslie Grainger

Paul Glover continues: 'the skills required of the Chairman of the enterprise were of a different order and embraced management of complex political and economic realities. This Memoir attempts to identify what qualities made it possible for Derek Ezra to undertake what will later be described by contemporaries as an "impossible job". Before tackling that daunting task, the narrative has to consider the final elements in the jigsaw: 'Skills, Staff, and Style.

'Skills': in including Skills in the McKinsey model, the authors had in mind the capturing of crucial attributes which had made the company what it was. The National Coal Board was created as a coal mining monopoly – the essential skills were related to the tasks involved in the mining of coal. The management of a mine required specific qualifications laid down by law, and the ability to motivate a labour force – with all that that entailed – training, discipline in a dangerous environment, and a rewards system. The way in which NCB developed systems to train and develop will re-appear in this short summary.

'Staff': Paul Glover, former Director General of Staff at the NCB, has written that 'when Derek Ezra became Chairman of the Board there were about 15,000 managers in the proper sense of the word - people responsible for making other people's skills productive – and there were about 300,000 other employees. It is hard to realise that an industrial employer of this magnitude then existed in the UK, alongside the NHS and the military. A leader for this size of organisation is today only found in the largest multinationals, or in the direct public sector. The NCB's Chairman had a responsibility for all, and in a sense was their 'Leader'. However, two groups of the managerial staff were more relevant to this enquiry than others: firstly, the Staff Officers working with him in his Private Office – their account is in Chapters 4 and 5.

'With few exceptions, those who served in the Chairman's Office in the NCB rose to senior positions inside and/or later outside the industry. They were, with one or two exceptions, graduates and were handpicked. The second significant group is composed of the Board members who served with Derek, and the 25 to 30 senior staff – Directors General, Area Directors, and Managing Directors of major off-line activities. In 1976, 30 years after nationalisation, of the 30 most senior executives only four had had substantial managerial experience outside the industry: 12 were mining engineers, all of whom had entered the industry after 1945. There were four accountants and three other professionals.

'The top team was the outcome of the necessity to develop, within the industry, managers recruited directly from the Universities or other professional training, and from the policy to first advertise all jobs internally. In the mid-1970s as many as 300 graduates of all disciplines were recruited annually. The composition of the Board itself altered during the 1970s. From the earliest days of nationalisation, Area Directors had been Mining Engineers. When Derek left the Chairmanship, all full-time Board Members were Mining Engineers – except for Brian Harrison, Finance Board Member. Changes of composition had begun in 1967 when on the retirement of Cyril Roberts, the Staff portfolio was taken over by the Board Member for Mining, W.V.Sheppard. When Derek succeeded as Deputy Chairman, he retained the Marketing portfolio; when he became Chairman, Donald Davies, an Area Director, was appointed to the Board and took the portfolio. Later, when Cliff Shepherd, a former NUM Officer, retired as Industrial Relations Board Member, he was replaced by Jimmy Cowan, another Area Director. Finally, on his retirement, the Board Member for Science, Dr Joe Gibson, was not replaced. It must be questioned whether Derek Ezra's vision and aspirations were shared by all the mining engineers. The composition of the Board certainly changed during his time.

'Style': from the start of his career Derek Ezra had realized that the traditional adversarial approach to industrial matters in the UK had to change – 'them and us'. He had first encountered that simple truth in his time in the army. Then, as outlined in the Introduction, he furthered that experience under the NCB's auspices for four years as their francophone representative at the ECSC in Luxembourg. (As an interpolation here, these were among the happiest days in his life, enjoying the embryonic, idealistic European atmosphere in the many regular discussions, all of which had to be reported back to the Board in succinct two-page monthly Reports. They also gave him and Julie the opportunity for a lifelong yardstick for good – but explicitly garlic-free! – continental cuisine at the "Cravat Hotel", and at the week-ends to explore many parts of Europe, as they emerged from the effects of a long war).

'He saw too in Europe how the trade unions had established a new role. The French and German coal and steel union representatives would attend Consultative Committee meetings but say nothing until the end. At Question Time they would invariably come out with a set-piece statement prepared well in advance, but would not disrupt the proceedings. Derek's amused conclusion was that this may not have achieved anything tangible in the short-term, but at least did no harm: indeed, it did good, because the workforce now knew what was going on, and could truly feel 'involved' with those leading them. This practice contrasted with what was then the norm in the UK. When Derek returned from his European detachment, John Garnett at The Industrial Society was stirring British Industry with the call for "bringing people together".[48] Consultation was implicit and required in the many Acts of Nationalisation; getting constructive arrangements for 'working together' became a hallmark of Derek Ezra's 'Style'. In the Coal Board's staff there were indeed two 'sides' that now needed to sing from the same hymn sheet – the historically predominant 'production' side, and the newly-blossoming 'Marketing' function. Even in the early days, when the emphasis was all on under-production, they certainly needed to be brought together for a common purpose: to sell more coal. The real chance to implement this approach to leadership in industrial relations would only come two decades later, when Derek was in direct communication with the NUM and other Unions, as Deputy Chairman, and then as Chairman.

'One key initiative was to give the Unions all the financial facts about every single pit, over and above the customary agreements to consult both about planned closures, and about all wage settlements. They were thereby at least party to the arguments for any proposed closure, without automatically being cornered into agreement with them for other reasons.

'He tried to apply this thinking wherever he could, notably when he was eventually – against precedent - invited by the NUM to attend their "Big Day": the annual Miners' Gala in the Durham heartland. Derek accepted – on one equally unprecedented condition: that he be allowed to speak. It was common ground that he would not exploit that opportunity by talking about the sacrosanct topic of wages – that was for the established negotiating machinery. Instead he used this heaven-sent but man-contrived moment to speak publicly about the industry's future prospects and the need to exploit its markets. He would take pains to introduce this same thinking – presenting a common front where it was relevant – to the coal trade dealings with Jack Charrington (Chairman of fuel merchants, Charringtons), Charles Clarke, and the Coal Merchants: (*this area will be covered in Chapter 6*)'.

Complementary viewpiont

Setting this thinking in the context of 2014 could be held to be a little anachronistic, but it could equally well be argued that any philosophy worth its salt should be able to stand the scrutiny of time. A number of complementary aspects of Derek Ezra's leadership thinking, as reflected in today's practice, are identified here by Dr Mark Pegg, an ex-NCB Staff Officer, and now CE of The Leadership Foundation for Higher Education, albeit from a time-frame which he modestly describes as 'limited and distant':

'Derek was a leader in business long before business schools and academic thinking had taken hold of the way business is done and business leaders judged.

'His army career introduced him, like many others in business, to thinking about leadership in a military context; this apart, it was relatively unusual for business leaders of his generation to consult business literature or study business as an academic discipline, beyond reading the "*Financial Times*" each day. Business leaders in the 20th century rose to the top without the aid of a business education. Business leadership was largely based on instinct, grounded in experience or adapted from other spheres of life – in political and military leadership.[49]

'Leaders learned pragmatically and from role models in business; even the management consultancy business had not then evolved to help leaders develop the strategy, structure or culture of their business. Leaders relied on their own counsel and social networks to guide them on the way to the top. Derek acknowledged that this was true for him as for many others at his level of responsibility in both the nationalised and private sectors.

'**How then does Derek Ezra rate as a leader? Has he been a great strategic leader in business? As subsequent chapters will reveal, he undoubtedly wins positive and enduring sentiments of admiration, sympathy and support from those who worked closely with him, and few detractors. What did he do to attract this strongly supportive network?**

'As an ex-military man he would understand John Adair's model of action-centred leadership – widely used in the armed forces at the time when he was a leader in business.[50] If one uses this model as a framework, one can examine his role as a leader – how far he succeeded in

managing the tasks he was set; and in working with the management team and motivating the individuals around him. This may help us to evaluate Derek's contribution as a business leader in today's terms. It is often said that leadership cannot be taught, but can be learned; that management is about doing things right and leadership is about doing the right things. Derek's career shows how he was born with many leadership qualities, but that at each stage of the career he evidently learned from his experience to build his leadership skills.

Fig.10: Derek Ezra's continuing emphasis on the whole coal industry's export possibilities, and on joint ventures with allied interests: launch, in Sept 1976, of Coal Processing Consultants, ['CPC'] a partnership company for coal utilisation and processing technologies, between NCB [Coal Products] Ltd, and Woodall-Duckham, member of the Power & Processing Group of Babcock & Wilcox Ltd. *Signing* (with NCB Chairman) John King (future Lord King and Ch, British Airways, and thus fellow-NICG member), Ch, Babcock & Wilcox. *Witnesses (l. to rt.)* R.Dean, Ch, Woodall-Duckham and Ch. 'CPC'; T.Carlile, MD, Babcock & Wilcox; L.Grainger (NCB Board Member for Science, & Ch., NCB [Coal Products] Ltd; D.Grey, ('CPC'); D.Davison, (MD, NCB [Coal Products] Ltd and Dep.Ch., 'CPC'). [Courtesy Babcock Power & Processing Group]

'His leadership style was modest and understated. He spoke quietly, rarely raised his voice, and was not given to emotionally charged interventions. In meetings, his chairmanship was dominant but low-key, quiet, not charismatic in the traditional sense, preferring to work away at the problem, involving and engaging the team, going round the table, hearing the arguments, and ensuring that a debate was summarised, decisions taken, actions agreed' (a view endorsed in later chapters). 'He relied a great deal on his powerful analytical ability – using his intellect, cleverness and quick-witted skills to unravel problems. From the beginning, he was interested in the bigger picture: not just the business itself or even the sector, but in where it fitted in the wider economy, in the UK, in Europe and globally – the political as well as the economic, social, and technological implications of decisions. And as a marketer, he has always understood the political and public relations impact of his leadership and decisions – the implications not just for Ministers but also for Parliament, for industry, and for customers. His political intelligence as a leader helped him considerably. In a public corporation it is an essential skill, and he knew instinctively how to manage the political dimension of business decisions, and how to promote the ideas contained in them to gain 'buy-in' and support for the implementation of his plans.

'Derek gave interviews for the Press easily, showing a reassurance, and confidence to inspire confidence, and to stand up to the rigour of cross-examination by journalists. He had a very effective voice for radio – a communicator one-to-one rather than to large groups – conversational style rather than soap-box. He regularly appeared on the BBC "Today" programme on Radio 4, known for setting the agenda each day for the decision-makers and opinion-formers. He wanted to lay out the case for '**Plan for Coal**' – to build the public profile for the coal industry. He had been a great believer that it is not enough to have a great case, but that you also need to promote it; that if you say the same thing often enough, people will begin to remember and believe it: for example, that major investment in coal made enormous economic sense; that productivity was improving; and that the coal industry was delivering performance improvement to justify the faith put in it by the nation. Soon journalists were quoting these arguments and data in their own commentaries on the nation's energy strategy.

'His upbringing, early years and military career showed him to be a resilient and determined character which became even more important for him as a business leader. It was not enough to have a '**Plan for Coal**', but you need huge persistence – to keep pressing an issue, with the power of repetition – in cogent, concise and memorable statements. You needed to lobby the key decision-makers such as Ministers, but also to convince the wider public, and particularly consumers, to have trust in '**Plan for Coal**'; and at the same time to persuade the Board itself, the management team, and the mineworkers, to deliver the security of the nation's fuel supply after the global oil crisis.

'His peer group, captains of industry of his generation, often preferred to have a low public profile – to stay in the background. Many of the more prominent ones, leaders of the large private sector industries, provided an interesting contrast – powerful in what some might say was an autocratic approach to leadership. He was a leader when there were different expectations about the accountability of business leaders. They tended to emerge through social elites, and from self-perpetuating oligarchies, and there was much less public scrutiny. Leaders combined the Chairman and Chief Executive roles, without fear of criticism; indeed there was then some expectation that leaders would take up all the powers of leadership and deliver shareholder value. Shareholder scrutiny, the power to challenge leaders, was limited. If anything, there was far more accountability for leaders in the public corporations.

'Derek's was quite different to this contemporary style; more empowering and engaging, bringing people with him, promoting a more involving kind of leadership to his management team, and very different to the prevailing orthodoxy, even in the more publicly accountable

Fig.11: New Selby coalfield, Yks, 1980: 23 km diversion of East Coast mainline to by-pass coalfield; (*l. to rt.*) Sir Derek Ezra, Sir Peter Parker (Ch., British Rail); F. Paterson, BR Eastern Region; G.England (Ch., CEGB). [Courtesy BR]

world of the nationalised industry. His peer group included some iconic figures – Lord Weinstock at GEC;[51] Lord Beeching at ICI and British Rail,[52] and, eponymously, Lord Sainsbury, and Lord Hanson. Derek could not have been more different. Lord Weinstock was, for example, the archetypal technocrat and industrialist of his age, ruthlessly culling uneconomic activities, taking on unions, and purging poor performing managers. He was a forbidding figure, a details man, high on control – his managers and Board members alike dreaded a call at home often late in the evening, as he scoured the books. His hands-on control enabled GEC to prosper, growing a huge cash mountain.

'His equivalents in Nationalised Industry were also very different people, for example Lord Robens and Sir Denis Rooke. Derek was almost the complete opposite of Rooke: a technocrat with an abrasive personal style, who nevertheless, as Derek was the first to acknowledge, achieved remarkable success in bringing North Sea Gas to the nation. Rooke admired practical people, especially those with experience of life outside the City and Whitehall; he often appeared unyielding, unsympathetic to the political world. Derek was at ease with metropolitan life, urbane and comfortable in dealing with political elites; he was also quite unlike the mavericks, the buccaneers of industry – a small group of flamboyant highly personal leaders.

'His generation did produce a limited few who set out to break the mould – like Lord Hanson and Sir James Goldsmith but they were really financiers. From the industrialists, leaders included Sir John Harvey Jones, Sir Freddy Laker of Laker Airways, and Sir Michael Edwardes, first at Chloride and later at British Leyland. These were the exception rather than the rule, in a world of anonymous grey suits. Harvey-Jones was a swashbuckler – a larger-than-life character in every sense, appointed Chairman of ICI because the Board wanted innovation and creativity, to breathe new life into a basic industry that was running out of ideas. What he did have in common with Derek Ezra was a military background (he was a submariner), a radically different vision for his industry, a steely determination to make it happen, and the skill to promote his ideas in the public domain'.

As has already been indicated in the Introduction, Lord Robens, in contrast, had set out his own philosophy in the first of his two books, **Human Engineering**, the main thrust of which was the conclusion in his Foreword: "There is no blueprint which will speedily and effectively solve the many vexed problems of man at his work, but there can be no doubt that where skill and care have been taken to solve these problems, great success has resulted".

The Team

Mark Pegg's analysis continues: 'Business leaders today are set a very high bar for their performance, and are expected to live with very high levels of public scrutiny by shareholders, consumers, regulatory bodies and the media – equipped not just to lead but to be seen to lead, and to be able to justify their position as a leader. Employees expect them to answer the question: "Why should anyone be led by YOU?"[53]

'In Derek's period of leadership, this level of scrutiny was relatively uncommon in business: the exception was for people in his role, the Chairmen of public corporations, simply because of their special status in the "commanding heights" of the economy and the accountability that went with them.

'Why did people follow Derek Ezra? Why did they see him as an authentic leader? These questions will be answered through the testimony of his younger NCB staff officers, in Chapters 4 and 5, but some broad comments can be made. Top Teams have a shared vision, they know where they are going, how to get there, and what the success factors are. Derek's strength was in building the strategic vision, forming the key features, setting the goals, and then bringing the team with him. It was not done through powerful oratory or persuasive tub-thumping speeches. His approach was softer, more thoughtful. He inspired loyalty, commitment and support by offering a clear vision of the way forward, a strong analysis, setting out a case clearly and cogently, bringing people with him, engaging with people. Derek was so well connected to his immediate management team that he earned their respect, and built up tremendous personal loyalty to his vision for the organisation. He commanded meetings with skill as a Chairman, gathering views and summarising the discussion, in order to reach agreement on the required actions, and share in this determination to see things through. At the Press Conferences to report the annual accounts, journalists in the audience would often try to raise issues that would get headlines: the 'misuse' of public money; the pay of senior staff; travel expenses; etc. Derek would always handle these coolly and firmly, and bring the discussion back quickly to the major strategic matters that Coal was facing: the Energy supply that the nation needed; plans for modernising the industry; investment; and never forgetting an emphasis on the skills and energy of the workforce. This was a clear and very public example of one of his leadership skills'.

Sense of direction

The abiding inference from the preceding analyses must be that Derek Ezra's style of leadership was in fact outstanding for its time; indeed that it can stand comparison with the best that today's business world has to offer. As will be apparent below in Chapter 9, it was not for nothing that his Lib. Dem. Peers in the House of Lords were subsequently more than delighted to be able to bring such talents to the benefit of the national debate.

The conclusion to this opening chapter rests with Paul Glover: 'At a Matriculation Ceremony at Oxford, Sir Richard Livingstone, a distinguished classicist, President of Corpus Christi College, and Vice-Chancellor of the University from 1944 to 1947, commended his supplicants to the study of Leadership with these words (translated from his Latin): "The History of civilisation is a catalogue of expeditions led by people with all the qualities of leadership except a sense of direction".[54]

This remark requires consideration in the case of the coal industry during the Ezra chairmanship. Whatever the arguments advanced here, it will be for later generations to decide whether, as a fundamental aspect of Derek Ezra's leadership, his judgment about the long-term future direction for Energy might well be right after all'.

Contributors: Dr Paul Glover, Dr Mark Pegg

CHAPTER 2: COAL AND ENERGY – WRESTLING WITH THE PRACTICALITIES

After a spell on the Board's management training scheme, Malcolm Edwards worked for Derek Ezra as soon as Derek returned from Luxembourg; he subsequently managed the industrial coal market and then added the selling and promotion for home heating. He went on to become Director General of Marketing in 1973, responsible for coal sales to all markets. Later, he was appointed Commercial Director of the reorganised Board of British Coal. He has contributed the following commentary:

'It is not possible to over-estimate the shock that the collapse in oil prices in 1957 gave to the British coal industry. For nearly twenty years before 1957, the industry, the Government and the whole country had only one thought in mind about coal: how to increase production. At the beginning of 1947, the new NCB had taken over an industry run down since the early 1920s. Wrecked by loss of markets overseas and industrial recession at home, prices and income fell, leading to acute labour problems, many public enquiries, changes in organisation, and the collapse of the capital investment vital to sustain an extractive industry. After 1945 it had all changed: access to abundant energy was recognised as the key, first to economic recovery and then to growth for the whole economy. Abundant energy was synonymous with abundant coal.

'The NCB was single-minded in its pursuit of increasing production. It had to sort out the mountain of miscellaneous assets it acquired in 1947: nearly a thousand working pits, and associated operations ranging from coke ovens and chemical plants to firelighters and bricks, 1800 farms and 145,000 houses, and a big interest in the 'National' petrol distribution Company. It was not allowed by Government to raise coal prices to the European level.

'Despite all the practical problems of creating a large new organisation (always underestimated by politicians) it did succeed and by the early 1950s production had once again recovered to the level of the 1920s. Reconstruction of the pits proceeded apace within a coherent **'Plan for Coal'** and a lot more: a serious start was made on fully mechanised mining; a pricing system designed to reflect the 'value in use' to the consumers of thousands of very different coals produced was put in place, and stood the test of time.

Clean Air

'Just as production reached a post-war peak, then within the space of six months the market fell apart. Already the Clean Air Act was starting to take its toll on what traditionally had been coal's largest and most lucrative market, for home heating. The industry struggled to produce the additional smokeless fuel that would now be needed for the new smokeless zones.

'However, it was the collapse in oil prices that wreaked havoc on the business. Not only did the price of heavy fuel oil halve but cheap naptha enabled the gas industry to jettison coal as its feedstock and reduce its costs. Within 18 months, the coal industry lost virtually all the 20m tons a year it had supplied for gas-making, and it had to face intense competition for home heating from rejuvenated gas. Coal distribution had not been brought into public ownership along with coal production due to the resistance of the Co-Op, the biggest coal merchant. Now, instead of having to buy the product of a state monopoly struggling to meet demand, the coal trade could access abundant, cheap and consistent quality oil for its many industrial consumers, and conversion started in earnest, the NCB having sold their interest in the oil business for a trifle to Shell.

'The railways displayed a new enthusiasm to replace steam with diesel ("just for a year or two before electrification"), and quickly another 12m tons of business disappeared. Most seriously, the electricity producers started to plan their new generation of stations, outside the central coalfields, on oil. Stocks of unsold coal at the pits were growing rapidly, to over 36m tons, and total national coal stocks touched the magic figure of 50m tons. It was a major crisis for the industry – the scale was vast, the outcome quite unpredictable, and it was nigh-on impossible to manage, now that every wiseacre in politics and public life pronounced that the NCB must immediately reverse what it had devoted all its efforts to achieve for all its ten years in existence. Viewed with hindsight, the reaction under the leadership of the then chairman, James Bowman, was surprisingly fast and decisive. Indeed, rationalisation was to be much simpler and more efficient within a single organisation. Management started to close the least productive mines to reduce surplus production but worked hard to ensure that, at the same time, the best pits could continue and then grow.

Ezra to Marketing

'If major changes were essential to bring production closer to demand, a total transformation was needed in marketing coal. The sales staff of the NCB were a mixture of old-fashioned salesmen, hardened by the intense competition of the interwar yeas, and a sprinkling that had come into the Board from the joint selling organisations, first voluntary and then in 1930 compulsory, backed by quotas. That experiment had become an unresolved struggle between 'fair shares for all' and 'freedom for the more efficient to prosper', but a great deal had been learned in the process. Overall, the reaction of this mixed bag of staff was enthusiastic for the chance to sell again, to finally get rid of the last remnant of rationing and the blight that this brought to the relationship between the coal industry and all its customers, large and small.

'The change of direction was remarkable. A policy paper by the then Inland Sales Manager, Jim Barratt, was accepted in its entirety by the Board. Not only did it insist that standards of service to all customers needed to be transformed – greater consistency of product, better quality, ready availability and active response to coal's customers throughout the supply chain – but first of any nationalised energy industry it recommended that large consumers should be offered binding contracts with fixed prices, and in some cases discounts from list price. These contracts would be negotiated directly with consumers outside, but not displacing the wholesale trade. The signs of change did convince staff and customers that despite all that had happened for the previous 20 years, the coal industry was still alive to its markets and could once again respond. The Marketing Department was reorganised and instead of representatives of the separate coalfields doing their own selling, all the coal supplied into a single sales region was sold by a single sales team and they were responsible for ensuring that the customers received the right service. The objective was to establish a clear responsibility for delivering the right product to the customer.

'All these were vital changes but they were not enough to manage the upheaval in the market. New blood was needed both to introduce modern marketing, and to ensure future continuity of experience. Now, graduates from the Board's respected training scheme were encouraged to go into sales rather than, as before, into personnel. Then it was remembered that an outstanding graduate had already been working quietly for years in an outpost of the NCB empire. So, Derek was summoned back from an idyllic experience as NCB representative to the new Coal and Steel Community in Luxembourg. His first job in London was as Deputy Inland Sales Manager, trying to establish just what coal we were supplying to the big industrial consumers with several plants (and most of these companies did not know either). Then he was transferred to the London and Southern Sales Region as Deputy to Frank Wilkinson, an old-stager in selling coal in hard times. Quickly afterwards, when Frank was promoted to the Board to take overall charge of marketing. Derek succeeded him as Manager in London and the South.

'London had been the richest market for coal, particularly for home heating. The leaders of the distributive trade there, led by Jack Charrington, enjoyed very high status. They were careful to maintain excellent connections particularly with Conservative politicians, whether in power or in opposition. Derek found that he got on well with the leaders of the trade and this continued throughout his career, for many years meeting them every month, consulting, explaining.

'It came as a distinct surprise to the staff that very soon afterwards, Derek was brought back to Head Office in 1961 as Director General of Marketing, responsible for all the executive operations. This changing scene was soon overshadowed by the arrival of the larger-than-life Alf Robens. Persuaded by wily Prime Minister Macmillan, calling on him to perform a national service to pilot the coal industry through its latest troubles, somehow Robens had to develop the morale necessary for a healthy, vibrant, modern coal industry, confident in its future at just the same time as many pits had to be shut and manpower reduced. It required a very large public figure to pull this off and it has to be said that living in the court of Alf Robens brought to mind what life must have been like living with Henry VIII. With a non-stop public presence on radio, television and in the newspapers, Robens was full of ideas about every aspect of the Board's operations, some before their time. His ideas about how modern marketing could be applied to promoting coal never stopped coming. Derek Ezra, he judged correctly, was the ideal person to put the programme into practice. Derek presided over years of heightened marketing activity.

'So, what happened? It may have been defensive all the way for the 15 years of low oil prices. Facing such a difficult market, it was a remarkably successful performance. Sales did contract but slowly. Backed by an intense drive to control costs – "three (old) pence per therm" was the watchword – every threat provided a sales opportunity. New smoke control zones required all old open fires to be replaced, but active selling at all levels of new high-efficiency glass-fronted stoves allowed so many homes to enjoy not only ample hot water on tap: the same fire could provide full central heating for the ordinary council house. After all, the new pumped small-bore central heating that made this practical had been an invention of the coal industry's laboratories. For the private householder, finance was made available by the NCB in association with Forward Trust. All this provided another opportunity to solve another challenge. A fall in orders from the steel industry for blast furnace coke, produced by the Board's coke ovens, led to the most vigorous drive to persuade customers to burn it in those glass-fronted stoves, under the new brand name "Sunbrite". There were disappointments: efforts to develop a stove burning ordinary coal smokelessly just failed to overcome problems in practical operation by ordinary people in ordinary houses.

'In 1962, the Approved Coal Merchants Scheme was introduced, and this was followed by Approved Installers and later by Approved Chimney Sweeps. To sell coal required first the sale of the fires to burn it. With no showrooms of our own, the builders' merchants pressed the Board to subsidise the sale of coal fires and boilers. This had the quite unexpected result in 1965 of a direct NCB investment in the builders' merchants, J.H.Sankey. This grew into a country-wide operation; it eventually formed a major component of the Wickes chain. Robens was always suspicious of the coal distributive trade and when the opportunity arose he decided to buy into the distributive business of one of the most enterprising pre-war colliery combines,

Amalgamated Anthracite Holdings. This soon grew into the very large British Fuel Company. These extensions of the NCB's interests caused such major perturbation out in the marketplace that it required all Derek's credibility and honesty to calm nerves.

'The switch to high-rise flats by many town councils led the NCB to look abroad for solutions in a programme to promote district heating from a central boiler plant, coal-fired. This programme was not without its difficulties in implementation, with problems in the design of pipework and in metering, and not least because of the abrupt changes in local government organisation, but the drive went on to find ways round these obstacles. Supporting all this effort with home heating was, for the first time for coal, national advertising vigorously promoting the benefits for everyone of continuing to enjoy a "living fire", at the same time as enjoying economical whole-house heating. Coal for industry featured prominently as well. Backed by a strong promotional campaign ("Every Ford Starts on Coal", "Tate and Lyle are Sweet on Coal". etc) contract cover grew and grew until it included the best and biggest in British industry: ICI, the cement companies, Courtaulds, the paper industry, Fords, and many hundreds of other coal consumers. They felt at last that they were being valued by a nationalised industry and treated as individuals. Behind all this work in the marketplace was a research and development programme developing modern ways of burning and handling coal which was cleaner, more efficient and which did not require constant attention. The NCB Technical Advisory Service was second to none in the field. The huge changes brought about by Dr Beeching required a major response from coal – after all, the railways had been first created to transport coal and it remained their greatest freight. Together with CEGB and British Rail, changes at the pits allowed whole trains of large wagons to be loaded on the move. The end of so many railway sidings brought investment by the NCB in concentration depots, away from the coalfield, offering small customers the full range of its products.

'The sales challenges and the responses went beyond the NCB's core coal business. The Board was a large brick producer, second only to London Brick. The new enthusiasm for industrialised building endangered demand for our product, so the NCB turned to develop prefabricated brick panels, combining the good looks and wearing properties of brick with the size and efficiency of large-scale modern construction. Most coal was now conveyed underground by belt and that had resulted in another problem: what could we do with worn-out belting? That was solved, at least partially, by using it to make a flexible damp course seal. Then interest in damp courses led the NCB laboratories to pioneer the injected damp course now widely used to damp-proof old buildings.

Sublime struggle

'Much of this frenetic activity may have seemed quite a sublime struggle at the time but it did have its ridiculous moments. A paint was developed in an NCB laboratory capable of transmitting electricity and therefore, given a little adaptation, it was enthusiastically declared that here was a way of providing very low capital-cost background heating. With great excitement, an office in the NCB headquarters was treated with the new wonder paint, and an obscure section of the Finance Department moved in. Somehow, in spite of its admirable qualities, it overdid the heating. About to catch fire, it required the urgent attention of the fire brigade. Also, the notorious incontinence of koala bears had disastrous consequences at an elaborately prepared photo shoot, praising the pleasure of a real fire, featuring the Chairman's wife in her new high fashion suede boots.

'Despite all this effort, the real key to successful long-term coal sales lay with the new generation of base-load power stations. Coal in the central coalfields was both abundant and still competitive, and slowly but surely the stations were built. For the NCB the price of achieving this was that the prices for central coalfield coal hardly moved in the 1960s; indeed, for East Midlands coal they were unchanged for nine years. However, coal was still in surplus throughout this period, and to try and mitigate that problem, there were annual wrangles about excess stocking to be negotiated with Arthur Hawkins of the CEGB. These cast a shadow over all Derek's marketing activities.

'Encouraged by Prime Minister Harold Macmillan, the first deal was negotiated in 1962. In exchange for more tonnage and a decision not to convert two stations to oil, a particularly complicated way was found to effectively reduce some coal prices. Each of these deals was for a year only, so every year thereafter the same negotiating process had to be endured. As the price of heavy fuel oil showed no signs of increasing, it was very difficult to keep the show on the road, but it did stay there and as a result, when oil prices rose in later years, the country benefitted greatly by the string of very large low-coast coal stations.

'Relations with the CEGB were not helped by the very public row about the nuclear AGR programme and in particular the proposal to build a nuclear power station close to the Durham coalfield at Seaton Carew. Robens cast serious doubts on the station's economics, countering with the offer of Durham coal at low prices on long-term contract. It did not succeed. It took electricity privatisation 25 years later to reveal that the coal stations had been cross-subsidising nuclear on a grand scale – equivalent to the total cost of the coal which would have produced the equivalent power, the cost of transporting it to the power station, and even then there would be £10 a tonne left over towards the cost of burning it. Exasperation at the failure to secure this investment for the North-East led Robens to be even more determined to secure one of the aluminium smelters promoted by the "white-hot technology" Labour Government. The NCB provided a site and it would have had a dedicated coal-fired power station supplied under a long-term contract with guaranteed prices. The optimistic projections of the cost of mining the coal needed were not borne out by experience and it required many hours of negotiation in changed market conditions to bring the relationship between buyer and seller to reasonable balance, but it did make a significant contribution to the economy of the North-East for 40 years. In Scotland, another long-term deal had been struck. Again, PM Macmillan had indicated that the Government would like to see the new base-load station at Longannet burning coal rather than oil as was planned, and here, uniquely in the UK, a power station was built, taking coal direct from a new mine next door.

'Not to be forgotten was a very attractive project which sadly the politicians aborted: the NCB investment in North Sea Gas. After initial reluctance, the NCB took a direct interest in exploring for gas in the southern North Sea. After all, the NCB knew about drilling offshore: they had done it for years for coal, and from that and through investment in International Mining Consultants, they had developed unrivalled expertise in seismic assessment of mineral reserves, which in turn has been deployed around the world. A small investment started to produce gas in 1972; it was very profitable, despite selling to a monopoly buyer. Unfortunately, the Government decided that this deviation from the coal business was not to be permitted, and it was taken away from the NCB with the only compensation being the amount of our investment, and no consideration of the loss of future profits.

Robens and Ezra

'Everything about the Robens era was high profile and public, and he managed to override any opposition. However, the harassment, mainly on financial matters, that he had to endure from the civil service, he found particularly irksome. In this way he appreciated in many ways perhaps the greatest quality of Derek and he became his Deputy. At his side he had an intellectual heavyweight who was more than a match for the debating skills of the best civil servants. Derek was given a major role in counter-attacking, resisting the enthusiasm in the Department to try to run the industry from a back seat, (a talent found seriously deficient when they did take charge of the last round of colliery closures in 1992). Robens could concentrate on what he did best – getting across a contradictory message: the industry had a splendid future because it was making great progress, but he had to close losing pits at the same time. At the end of the Robens era, there was no contest for his successor and Derek took over in 1971.

'It proved to be a baptism of fire. From 1957 to the end of the 1960s, the NUM under Will Paynter had been persuaded to accept relatively low wage increases so that UK coal prices could be kept low, more coal could be sold, and therefore more jobs preserved. Only the political astuteness and sheer dominance of Robens kept things under control for so long. In the process, from the top of the industrial wages league in 1957, mineworkers slipped right down the ladder. In particular, resentment built up in the most productive and moderate part of the industry. Traditionally, high productivity had been rewarded with high wages through piecework. However, day wage became all the fashion in British personnel circles in the 1950s and 1960s - machines determined the workload, everyone should be paid the same for the same job, regardless of what they produced. So, for years, wages in the moderate, most productive central coalfield were held down while the rest caught up. Added to this mixture were the activities of the hard left from outside, like Bert Ramuelson, identifying and grooming young recruits to undermine the old guard of the Union, spectacularly successful with Scargill in Yorkshire.

'The mixture finally boiled over late in 1971. The 1971/2 strike caught out everyone in the authority. There was public surprise at how far the mineworkers' wages had fallen behind and sympathy for them, and with the support of the media which had a distinct distaste for the new 'Selsdon style' of Conservatism; the mineworkers won, much to their surprise. Their victory was total. All the elaborate Government contrivances to restrain wage inflation collapsed, mineworkers' wages soared after years of containment, costs shot up, and the NCB faced nothing sort of financial chaos – large losses, with no solution in sight. It was impossible to manage.

'After little more than a year trying unsuccessfully to understand the implications of what had happened, equally surprisingly a solution began to emerge. It was indeed notable that the even more decisive 1974 strike, with its three-day week, and the fall of the Heath Government, coincided precisely with OPEC's decision to raise oil prices five-fold and to double prices for the all-important heavy fuel oil. Notwithstanding all the doubts, the new prices held. So, by autumn 1974 the NCB had been able to cover its greatly increased costs by big price increases for central coalfield coal. NCB prices rose by 80% in total, but British coal ended up more competitive than a year before. In following years, high oil prices continued and then in 1979 were doubled again. This increase did much damage to the world economy and pushed it into serious depression.

'New factors dominated the British coal industry in the years after 1974. The NCB under Derek's leadership set out what investment would be required to produce the coal which they believed the country would need in the changed market. The new '**Plan for Coal**' had the advantage of all the knowledge gained over the previous 25 years. The assumptions were optimistic but not unreasonable. The 1979 oil price rise, however, produced an even more enthusiastic response from the NCB in '**Plan 2000**' and then the targets for the industry did become unreasonable. A serious start was made immediately on persuading industrial consumers to convert back to coal plants lost when oil prices were low. This gathered momentum and ingenious ways were found to get around the virtual ban on capital investment in the late 1970s. Conversion was helped later by a government grant.

'Most important, the new market conditions produced a new and much more fruitful relationship with the NCB's biggest customer, the CEGB. The first of these arrangements in 1979 exchanged a willingness by CEGB to buy 75m tonnes a year for the next five years, in return for the NCB keeping its prices in line with the Retail Prices Index. This matched the movement in wage rates which the NCB would probably have to grant with the electricity prices that were likely to be acceptable to the public. The original agreement was modified several times in the following decade, most importantly to provide an answer to the increasing availability of international steam coal, and it provided a firm foundation for sales and income on which the NCB could base its operations.

'The oil companies decided that heavy fuel oil had no longer any future in power generation, and that they should move into the international steam coal business in a big way with characteristically very large investment in distant countries, backed by their skills in low-cost, long-distance transport. Shell, Exxon, Total and the rest may have had varying success with their new coal mines but in the process they transformed the international steam coal business. This was competition which the NCB faced increasingly but effectively in the 1980s to hold on to its all-important sales to power stations. The NCB was less successful in curtailing imports of coking coal by the British Steel Corporation (BSC). British reserves of medium volatile coking coal were becoming exhausted. Valiant efforts were made by the NCB to convince the BSC that careful blending of what was a wide variety of coking coal still left in Britain was just as good as the real thing. This failed. Now that steel plants had been relocated close to deep water, mainly to allow high quality iron ore to be imported economically, BSC concluded that they might just as well also import prime coking coal, especially as Australia was offering first-class quality coal from Queensland. Even so, the NCB did not give up – it made contracts for what coking coal it had left, and identified high fluidity as a special advantage of the British coking coal remaining. Not able to compete with the new supplies of Australian prime coking coal, it decided to join the opposition by developing a new coking coal mine in Queensland.

'At the same time the NCB made great efforts to get round a serious and increasing problem in their main market. The power stations might burn the bulk of its output, but the NCB had no direct involvement in how that coal was burnt. This was now becoming an increasingly contentious issue. The base-load power stations built in the 1960s and 1970s worked well. The problems of unreliability in the 1950s had been completely solved, but the concern about the effect of the emissions from these stations was now becoming serious. At first it was all about acid rain. For years, the CEGB contested that it was not a problem. It took the NCB to set up a large pilot plant in the 1980s at Grimethorpe to explore new ways of burning coal at high efficiency and with much reduced noxious emissions. This was ten years before this issue seriously crossed the public mind in the shape of global warming. The start that the NCB made to identify ways of mitigating emissions from very large coal plant gave the wherewithal for the coal industry to respond constructively to increasing public concern about the burning of coal. It is one of the unfortunate casualties of privatisation that this accumulated experience and effort ceased totally and abruptly just when it was needed most.

'Politicians of all varieties were determined not to risk a repeat of the 1974 dispute. Certainly the Labour Government which came to office in 1974 would never have countenanced any move by the management to confront the NUM by trying to close pits which were still losing money despite the much increased coal prices justified by the market. The management had no option but to face this fact and to deploy their main technical efforts to develop new methods of underground mining which had the potential to deliver much greater productivity and lower costs. So the concept of heavy duty mining was developed. They had the advantage of working in an industry which had only rarely resisted the introduction of new production techniques because they brought greater safety and required less effort. For the time being, however, the NUM were in such a strong position that they could capture most of the 'economic rent' of this new investment. Productivity failed to rise in the early 1970s despite the investment and Derek's vehement urgings. It is worth recalling that other parts of British heavy industry shared the same problem. Technical progress went ahead - the commercial benefits lagged behind. In the British coal industry the potential was not realised until the 1980s.

'Thoughtful caution in general and a determination not to risk a repeat of the 1974 dispute in particular characterised the early years of the incoming Conservative Government under Mrs Thatcher. The public reaction to the winter of discontent, and the arrival of North Sea oil in quantity they believed offered a once-in-a-lifetime chance to sort out the British economic malaise. They were not prepared to see this opportunity derailed by the NUM unless and until they had overwhelming public backing, and in particular a solid blue-collar vote behind them to go ahead with economic reform and, especially, reform of the Trade Unions.

'Throughout Derek's tenure as Chairman, the NCB were having to deal with one of the most artful union leaders in modern British history. It was a creative form of artfulness, an instinct to make the best of almost any turn of events, however unexpected or indeed unwelcome. Joe Gormley was intent not to allow the hard left to make any more progress than they had already. Determined to remain in charge of the situation, he would take any opportunity to do so that was available. Perhaps his greatest service was in 1977 when he was able to manoeuvre the resumption of incentive payments despite intense opposition from the hard left. It was the breakthrough, at first only in one small coalfield that the management pursued with vigour and it contributed greatly to the Union splitting in 1984. Gormley was quite realistic about the problems that the British coal industry faced, in particular from the new international coal trade and he made this an important part of his final public performance.

Last performances

'Right at the end of Derek's tenure, the crisis of 1981 showed all the elements in play for the last time before the changes in leadership of both NCB and NUM. The 1979 oil price rise had driven the world economy into a major slump, and Britain was hit even further by the exceptional strength of sterling, following the arrival of North Sea oil. The traditional British heavy industries, never the most profitable end of private enterprise, were badly hit. In the space of six months the NCB lost over two million tonnes of business just because of permanent factory closures, and this was in addition to the reduced coal demand following lower activity generally throughout the economy.

'So it was decided that preparations should be made to accelerate colliery closures already scheduled. Gingerly this was presented to a meeting of all the Unions in February 1981. Gormley signalled that he did not see what all the fuss was about as this did not seem much different from the normal round of closures of "exhausted" collieries which took place every year in such an old extractive industry. As the meeting became more heated, Gormley announced that he would come round to the management's side. Soon everyone decided that they should talk urgently to the Minister, David Howell. The Government were alarmed at the prospect of a dispute in the coal industry once again getting out of control in a repetition of 1973/74. As the excitement needed to be reduced while the Prime Minister went away on her first visit to President Reagan, Howell was told to convene a big meeting of all the parties to calm things down; to assure everyone that the Government viewed the coal industry as important to the economy the Government would carefully study the proposals put forward to deal with what was a difficult situation arising out of the state of the world economy.

'The meeting duly took place in a characteristically gloomy room in the Department of Energy. The Minister spoke at length to a carefully worded ministerial script. At the end of this, Joe Gormley asked to be excused. Everyone assumed that he had had an urgent call to the gents and helpful directions were given. In fact, while all the press were corralled in the Department's Press Room, awaiting the official statement, he descended to the back of the building to meet a couple of TV crews and give his version of events. He was pleased to assure the public that the Government had understood the seriousness of the situation and the wisdom of the case put forward by the Union to help the coal industry through. They had conceded all the issues that the Union had raised; in particular the Government would help solve the financial problems facing the industry and coal imports would be cut. Most important, in recognition of what the Government had done, he could now tell the lads that there as no need for any industrial action. Within a few minutes this was out on the 7 pm news. The wrath of the PM may have been palpable but the Government could not possibly contradict what Gormley had said. It was the last performance of a great character actor. It also spelt the end of the political career of David Howell, and various members of Coal Division were soon banished to distant parts of the civil service. Those who have referred disparagingly to the "Derek and Joe" show forget the circumstances of the time. In fact, that was the only show practicable.

'However, all this time Derek was wrestling with the practicalities of managing an industry which, despite the problems inside and out, technically was progressing rapidly, was holding on to its key markets, and was getting organised to respond to the emerging concern about the effect of emissions from large coal plant on the environment. Derek left no doubt in anyone's mind, inside or outside the industry, of the commitment of the Board's management to the future of British coal, which the public was still convinced was a great British asset, to preserving the physical access to the best part of those reserves, and to the accumulated skills which were required if the coal was to be produced efficiently and in the quantity needed. The tactics of the management may change to match the market but that was only to preserve the business.

'Derek Ezra's self-evident sincerity and long and single-minded pursuit of his objective laid an excellent foundation for his successor, Norman Siddall, when he put the Board's management to the ultimate test. Not only did he persuade the workforce to back the management's proposals and reject the Union's recommendation once, but he did it twice'.

Contributor: Malcolm Edwards

CHAPTER 3:
THE NCB CAREER – 'OUTSIDER' TO 'INSIDER'

Derek Ezra's time at the helm of the NCB could be depicted as an evolution from an initial status as very much an 'outsider', to the ultimate perception of him as a committed 'insider' to the industry he loved. (The tight regime, and the impact of 'The Office' – explored below in Chapters 4 and 5 – whereby he ran this industry's Board, raise some interesting questions for management observers).

These recollections come from two senior members of his management team who worked closely with him, through the words of Dr Paul Glover, but also embracing comments by Brian Harrison, NCB Board Member from 1976 to 1985. (They need to be read in conjunction with the summary of the main events of the Ezra decade, in 'Timelines: 4'). Included also are the observations of a leading contemporary politician. Each saw different aspects of Derek Ezra's instinctive 'leadership philosophy', outlined in the opening chapter. (Paul Glover was NCB Director General of Staff from 1974 to 1985, reporting functionally to the Deputy Chairman, Paul's experience of his Chairman extended in total over fifteen years. His relationship was rarely day-to-day, but ranged from the politically charged to the purely functional. Occasionally – and by comparison with other testimony in this Memoir, quite rarely – it took place on a social level too, involving his wife, Angela, and Derek's wife, Julie:

Chairman of the Board, Chairman *and* 'Chief Executive'

'The way Derek Ezra executed a *de facto* 'Chief Executive' role combined with his titular "Chairmanship", in today's jargon, is central to understanding how the NCB worked under him and his 'Office'. Even if this demanding dual role was then quite normal, it was all the more important to Derek Ezra that he did his homework. His Staff Officers (*Chapters 4 and 5*) and other colleagues will observe later how for weeks in advance Derek would work diligently on any case that needed to be argued. Around the Board table, Derek was fully in control of an agenda, and ran meetings strictly in accordance with it. Derek's own view of what he himself termed his "style" at the Board table was simple: "I set myself the aim of not being a 'bumbler' at Board meetings, ensuring that clear conclusions were reached on each item. This avoided the practice of 'seeing what the Minutes said', leaving some agenda items 'in the air' until Minutes appeared. I always listened to the viewpoints that those round the table wanted to express. I then summed up at the end of each meeting. In this way, everyone now knew where I stood on any particular issue, and just as importantly, everyone knew where the Board's collective judgment now lay." (This same approach, bearing all the imprint of a sound early army training, will also be apparent later, in the recollections of Derek in his role as a contributor to House of Lords debates).

'Derek Ezra recognized his role as Chairman – the man in charge. Possibly because of that, he sometimes came across, perhaps necessarily, as very much a loner. It will be evident that Derek chose only to unveil the softer and often humorous side of his nature to a limited few among his colleagues and friends. That side of him was still a real part of his complex personality, but was not a facet that he elected to present, or perhaps could afford to present, to the outside world.

'The setting in which the Chairman of this nationalised industry in particular had to operate was lonely – always political, ever critical and media-dominated, and often downright hostile.

The early years of nationalisation

'Over its first 15 years, the pattern of relationships and management structure in the NCB under the successive chairmanships of Lord Hyndley, Sir Hubert Houldsworth and Sir James Bowman was determined by the need to maximise production. Initially, Board Members came largely from outside; DGs were appointed to manage major functions. Divisional Boards were established for the major coalfields, and supervised the General Managers of 48 Areas. In the early years, an initial precedent had been set in the politically stable post-nationalisation era by Lord Hyndley, through a weekly 'Chairman's lunch' with his Minister, "Manny" Shinwell. Derek recalls that in the 1970s he preferred to maintain regular contact with the Ministry through its ongoing cohort of civil servants, rather than with their flux of constantly-changing political masters. 'In the immediate post-war years, the newly-nationalised industries attracted into their service many who had seen the war years through in the armed services. In the Coal Board these included Derek Ezra (introduced into the industry by Val Duncan – *see Chapter 11*) and whose career in marketing was settled by the then Secretary of the Marketing Department, Harold Hodgson. The intake also included Cyril Roberts who became the Board Secretary, and later the Board Member for Staff.

Fig.12 Birth pangs of new production-oriented NCB (represented by 'Shinwell & Co., Best Coal'). (*top l.*) winter 1946/7: weather crisis and transport failure, causing fuel shortage. Illingworth political cartoon of Labour Govt: (*top rt.*) Aneurin Bevan; (*rt.c.*) Stafford Cripps; "Going to the Dogs"; (*lower rt.*) Hugh Dalton
[Courtesy, **"The Fueller's Tale"**: Editor's collection]

'The foundations laid down in those early years of the NCB had a profound effect on the freedom of action of those who succeeded. The '**Plan for Coal**', published in 1950, created the framework for capital investment for 20 years. The price structures for industrial, carbonisation and domestic coals – based on 'value in use' – had a major effect on the market. The negotiation of the first national day-wage agreement set the pattern of wage negotiations for decades to come. Research facilities covering miners' health, mechanisation and coal utilisation, were all established in the early years, and managers, officials, and administrative staff today still know the benefits of the fully funded Superannuation Scheme inaugurated in 1949. The management framework of the industry in the early years was profoundly influenced by the work of the Deputy Chairman, Sir Arthur Street, a former Permanent Secretary of the Air Ministry. Alfred Robens became Chairman of the National Coal Board in 1961; Derek Ezra was then DG of Marketing at Hobart House, the Board's London HQ. He had succeeded to this post in 1960, after a career centred on marketing in the London Office after 4-5 years in Europe. In 1965 he became Board Member for Marketing. *(In 1961, I was Assistant Secretary to the West Midlands Divisional Board, having entered a more formal Administrative Assistant [the 'AAs'] Scheme in 1953).*

The marketing revolution and the Organisation

'Robens' "ten-year stint" saw many changes in the industry. A major reorganisation eliminating Divisions, creating new, bigger Areas, was announced in 1966. During his years as DG and Board Member for Marketing, Derek had already made many changes to the marketing organisation – creating Sales Regions and Districts. His changes in some respects anticipated the major reorganisation of the mining activities in 1967 but he certainly saw their effects.

'As the new organisation took shape, he became Deputy Chairman, succeeding Sir Humphrey Browne, who, with Cyril Roberts, then Board Member for Staff, had seen the reorganisation through. Sir Humphrey, a mining engineer, as DG of Production had produced the first '**Plan for Coal**'. The Plan, coalfield by coalfield, outlined the ways in which output could be built up to over 200 million tons per year, and was the starting point for the strategic aim of creating a viable industry of this size. Robens and Browne were not, however, happy bedfellows – they came from different worlds: Robens from Trade Unions and Politics – Browne from Management and Mining Engineering. They were, however, essential complements in an industry which was changing fast. Robens paid tribute to Browne in fulsome terms in his autobiographical study, **Ten Year Stint**. He also recognised the considerable contribution over the years of a true mandarin – Cyril Roberts – a close ally of Browne's who left the Board as its Staff Member at about the time that Browne moved on.

'In suggesting Derek Ezra as his Deputy (the appointment made by Richard Marsh, the Labour Minister of Fuel and Power), Robens clearly had in mind someone with whom he could work - a potential successor. But Derek didn't inherit all the influence and power which Browne had exercised. The Staff portfolio was transferred to W.V.Sheppard – a mining engineer and newly appointed Board Member, the driving force behind mechanisation. He had travelled the country with Robens – popularly known as "The Lord and my Sheppard". He must have aspired to the Deputy Chairmanship himself. Learning of the Ezra appointment from the seller of the "*Evening Standard*" in the entrance hall of Hobart House, news of his fury spread quickly through the building. Relations between Robens and Sheppard were never quite the same again. Sheppard, however, by adding the Staff portfolio to his Production responsibilities, had acquired a formidable power base, which Ezra accepted. On Ezra's elevation to Chairman after a couple

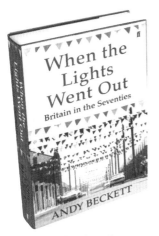

Fig.13: '**When the Lights Went Out. Britain in the Seventies**'; review of the 'Ezra decade', by Andy Beckett (refers to three-day week under the Heath Govt)

of years, Sheppard was appointed Deputy Chairman. Ezra and Sheppard were again complementary, not close; again with differing backgrounds.

'Derek Ezra's appointment as Chairman was made by John Davies, the Minister of State for Trade and Industry in the Conservative Administration of Edward Heath. He was clearly a 'safe pair of hands', able to continue the Robens' tradition of firm management for a fast-changing industry. His appointment was offered to him over the telephone. There were major marketing challenges.

'The Unions were, however, beginning to become more restless. The management had just undergone a massive reorganisation, and Ezra had seen at first hand the diversion from more essential goals which this had occasioned. He was resolved, as he recounted in 2012, not to make "the organisation" a continuing issue. (As a classicist he had probably read Gaius Petronius [AD 65] – a Roman General – who had concluded: *"every time we were beginning to form up in teams we would be reorganised. I was to learn later in life that we tend to meet any new situation by reorganisation, and a wonderful method it can be for creating the illusion of progress while producing confusion, inefficiency and demoralisation"*). Robens' advice to Derek on taking up his appointment was to do things in his own way – "the last thing you should try to do is to do it my way!" During Derek's years as Chairman, organisational change was minimal. The Committee structure was largely maintained, and as Chairman he presided over a well-organised administrative machine. Board Members and senior executives who served with him have remarked on the efficient and courteous way in which meetings were conducted. A fellow Board Member described Derek as "honest, fair and hard-working, with a proper sense of balance between the workforce and the nation".

'On his appointment as Deputy Chairman, Derek had retained the Marketing portfolio, with Jim Barratt (who was appointed DG of Marketing when Derek became Board Member), continuing in that role. Barratt had, I think, expected the elevation to Board Member and was disappointed. (In 1967, as Divisional Board Secretary, I was redundant when the Divisions were taken out. I had had some early marketing experience; had been sent by the Board on a Harvard Business School course; and was known to both Sheppard and the Board Member for Finance – David Clement – through my work in the West Midlands Division. John Brass, the Divisional Chairman, who himself became a Board Member in 1967, must have been my real saviour. I was not then known by Derek, but he and Jim Barratt were clearly agreeable to my being appointed to a key marketing job which had become vacant, Deputy Regional Marketing Director in the North-West. I was not seen on my appointment by Derek Ezra, but within weeks found myself deeply involved with his work).

'Although there was a growing shortage of smokeless fuels, production overall in the late '60s was beginning to overtake the market. Mechanisation had improved the quantum but reduced the quality of many of the industry's products. Changes were being made to the rail network, making concentration of merchant activities necessary. As Chapter 6 will amplify, Derek had instituted a review of the general arrangements in the domestic market. Common ground was sought for plans to rationalise the domestic coal trade: I became the prime mover in the North-

Fig.14: NCB Chairman's regular pit visit programme, 1970s; keeping in touch with the miners' concerns, Kellingley Colliery, Yks., now one of the few collieries still in operation

West where the Board was the leading player in the domestic market, with a large retail coal business. Derek Ezra was the driving force behind the many changes effected nationally in just a few years: rail depot rationalisation; train-load working from pit to customer; mechanisation of domestic coal handling; containerisation and pre-packing; advertising the benefits of the open fire; and solid-fuel fired central heating, and even district heating.

'Wherever possible, developments were by partnership with the private coal and allied trades and many new ventures were started. Although Robens was clearly behind Ezra and gave him valuable support, often taking centre stage when advances were made, Ezra was, in my view, responsible for most of the progress made with the rationalisation and modernisation. Very often Marketing Department had to respond to the many initiatives, which manifestly had the full authority of the Board and which at times ruffled many feathers. (Something of the manner whereby appointments were made at that time is illustrated by the way in which, after two years, I became the Marketing Director in the North-West. The interviews I attended did not involve Derek – who probably knew more about my work in the North-West than anyone else. Barratt and Essame, the Director General of Staff, interviewed me, although it was obvious that the die had been cast elsewhere. The night before my final interview, Bill Hindley, the Senior Regional Sales Manager in the North-West, telephoned me to say that he had been appointed to my job as Deputy and I was either up or out. My appointment was confirmed the next day by Sheppard who handed me my letter of appointment. Derek rarely got involved directly in appointments in the mainstream; he was much more involved with appointments in the growing number of joint ventures. In a way this was the natural reaction of a boss who had only limited knowledge of the mining men, but perhaps strange when he stood away at this point from marketing appointments – leave well and Sheppard and the DGs to get on with it.)

New horizons and challenges

'(After two years as Director in the North-West, I was summoned to London to be told by Barratt that the Board were mindful to appoint me as Principal of the Staff College, and that on the morrow I was to meet Essame and Sheppard – and, if I accepted – Robens; again, there was no message from Ezra. The move took me by surprise. I was happy in the North-West and still had much to achieve. I was told that if I succeeded, in five years or so, I should move on. I could in theory take on a few of the senior available roles. I accepted the appointment and agreed to start within a few weeks).

'My relationship with Ezra entered a new phase. Almost the very day I entered the Staff College, I was faced with a Kepner-Tregoe Course for potential members of the 'Performance Improvement Teams'. The idea of the Course and, I think, the PITs, had been hatched up by Robens and Ezra as a way of identifying future strategic alternatives. I was asked to lead a team which included Norman Woodhouse, the Deputy Public Relations Director, a man to succeed to the Directorship a few years later. The Team was to look into 'The Image and Attitudes within and towards the Industry'. The project involved quite a lot of imagination and extensive attitudinal surveys. It did, however, result in a number of interesting options being brought forward. The PIT Report was completed after Robens left the Chairmanship. The idea that the NCB should become British Coal was not taken up until 15 years later; the idea that Regional Groupings would allow more flexibility – that 'Scottish Coal', and 'North-Eastern Coal', for example, might lead in the longer-term to a less rigid organisation – was put to one side. Derek, as Chairman, has confirmed that organisational change was not to be his priority. Of the recommendations in the Report only those relating to appearances – house styles and liveries, and the refurbishment of Hobart House – were pursued by the new Chairman. In a sense, the change of style became one of the most significant aspects of the Ezra regime. Almost his first act was to have the nameplate NCB 1 – presented to Robens by the Local Authority holding it - taken off the Daimler limousine used by the Chairman, and transferred to a Hobart House delivery van. The attitudinal surveys were, however, a valuable entrée to the problems arising in managerial remuneration which faced us later.

'On taking up the Chair in July 1971 Derek embarked on a programme of pit visits which continued throughout his period of office. He tried to be in the coalfields at least one day a week; the visits gave him insights into the reality of life at the coal face, and the geological risks in mining investment. He became a regular visitor to the Staff College at Chalfont St Giles, and, like Robens, addressed most of the courses. One of the first special arrangements I had to make for him at the College was a Dinner for the Chairmen (and their wives) of ICI, the CEGB, British Rail, British Gas, and other major customers. Derek and Julie and I and my wife Angela – with a Staff Officer ('SOs', see Chapter 4) – were the only NCB hosts. Some guests accepted invitations to address senior courses; a number later sent managers to attend the Advanced Management Course. One of the advantages of inviting the great and the good (and not so good) to the College was that it provided opportunities for exchanges of views between interested parties. Government Ministers and Opposition spokesmen were particularly welcomed. Shortly after he became President of the NUM – in succession to Sir Sidney Ford – Joe Gormley made the first of his visits to the College.

Fig.15: Throughout his time at the helm, Derek Ezra had seen it as his job to fly the flag internationally for the UK coal industry: here, he represents the NCB, and asks a question, at the Annual Convention of the US National Coal Association, Washington, DC, 1960s. As so often, Julie accompanied him on this visit. [Courtesy, NCA]

'Informal contacts did not, however, prevent the major confrontation in 1972 which led to the three-day week and, and brought down the administration of Edward Heath. The new Labour Government brought a new sense of optimism to the industry, but the market for British coal was still being eroded by competition from oil, gas, nuclear power, and cheaper coal from abroad. Ezra's Chairmanship was to be dominated by the consequences of the marketplace, mechanisation, the threat to employment, and the fact that Britain was no longer creating jobs, which were being threatened by the Wilsonian "white heat of the technological revolution".'

The Nationalised Industries' Chairmen's Group

As two of the NCB SOs, Peter Jones and Colin Ambler, have written, "in the 1970s and early 1980s, the Nationalised Industry Chairmen were a significant force (some might say, lobby group) in the land. The industries under their control represented a sizeable share of GDP and of employment. Initially an informal luncheon club of the 'big seven' (coal, gas, electricity, steel, the Post Office, the railways and British Airways), this developed into the Nationalised Industries Chairmen's Group (NICG) … Derek was an increasingly influential member … and was the driving force behind the setting up of an off-shoot (NIOG), formed to promote the export of goods, services and expertise". Here were the major markets for coal, and relations with the Heads of these enterprises had to be a prime concern to the NCB.

Relationships with Government varied with the political mood, and former SO, Colin Ambler, has added: "Coal and rail, whilst modernising, were struggling … Richard Marsh [Chairman, British Rail] and Derek Ezra, aware of their industries' relative vulnerability, possibly had greater 'need' of the NICG, but, I believe, also recognised that … acting as a group, [they] had considerable unexploited 'clout'. From time to time they invited a guest to their lunch … After the then Mrs Thatcher had been elected leader of the Conservative Party, she too was invited … she used the occasion to attack the coal industry … describing coal-fired power stations as 'nasty, dirty things' … a cold chill suddenly descended on any aims of a long-term coal renaissance. After the return of a Labour Government in 1972, NICG had brought in the smaller public sector; these 26 industries now represented some 40% of GDP. PM Harold Wilson suggested to Derek Ezra that the grouping should be put on a more formal footing, to enable Government, in Wilson's words, 'to know better what we are dealing with'; however, the pay-off for NCB meant trying to keep Government intervention at the minimum level possible, compatible with its special circumstances of relying on an annually reviewed Government Grant for its heavy future investment programme. Government was pressed to take a long-term view of investment … the concept of counter-cyclical investment was also pursued … such concepts were cogently argued by Derek Ezra, deriving from his extensive knowledge of the European situation and the evidence of superior performance by the continental countries".

There were, however, inherent day-to-day interests at stake between themselves. Each Chairman needed to fight his corner, if necessary at fellow-Chairman level, despite the fact that they might also be sitting periodically round the same table. Thus Coal, from its then historical monopolistic position *vis-à-vis* the other nationalised industries – who, through government policy, had to buy their fuel from it – always appeared to them to be bargaining from unfair strength. Comments elsewhere (*see Chapter 6*) might suggest that Derek Ezra could seem to be too flexible as a negotiator. That did not appear to be the view of at least one of his fellow-NICG personalia, Sir Denis Rooke, of British Gas. (*Denis had started out as a fairly humble chemical engineering manager on the coal tar works, Ordnance Wharf, the Chemical Products Department of South Eastern Gas, in the grounds of the old Greenwich Gasworks – site of the smart millennial O^2 Dome, and a part of the 2012 London Olympics. From the insular culture of the then regional Gas Industry, this tough, down-to-earth engineer rose to fame and success through his creation and development of the National Gas Grid for North Sea Gas, and thence to the Chairmanship of the British Gas Corporation itself*).

Perhaps compounded by Denis Rooke's view of non-engineers as a breed, John Demont will relate later (*see Chapter 10*) that there was an inbuilt memory of Coal exercising too tough a role in supply and price negotiations. Rooke told his colleagues: "I'm just a gas industry man", and he manifested a healthy prejudice against urbane, over-civilised, 'foreign' non-engineers, like Derek, running engineering-based industries, which is how he simplistically saw Coal. Here were two very different personalities, representing opposed interests, although Derek never expressed any antipathy towards Denis himself. These difficulties were just part of the job, to be dealt with as best he might. Derek's task was to maximise the price for his products, and in those Government-protected days he often prevailed. In short, he and Denis did not exactly get on, and for all its benefits to the NCB, the NICG could sometimes become yet another of his unsought personal battlegrounds.

Looking out

Paul Glover continues: 'From the beginning of his Chairmanship Derek Ezra sought to increase NCB's contacts, ensuring that its interests were well presented and better known. In this context, his Chairmanship of the British Institute of Management (today's Chartered Management Institute), and of the "Keep Britain Tidy" campaign, can also be judged, although there is no doubt in my mind that he believed sincerely in the need for better managers, and in a cleaner environment, not least in the pithead areas. It is not my intention to attempt to recount the events of the eleven years of Sir Derek's Chairmanship – in many respects I was only an observer of a passing show. My contacts and activities, however, provided insights into the life of the Board and its changing *personae*. Becoming Chairman in 1971, his appointment was renewed in July 1976 by Tony Wedgwood Benn, the Secretary of State for Energy in the Labour Administration. Reports at the time indicated that the further three-year term offered to Derek was not what Benn really wanted and that there was little grace on the occasion of the hand-over of the letter of appointment. One essential quality required of a nationalised industry Chairman was the ability to work with a succession of Ministers, each with his own sense of priority and political necessity. Sir Derek demonstrated the ability to work with Administrations of very different hues.

'In 1973, Norman Siddall became a second Deputy Chairman, and Donald Davies, a mining engineer and South Wales Area Director, joined the Board as Marketing Member. The long-serving DG, Jim Barratt, died soon afterwards in tragic circumstances. He was succeeded by Malcolm Edwards, who was clearly Derek's choice. The Board also acquired in 1974 a further mining engineer Member in John Mills. The influence of the mining engineers was checked by the Board Members for Science (Leslie Grainger in 1978 – then Dr Joe Gibson), Finance (David Clement to 1977 – then Brian Harrison), and Industrial Relations (Cliff Shepherd to 1981). Regional interests were served after the '67 re-organisation by the appointment to the Board of John Brass and Wilfred Miron – previous Divisional Chairmen. There was also a succession of part-time Board Members, of which the most influential appeared to be John Peel (to 1973), John Marsh (to 1974), and Sir Jack Wellings (to 1978). 1974 was to be a testing year, as is revealed in Chapter 5. (Almost five years after I entered the Staff College, I was appointed DG of Staff, in succession to Sam Essame, one of my earliest mentors, and predecessor at the Staff College. I took up office on December 1 1974: my briefing came from W.V.Sheppard, to whom I reported. My letter of appointment came from Sir Derek, who thanked me warmly for my work and hospitality at the Staff College. I was in the middle of my year as Chairman of the Coal Industry Society (CIS), and on my way to becoming Chairman of the Coal Trade Benevolent Association (CTBA). These activities gave me greater contact with the Chairman than did my functional responsibilities).

Fig.16: Lady Ezra entered into the spirit of Derek's frequent pit visits and was popular with the miners and their wives; here she is enjoying being carried away on a conveyor belt, at Calverton Colliery, S.Notts

'When W.V. Sheppard retired, Norman Siddall continued for a time as the sole Deputy. Throughout his career Sir Derek maintained close contacts with the CIS – he was Chairman in 1961-2 – and became President in 1981, giving him a strong voice in the affairs of the industry after his retirement. He was President of the CTBA in 1974, and took particular interest in its activities during the Presidency two years later of HRH the Duke of Edinburgh (*see photographs p.56*). His Royal Highness had accepted my invitation to become President during my year as Chairman; the Festival Dinner, attended by over 700 on November 16 1976, was a glittering occasion. Sir Derek, seated between the Earl of Lanesborough (Past President) and HRH – with the Duke of Devonshire (President-Elect) on his left –

responded to the toast of 'The Guests'. The dinner was attended by managers, union leaders (including Joe Gormley), political figures (not including, as I remember, the Secretary of State for Energy, Tony Benn), and, for the first time, wives. Derek's wife, Julie, and Angela, my wife, renewed the contact they had previously enjoyed at the Staff College. In his response, Derek referred to '**Plan 2000**', which seemed to provide the blueprint for the future. New capacity would expand coal's contribution to the economy; coal had been the springboard for the first industrial revolution, and home-produced coal was now helping in a major way to strengthen the balance of payments by meeting nearly 40% of the nation's energy needs. These were indeed heady days. At the Dinner, HRH was invited by Sir Derek to lunch with the Board at Hobart House, following which the Board became an active supporter of the Duke's Award Scheme (*see also Chapter 5*).

"An impossible job"

'Early in 1977, I was introduced to Jim Prior MP, who in Opposition was shadowing the Department of Employment; (*a brief résumé of his views appears in a later paragraph*). The contact was welcomed by Derek, and developed over the next few years, through my having regular briefing meetings with him.

'Following the return in May 1979 of a Conservative Administration under Margaret Thatcher, Sir Derek's term of office was renewed for a further three years by David Howell, Secretary of State for Energy. Jim Prior became Secretary of State for Employment, and retained interest in the delicacy of industrial relations (IR) in the coal industry. Very early on, the composition of the Board and the possible succession to the Industrial Relations portfolio were on the agenda for my meetings. I was able to introduce Jim Prior to officers of the Management Union (British Association of Colliery Management – BACM) and to moderate members of the NUM Executive. On one or two occasions Sir Derek joined my meetings with Jim Prior, and briefed the new Secretary of State on the overall situation in the industry'.

By way of an external perspective on the NCB at this time, and an interpolation on the varying degree of 'protection' that Coal might or might not expect from Government in the 1960s/70s, the following account has come from Jim Prior himself, thinking back to the time when he was the Minister responsible for the Conservative Party's interface with the nationalised industries and with the wider field of IR – and particularly with the Unions, (Jim Prior was MP for Lowestoft and then for Waveney, Suffolk and had served as PPS to Edward Heath, before becoming Lord President of the Council, and Leader of the House of Commons from 1972 to 1973. As already outlined, he was Front bench spokesman for Employment in Opposition up to 1979, and was then appointed by Margaret Thatcher as Secretary of State for that Department until 1981. After retiring from active politics he was raised to the peerage, and became Chairman of the Arnold Weinstock industrial conglomerate empire, GEC, in 1984). Lord Prior's broad and experienced views on public ownership, and the leaders of both 'sides' of industry, command a special importance in this Memoir. He had written in his autobiography, **A Balance of Power:**[55] 'The nationalised industries therefore not only suffered from constant interference from Government, but their accountability to Parliament also made the position of the chairmen almost an impossible job'.

Looking back on that era from the different economic and political vantage point of 2012, Lord Prior further endorsed that view: *"Although I found Ezra a very reasonable man to work with, doing a good job, my conclusion now is that that job was an impossible one to do. The Party's mistake in the 1960s had been to rely too much on Robens at the Coal Board, who certainly had his own way of doing things, but appeared to be keeping the miners in good order. In the light of subsequent events, we should have paid more attention to the trends within the Unions, and to the underlying, longer-term problems of the fuel industries. Robens had of course been appointed Chairman under a Conservative PM, Harold Macmillan, and often seemed to be taking a stance against his own Labour Party, which pleased our side! …*

"Up to that time, Government did not seek to get too involved with industrial matters, and Nationalised Industry Chairmen were expected to manage as best they could. I nevertheless made it my business to meet the Union Leaders, above all the NUM figures, such as Joe Gormley, Mick McGahey and Laurence Daly. Mining leaders seemed to appreciate this, and would look at my hands and compliment me on not having a politician's hands! (Having been a farmer, mine were inevitably pretty large and tough! I also knew Robens quite well and he kept in touch, but I did not get very close to Derek Ezra, after Robens retired in 1972. I did spend some time as the guest of Dr Paul Glover at the Board's Management College, learning about the industry's current aims and problems, but Ezra himself did not seek to get too close to me as the Secretary of State.

"The second Conservative regime from 1979 was a different kettle of fish. The think-tank behind Margaret Thatcher – John Hoskyns, Keith Joseph, etc – had for long been counselling the Party to reduce the power of the unions, highlighted by Ted Heath's three-day week and the consequent loss of the General Election. Later, when Nigel Lawson became her Chancellor, the manufacturing sector became unfashionable, it being assumed that the financial and service sectors could see the country through. Nevertheless, Margaret was not 'all for confrontation', least of all with the public sector Unions, but she did allow herself to be persuaded to develop the strategy of strength which Ian MacGregor finally implemented vis-à-vis the miners".

A personal summing-up

These highly condensed recollections by a prominent Minister of the 1970s/1980s underline the gap which existed between Government and Boards such as the NCB, making the already complex task of running it more and more difficult. Sir Derek Ezra – as he had by now become – still had to do the task allotted to him.

Paul Glover here resumes his overview of that task, at that time - both light and serious - and the kinds of problems Sir Derek Ezra personally had to deal with. 'I was a regular guest of the moderate COSA (Colliery Overmen and Shotfirers Association) branch of the NUM at the main Union conferences, where on occasions Sir Derek and I, with our wives, were the only NCB guests. (I remember with particular pleasure the occasion during an NUM Conference in Jersey, when Timothy, our small son, was invited by Julie Ezra to check the money in her purse to assure Derek that she needed more cash!). NUM Conferences during his Chairmanship always involved him in a major review of coal's prospects. His messages were always listened to and he was regarded as a champion of the industry.

'The announcement in February 1981, however, that between 10 and 20 pits were in serious trouble and that 20 to 30 were nearing exhaustion – that possibly 20,000 jobs might be at risk – seemed to take the Unions by surprise. There was an immediate reaction from the NUM who had clearly not been listening to the warnings of over-capacity which were there for all to see – a national strike became once more a real possibility.

'I advised Prior of the likely solidarity within the NUM, and of the prospect of the National Association of Colliery Overmen, Deputies and Shotfirers (NACODS) - the first and second line management – becoming involved. In the event of a strike only the management represented by the BACM and a minority of clerical staff might stay at work. The NUM seemed to be united behind their benign leadership. I was far from certain of the outcome: a repeat of the constitutionally interesting downfall of the short-lived Conservative Government in 1974 was on the horizon. The prospects of this led the Government to reduce pressure on the Board to cut back capacity. New arrangements for the Government, the Board and the Unions – a Tripartite – to work out a way forward were established. There was, however, only limited recognition of the new reality; a market no longer dominated by coal, but one in which oil, gas and nuclear were each major players, and where the inevitability of economic exhaustion after 200 years of over-intensive mining had meant that the best and easiest coal had long gone, and there were no longer a quarter of the viable mining jobs to be had.

'Sir Derek's role in finding a way out of the crisis was crucial. It was he who saw the need for all parties to work together. He survived what was probably the most challenging time of his career. He suffered a minor coronary event, but went on to see the industry through to his retirement 18 months later in July 1982. In September 1981, Jim Prior moved to the Northern Ireland office; he was blamed by the "Daily Express" for what they regarded as a surrender to the demands of the NUM. In November 1981, at the Mineworkers National Art Competition in Blackpool, I had an interesting meeting with Derek, and with Roy Mason MP (a one-time Secretary of State for Energy). We discussed the problems that Derek's successor would face when he retired in eight months' time. Scargill was on the point of election to the NUM Presidency and would certainly be a new force to be reckoned with. Roy Mason was a man likely to be able to provide the strong leadership the NCB would require, and I was asked to proposition Jim Prior on the possibility of his appointment.

When I saw Jim Prior it was clear that the Government was thinking of Ian MacGregor, then Chairman of British Steel, as a possible successor. A few months later I was the only NCB invitee (courtesy of NUM / COSA) at the first NUM Conference under Scargill's Presidency, at Inverness. I duly reported the gathering storm to the new Chairman, Norman Siddall, and to Jim Prior.

'My relationship with Derek Ezra over the years was a happy one. I was always aware that the Deputy Chairman, who stood between me and him, was possibly suspicious of my loyalties, but Sir Derek never intervened in any matter which was properly within the portfolio of his Deputy. Indeed he always had his eye on his main problem – reconciling the demands of Government on the one hand, and the longer-term needs of the industry on the other. On assuming the Chairmanship he followed the Robens' practice of regular Monday morning meetings with Board Members and DGs. The meetings were dominated by IR issues. I never remember being questioned about any aspect of staffing policy at these meetings. Indeed I cannot remember any serious discussion of my portfolio at any meeting formal or informal. I was left to get on with the job for long periods – sometimes for months – without any formal or informal accountability. Sir Derek left his subordinates to carry on their jobs, but was always accessible. He had had to cope with almost intractable problems - to deal with political masters as different as Margaret Thatcher and Harold Wilson, Edward Heath and Jim Callaghan, and Secretaries of State as different as Wedgwood Benn and David Howell. I was able to pay tribute to this outstanding level of leadership when I proposed his health at the Hobart House farewell party on his retirement in June 1982. The industry which Derek left behind was still a major contributor to the energy demands of the country. However, production exceeded demand by over 10 million tons a year. Downsizing was clearly a major problem, but no one could have foreseen that in 30 years time deep-mined production would only be 5.5 million tonnes a year – just a good week's output when Derek became Chairman. Sadly, the balance of the UK's coal requirements of about 50 million tonnes is now imported through ports designed originally for the export of coal. In 1981-82 – Derek's final year as Chairman – the industry exported nine million tonnes of coal, contributing £350M to the national exchequer.

'Sir Derek did not blindly believe in and work for a large coal industry irrespective of the consequences. He had lived through the trauma of Aberfan; he knew the environmental results of mining and burning coal; he had worked constantly for a safer workplace and for better protective clothing; he had done his bit in tidying up colliery operations. In his final year the number of fatal accidents underground was the lowest ever recorded, as was the total accident rate per 100,000 manshifts. He had fostered better management practices, doing his time as Chairman of the BIM. Probably most importantly, he had consistently supported substantial investment in

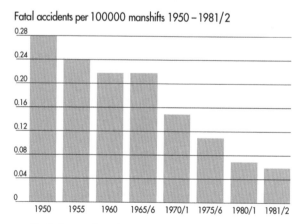

Fatal accidents per 100000 manshifts 1950 – 1981/2

Fig.17: Outstanding safety record during Derek Ezra's time with the NCB: bar chart from the Annual Report of his final year as Leader shows decline in Fatal Accidents per 100,000 manshifts

Research and Development, which in 1981-2 was over £48M. The record here is clear. In terms of health and safety, mining technology, and efforts to make coal cleaner in use, Britain led the world. Quietly and without fuss, Sir Derek tried to take the long-term view and make the industry and the country around it a better place to be in'.

Derek's generation of leaders did not work from any background of academic theory about business, yet some of his inner convictions could well be gleaned from **Advice from the Top: Business Strategies of Britain's Corporate Leaders,** which he co-edited and to which he wrote the Introduction. His comments may well be unintentionally illuminating about himself: "this book is about people who have put their unmistakable stamp on the businesses they have led … I have been struck by one thing above all – their air of calmness and detachment when dealing with the many difficulties large businesses inevitably bring in their train … This is more than just a record of achievements by a selection of successful business leaders. It is a testimony to the enormous changes taking place in British industry today and to those who helped to shape those changes". Perhaps tellingly for Derek Ezra, the compendium ends with the editors' choice of a quotation from one of the contributors, Lord King, Chairman of British Airways: "Young men see visions – old men dream dreams … It is the vision which generates the determination, and the dream which sustains the years of hard work".

A further factor complicating Derek's tenure at the NCB is evidenced in an article by his 'opposite number' at the Department of Energy, Sir Jack Rampton, which appeared in the Autumn 1975 issue of the **Journal of General Management,** the voice of Henley Management College; (Sir Derek was by now a member of its Editorial Advisory Board). Focussing on the "special nexus" of the energy industries, the PUS highlighted the emergence of "the great divide" of the late 1960s whereby "successive Governments felt the need to exercise a further control and to widen the strategic and tactical purposes of nationalised industry as an adjunct to national policies – in short the point at which the Morrisonian [arm's length] concept ceased to provide a wholly acceptable answer… Occasionally the conflict of interest is too sharp, and often there is much frustration on both sides over what each tends to regard as the capricious or undiscerning attitude of the other". This underlying and irreversible revolution in Government policy did not make the Ezra years any easier. Paul Glover concludes: 'whether Derek retired satisfied with his own record of achievements and years of hard work in the face of this conflict, or disappointed with the outcome, I do not know. In later discussions he only emphasised one of the main instances of his own set of "difficulties" - working with the inconsistency of the "mining mafia". On the one hand they displayed over-optimism for a given mining project, such as the new Selby coalfield in Yorkshire, but on the other hand pessimism for Derek's longer-term "vision" and macro targets for the industry as a whole. Certainly, talking to him during the preparation of this Memoir, in his 96th year he had lost none of the mastery of the detail of his job nor of his memory of its most challenging days, and of the idea of the world he sought to serve and improve. He assuredly did his best, and expected the same of his staff. He went on doing important things for another thirty years'.

Contributors: Paul Glover; also Lord ("Jim") Prior, Brian Harrison,
Peter Jones, Colin Ambler, John Demont

CHAPTER 4: HOW DID HE DO IT? -
THE 'CHAIRMAN'S OFFICE' FACTOR

The studies of all great leaders – political, military, industrial – assess both the internal background and external achievements that made them and their reputations what they were. There is often objective evidence for both factors, usually through the perceptions of their equals or opponents – the what?, the when and where?, and, if possible, the why? There is never any real data for that missing fifth wheel on the coach – *how* did they do it? – because the witnesses that might have supplied it were not around to be asked at the vital time. If there is justification for that overworked commentator's claim of 'uniqueness', advanced with some temerity at the outset of this Memoir, it lies above all in the next two chapters, for their contributors address that 'how' factor which the published works on the other industrial contemporaries with whom Derek Ezra has been compared – Weinstock, Beeching, Robens himself – have had to forego. The record at this point also provides the opportunity to explore what are here advanced as four of the 'covert factors' that were to affect his role at the NCB.

It has become clear that for Derek Ezra there was of course both a public and a human face. There could also be an intermediate personality, seen through private close-ups of the public man, talking and acting informally. It was the insight of Paul Glover that this Memoir should reach out to surviving former members of the NCB 'Chairman's Office', so that this chapter could examine the "How?" of this very private Chairman. This could only be done through the eyes of those working closest to him, this succession of high-flier graduate Staff Officers that before and beyond his time formed the first rank of the 10-person strong 'Chairman's Office'. They could almost be seen as NCB 'guardian angels', exercising a wide albeit non-statutory influence. Andrew Horsler, who served six years as SO and PPS, before moving on to other roles, finally as British Coal Marketing Director in 1991, has here co-ordinated the observations of Christopher Pennell, Colin Ambler, Peter Jones and Simon Kermode: Christopher Pennell's principal output follows as Ch.5 This testimony is enhanced by the writings of Mike Parker:[56] he worked closely with the Chairman in his then role of Director of the Central Planning Unit.

The 'covert factors'

Inevitably, these men – always men in the Robens/Ezra era, women only reached this inner 'core' later on – were chosen, and finally, on recommendation, by Derek himself, because they were of the calibre to offer wider, even contrary, advice. Much of the strategic aspect of their commentary has been subsumed in the three preceding chapters. Those parts of their input will not be lost to future students of industrial management, but are now preserved in the Archive to this Memoir. Their observations may also be read in conjunction with the *résumé* of the main events of Derek's chairmanship (*see* 'Timelines: 4') , in relation to some of the vital, longer-term 'covert' factors; these worked beneath the more obvious overt forces that influenced the actions of Derek and his Board. Of such fundamental 'covert' factors, it would be possible to discern at least four, three of which could not be 'overt' to Derek at the time, although they were to become all-too evident in due course. These included determinations that entered the minds of two of the major actors in the coal industry's drama over this decade – Margaret Thatcher, and Arthur Scargill. Although neither could express their thoughts publicly, the spate of later memoirs has implied that each had set their sights early on for a course of future action that would challenge one nationalised industry above all – the NCB, and thus Derek himself – given the right opportunity.

Margaret Thatcher's credo was to break the trade union grip, to smash the "Holy Grail" of nationalisation, and so, on the way, break up what she saw as the NCB 'monopoly'. Nicholas Ridley in his memoirs attributes this to at least 1978, reflecting a third factor: the Tories' sense of defeat at the miners' hands. Arthur Scargill asserted that it went 'right back to 1972'. Scargill's own highly politicized path was discerned by Ted Heath and others as also going back to the 1972 time: it lay in establishing the mineworkers as the dominant force in British industrial – and by extension – political, life, by any means, democratic or otherwise, and thus to outwit the traditional moderate wing of the NUM.

A fourth 'covert' factor must have been latent within Derek's own mind, not explicit, but inferable by those closest to him: idealistically, to do the best job he could, in the face of all the difficulties, foreseen and unforeseen, for his industry, for his workforce, for the cause of long-term Energy Policy, and thus for the nation. These four hidden agendas could only result in a clash of the titans, with coal in the middle of the crossfire. Andrew and the SOs worked within the 'Office' model imported directly by Robens from his Ministerial experience, well able to deal with their "oppos", the Civil Service's Admin Class; they can now provide the insider background to *how* Ezra managed that process, first here in Andrew's own words:

'The Office'

'Derek Ezra, like Lord Robens and others before him, was in effect both Chairman and Chief Executive of the NCB. Central to the way in which he carried out these roles, and indeed his other appointments and activities, was the operation of his private office, usually described by him as "the Office" … Next to the Chairman's own office was that of the Private Secretary, whose principal responsibility was organising the diary – no small task given the range of Ezra's interests and the volume of meetings and functions that he attended … Close by was a room occupied by three Staff Officers … Apart from dealing with the internal business of this large and diverse organisation, the Private Office also supported Sir Derek's wide range of external activities'. At any one time there were three such posts – junior, middle, and the senior' [the 'PPS', in another echo of civil service practice] … 'The three young men occupying these positions had unparalleled access to Derek Ezra and shared his confidences and trust … With very few exceptions all correspondence … passed through one of the SOs … The amount of paper … was immense, and a collective effort by the Chairman himself and all his staff tried to ensure that it was kept moving. One SO would attend nearly every meeting at which the Chairman was present … they wrote or commissioned detailed briefings for all his meetings, engagements or visits … he liked every aspect to be covered, even to finding out who he would be sitting next to at a lunch or a dinner – except for functions at Buckingham Palace!' Peter Jones worked in the Office from 1978 to 1982, having joined the NCB in 1974 as an 'AA' … "The appointment was made after an initial competition … My exposure to the man for whom I was to work for the next four years came only at the final stage, when I was presented to him as the preferred candidate. I was ushered into the Chairman's private meeting room … After four or five minutes the connecting door from the office of [Doris Proctor] the Personal Secretary, opened and Sir Derek entered and sat down in another armchair. After a brief pause he looked at me and said: 'So, you are going to join us?' As this did not yet appear to be a foregone conclusion, I was a little uncertain as to how to respond and I do not remember my exact words. Whatever I said appeared to be the right answer. There was then a short exchange which concluded: 'We are very busy in here. We have a lot to do. When can you start?' As far as I can remember after 34 years, that was about the extent of my final interview, which was perhaps less challenging than I had expected". Peter continues: "on reflection, this brief initial encounter demonstrated two important aspects of Sir Derek's outlook and way of working at the time. The first was signalled by the words 'you want to join *us*', and the second by the brevity of the interview. '*Us*' represented the small core team which facilitated the carrying forward of Sir Derek's objectives and strategies in the face of possible opposition or inertia from other parts of the Board's large, and mining engineer-dominated organisation.

"The brevity of the interview reflected Sir Derek's complete confidence that if the core team and the few senior executive that he regarded as essentially competent (in this case David Brandrick [Company Secretary] and Paul Glover) made a recommendation on a significant organisational or administrative issue, then it was not necessary to spend time second-guessing the recommendation because it would be fundamentally sound and could be relied on. Sir Derek's management style has been described elsewhere as 'inclusive'. The Board's organisation and governance structure [*covered later in this chapter*], in which full-time Board members had functional responsibilities but where Headquarters Departments also had Directors General who were not on the Board, did not foster clarity or accountability … Board Members and senior officials were thus required to spend a significant proportion of their time in meetings during which they were left in no doubt as to the Chairman's views on current issues, and loaded with remits and requests for information (some of which the Private Office would subsequently seek to modify or clarify, to avoid unproductive effort or confusion). Changing the Chairman's views or position on issues was, however, more challenging, and often required a degree of courage. Arguments needed to be presented rigorously, concisely and rapidly, and any deviations from currently established orthodoxy had to be cogently advocated. Any logical inconsistency or inadequately explained deviation from the Chairman's view ran the risk of a speedy, often unanswerable and sometimes unintentionally cutting response. Many senior colleagues did not, therefore, find Sir Derek an easy man to work with, leading to a progressive widening of the gap between 'them' and 'us'.

"Sir Derek was, however, intensely loyal to those who were prepared to work with him in the way he wanted (and whom he considered to be 'sound' both intellectually, and preferably supportive of his views on major policy issue). He worked hours that were long in the context of the time and was appreciative of a similar approach in others (including the Private Office)." Peter Jones notes that it did prove possible to rationalise the amount of briefing … "Andrew and I agreed that it would be useful to try to institute a regular meeting at which we could briefly discuss each engagement with Sir Derek and clarify what, if anything, was required. Sir Derek agreed … These meetings proved invaluable … We often also spent a few minutes at the end … discussing how we should be approaching some of the key issues of the time … Once his trust had been gained, Sir Derek was always prepared to listen to a well-argued view … I learned that it was often necessary to argue robustly but (he) was always prepared to be challenged in private".

Andrew Horsler adds that 'speech writing was also a significant activity, with … several speeches a week to different audiences. He was widely and rightly regarded as an accomplished speaker and was in much demand'. Christopher Pennell puts it elegantly: "[Derek] created whole cathedrals of carefully fashioned thought, founded on a nave soaring to a vaulted roof, given extra interest by wandering into side aisles and transepts which always led back to the central point, and where there might be weaknesses in the argument, flying buttresses supported the whole edifice, so that listeners hardly saw the joints – all delivered in that deep rich impressive voice that my wife once told me she could listen to for hours!" Interestingly, from a latter-day 'transparency' point of view, Andrew comments: 'the Chairman's Office played a role in seeking to ensure effective communications between the Chairman and the management of the NCB. Through informal liaison with Board Members and senior managers, the SOs were able to act as a two-way conduit of information and advice. On the one hand they acted as "eyes and ears" for the Chairman and could gain a better feel for the views of managers who might be reluctant to speak out frankly at meetings. On the other hand the SOs could explain to others why the Chairman was taking a particular view … This process of communication required a high degree of discretion on the part of all concerned … Derek Ezra almost certainly had a closer relationship with his own staff than with most other colleagues in the NCB. He would usually address the SOs by their first name although they properly addressed him as "Chairman".

'It was very rare for the Chairman to meet anyone, other than a member of the Private Office, in his own office, very much his inner sanctum … The SOs therefore had the privilege of direct access …' Peter Jones recalls: "On rare occasions … the Chairman would venture across the corridor to talk to us in our office about a specific issue, for example a draft reply to an MP with which he was not completely happy … occasionally, there would be a more dramatic entrance into our office followed by an explosion. This was rarely caused by a shortcoming on our part (those, when they very occasionally arose, were almost always dealt with in a quiet, civilised way in his office) – rather by perceived incompetence on the part of a senior official who had failed to deliver what was requested, or perhaps by some unhelpful, and in Sir Derek's view, illogical communication from a senior civil servant or Minister. Early Friday evenings were frequently a time for an informal gathering of Derek and the SOs … to talk about current matters … Such gatherings took place in [what was] known as the "Green Room" from the colour of the décor, and which was furnished with armchairs rather than the office chairs … At some point in the mid-1970s Derek met sculptor Henry Moore and as a result of that meeting Moore offered to lend a collection of his sculpture sketches (*see Fig.2 and back jacket*) on permanent loan for display in this room. Henry Moore himself attended the launch of this exhibition. This rare example of culture in Hobart House did not appeal to everyone in the upper echelons of the NCB'. Christopher Pennell, as the attendant PPS, recalled that "W.V.Sheppard was overheard to say that he could not see what all the fuss was about: they looked like naked ladies on lilos!"

Andrew continued: 'Derek would not claim to be a regular attender at cultural or artistic events, but he was clearly very well read. On one occasion he was discussing with the SOs an invitation from Sir Michael Swann, then Chairman of the BBC, and used the literary allusion "*Chez Swann*". The blank looks on the SOs' faces revealed that they had no idea what he was talking about, leading Derek to remark that he was astonished! that they had not read Proust'.

Governance and guardianship

The metaphor of a "guardian angel" role has been tentatively suggested here by the editor to embrace the kind of benign overview that the Staff Officers seemed to adopt, almost by osmosis. Neither they nor their boss would ever have asserted such a claim, yet to the outside eye it does seem to describe both the intimacy of their insights into everything that went on, but also more especially the moral, almost caring code by which they appeared to operate. However, Christopher Pennell wanted to qualify this thought: 'I hope and believe that the group of successive PPSs and their SO sidekicks performed really useful functions for the good of the NCB, but "guardian angels" exaggerates both our motives and our effect. Sure, we were a source of independent intelligence and occasional advice to Derek, provided without personal or departmental motivation, but … we were relatively junior and had influence because we were, in a sense, the *alter ego* ears, eyes, and sometimes the voice of Derek, not because we were necessarily brilliant operators in our own right. We also provided Derek with a loyalty … but we never lost our loyalty to the NCB itself, so we occasionally would be privately quite firm with Derek where we believed he might be tactically likely to make a mistake; but we had to have good reasons for doing so. We never let our loyalty to Derek blind us to the hopes and fears of other senior colleagues who needed guidance on what was in the Chairman's mind, so that they could act appropriately and positively'. This necessarily caused the SOs to think hard, as an essential cog in the machine; it would today be seen as the NCB's 'corporate governance'. Colin Ambler sets the scene in greater detail, from the vantage point of an SO in 'The Office', observing how 'DJE' had to manoeuvre his way via his legal remit. His comments dovetail with the broad picture set out in Chapter 3 above):

"So how was the National Coal Board, as one of the major nationalised industries, *run* during the 1970s after DJE had become Chairman in 1971?

"The formal position was that contained in the 1946 Coal Industry Nationalisation Act. In outline the Minister appointed the Chairman of the Board and other Board Members, not exceeding 14 in total. The Board had considerable freedom to organise and run the industry. It was obliged to submit to the Minister an annual Report and Accounts which was then presented to Parliament. The Minister had the power to issue directions to the Board which had to be published in the Report and Accounts. All fairly simple!

"In practice things were a bit more complicated … Governance in the 'pre-Cadbury' days was very different from the norm today. The role of the Chairman was full-time and he was effectively also Chief Executive; the mining engineering Deputy Chairman was in effect chief operating officer for deep mining. All the other full-time Members had executive responsibilities and were supported by departments headed by Directors General. The part-time Members, numerically in the minority, were the equivalent of today's Non-executive Directors. The Board (full- and part-time Members) met once a month. It had two principal committees – consisting only of full-time Members with officials in attendance – each with substantial delegated authority: the General Purposes Committee, and the Mining Committee. The former, chaired by the Chairman, oversaw the day-to-day direction and results of the industry; the latter, chaired by the Deputy Chairman, concentrated on deep mining results and projects, including the most major … even if full formal approval by the Board was required.

"This formal governance structure was only part of the story. Each Monday morning a 'Chairman's Meeting' took place not in the Board Room but in the "Green Room" [*see above*] at Hobart House. All full-time Members and the senior DGs attended. These were the occasions on which the real business of the Board was done. Results were scrutinised, future plans developed, tactics *vis-à-vis* the trade unions discussed, along with positions to be taken with a Press that was increasingly hostile as the industry found itself more and more on the front pages for the wrong reasons. The atmosphere at such gatherings was often tense. Although DJE gave unstintingly of his time at evenings and weekends to speak about the industry or to attend functions to press its case, he also used the weekend to reflect on the current state of play.

"We in his Private Office came to expect that by Monday morning he would have concluded that things were not going as they should on one front or another. He then used the meeting to generate discussion and action. His thinking cut across the whole spectrum of the industry's

activities: production and productivity, safety, sales and marketing including prices, finances and costs, wages, personnel, planning the future, Europe, co-operation with other coal-producing countries, relations with Government – the list was endless.

"These meetings exposed some very real problems, centring on the stubborn refusal of deep-mined productivity to improve to any tangible degree for several years, and this despite the massive investment being poured into the industry to renew existing collieries and open new ones. Linked with this was the continuing problem of making any meaningful progress with the mining unions towards a more effective pay system to incentivise the workforce. DJE's persistent questioning of mining performance brought him into conflict with the Board Members with mining engineering backgrounds. The questioning was taken as criticism of what they were or weren't doing. 'They' became defensive; communications were far from two-way, open and constructive. The mining engineering 'camp' on the Board encompassed several Members and senior executives. Possibly this Cambridge-educated, pro-European marketeer was seen as coming from a completely different culture, and therefore clearly unable to understand the realities of coalmining (despite having spent his career in the industry).

"Another way of looking at this was that, far from 'interfering', he was asking difficult questions to which there were few convincing answers. However, DJE's position was not as strong as it should have been. The non-mining engineering members of the Board (except for David Clement, who then retired in 1976) were less robust and able characters than their colleagues; it was often necessary for DJE to force issues through against opposition – taciturn perhaps but opposition none the less. In doing this he showed remarkable determination, but the Board was often an uneasy forum, despite the press of opposing external forces. In all this the position of the part-time Members did not help. They were regarded with some suspicion; were they placemen of the Secretary of State (or worse, of the civil servants?), there primarily to report back? Did they really have anything to contribute? With one or two impressive exceptions they seemed content to turn up to Board meetings and make limited or naïve interventions. They must have known that the monthly Board Meetings often skated over the real issues, including, for example, merely noting the Minutes of the two main Committees. Most spent little or no time getting to know the organisation. DJE could have encouraged them to get more involved and use them as allies but it looks as though he simply thought that the likely return for this would not have justified the effort, and, at that stage in the evolution of the concept of the Non-executive Director, he was probably right. In consequence he bore a very heavy load in identifying and pushing forward on the priorities … the Board was not a united team, and this probably detracted from its performance.

"The sudden arrival of a Labour Government in 1974 brought a new Secretary of State to the newish Department of Energy". [**This critical year, 1974, which also brought in as junior minister for Coal in the Department, Alex Eadie, a Scottish mining MP, is further detailed in the following chapter, Ch.5**]. Eric Varley, MP for Chesterfield, also from a mining family, was able and well-disposed … A new investment-heavy '**Plan for Coal**' was quickly agreed in 'tripartite' talks between Government, NCB and the unions … Within 18 months Varley was moved to head the Industry Department and Tony Benn became Secretary of State for Energy. To walk into his office in Thames House South was a memorable experience; a full-scale NUM lodge banner adorned one wall … DJE and Tony Benn got on pretty well, but it was apparent that the latter's focus was at least equally, and possibly more so, on the NUM …

"One final aspect of governance which we in the Private Office were less privy to was the

Donald C. | Robert B. | Sir Derek | Reginald H. | Joseph | Arthur M. | R. Peter | Roland W. | Colin D.
Berkey | Kurtz | Ezra | Jones | Gibson | Bueche | Davidson | Schmitt | Ambler

Fig.18: visit to USA, July 1977: top-level agreement between NCB and (American) General Electric, to collaborate on the development of advanced methods of coal conversion. Signatory group includes Dr J.Gibson, new NCB Board Member for coal research, and the Chairman's PPS, Colin Ambler. The GE team was led by Reg Jones, Chairman and CEO, and Dr A.M. Bueche, VP for R&D. (The desk for signing was Thomas Edison's, inventor of the incandescent light bulb. Edison's Company was the foundation of GE, one of the world's greatest global corporations) [Courtesy, Colin Ambler; GE; and "*Schenectady Gazette.*"]

role of the civil servants. The NCB was the concern of three senior officials in the Department of Energy: Sir Jack Rampton – Permanent Under Secretary; Brian Tucker – Deputy Secretary; and Jasper Cross – head of the coal division. Each month, Messrs Tucker and Cross lunched with DJE at Hobart House. It was one of the few meetings at which DJE did not ask for one of us to be present and was clearly an opportunity to keep the Department briefed about a whole gamut of issues. Being Chairman/Chief Executive can be a lonely existence at times, but we had the impression that DJE found these sessions helpful in ensuring that civil servants and Ministers were generally in the picture and not at risk of having sudden and unwelcome surprises. Perhaps he was also able to test the temperature on ideas and plans that were forming in his mind … Jack Rampton came occasionally for a one-to-one lunch and the conversation seemed to centre on appointments. It was interesting that at meetings in Tony Benn's office, Sir Jack was only occasionally present; either his priorities were elsewhere, or coal was just too tricky!"

DJE's strategy: overview from "the Office"

The team of SOs witnessed not only how 'DJE' managed the day-to-day tasks, but also, and more importantly, how he developed his strategic vision. Here one of the longest-serving members of the Office, Andrew Horsler, resumes his overview: 'The early part of Derek Ezra's chairmanship was dominated by the two mineworkers' strikes of 1972 and 1974 ... After 1974, industrial peace was rapidly restored, largely in the miners' favour. Derek seized upon the transformed` international energy outlook and the new political situation to develop and push forward what became known as '**Plan for Coal**' …

'The themes of many an Ezra speech were the three legs of '**Plan for Coal**': "investment, exploration and research". This illustrated a key attribute of Derek Ezra: that he was a man of vision and someone who has always seen the importance of developing a strategy. That the precise targets of '**Plan for Coal**' were always on the optimistic side (and, even more so, the later '**Plan 2000**') is of less importance than that the strategy existed, could be readily understood, and was bought into by all parties. A positive message was communicated within and outside an industry, and this was one of Derek's great strengths. Derek also strongly believed in another feature of that era, "tripartism". '**Plan for Coal**' was developed through a process of discussions following the 1974 strike – known, rather oddly, as the Coal Industry Examination – involving the NCB, Government and the three principal trade unions … The approach owed something to his continental experience, and Derek always had some admiration for the consensual German attitude to industrial management. The Western European coal industries were all members of an organisation known as *Cepceo* (an acronym from its French name). Derek was a leading personality in driving this organisation, and in developing a parallel strategy to '**Plan** for Coal' at the European level. On the wider international stage, too, there was action. The International Energy Agency was established in response to the 1973/74 oil crisis to monitor international energy developments ... the UK was a founder member and Derek was keen that the NCB should participate as actively as possible. The major oil companies began to invest in coal, which lent support to the view that coal was "the fuel of the future". The 1979 oil crisis reinforced these trends, and led the IEA to set up the Coal Industry Advisory Board to provide advice on coal industry issues. Naturally, Derek became a member. For a period in the 1970s there was therefore an overall sense that the tide had turned for coal, even in the UK. It was Derek Ezra who seized the opportunity, and it is difficult to think of anyone else from within the NCB who could have done the same.

'Not that everyone was as keen. Some at senior level within NCB management were sceptical about the ability to achieve the targets in '**Plan for Coal**' ... When news of someone's doubts reached Derek Ezra, his response would be that "X is so negative". Being "negative" was one of the harshest criticisms in his eyes ... Publicly and with Government, Derek Ezra remained an eloquent advocate for '**Plan for Coal**', emphasising the long lead-times involved in mining investment. Privately, especially in conversation with his Office staff, he became increasingly exasperated by the failure to achieve planned performance levels. There seemed to him to be no reason why this should be, and no obvious levers to pull to change the situation ... occasionally he would vent his frustration on his mining engineering colleagues, some of whom he felt were not sympathetic to the strategy. Various initiatives were undertaken including a Joint Production Drive with the unions, very much an Ezra-style response. Eventually performance did begin to improve, but then the financial results for 1978/9 were adversely affected by the problems and the weather of the 'winter of discontent'; before long another set of difficulties came along with the recession and consequent fall in demand of the early 1980s.

'Criticism has been directed at the management of the NCB during this period. Nigel Lawson in his memoirs describes it as "the archetypal public corporation where genuine business management is largely unknown" ... Apart from the fact that this is a gross caricature of the situation, it also ignores the political and economic climate within which the NCB was operating at the time. As Mike Parker, then NCB Director, Central Planning Unit, has written [in **Thatcherism and the Fall of Coal**], the NCB faced a dual dilemma: First, how to pursue a policy of major investment designed to consolidate UK coal's perceived strategic importance in the era of OPEC power, without at the same time consolidating the power of the NUM; and second, how to make progress with eliminating surplus, uneconomic production capacity while seeking to keep peace in the face of the annual cycle of large wage demands and strike threats. There is room for honest disagreement as to whether at all times the appropriate balance was struck ... but there is no denying the great difficulty of the task." Andrew Horsler adds: 'In fact, nearly 50 deep mines were closed between 1975 and 1982, and industrial manpower fell significantly. Many of these closures followed protracted negotiations at local and sometimes national level, often involving a considerable degree of semantics as to whether collieries had genuinely run out of workable reserves, in which case the NUM would acquiesce in closure. The "Derek and Joe show" may have been imperfect, but it may have been the only show in town which could deliver results in the circumstances of the time. Derek Ezra was undoubtedly conscious of all the dilemmas and conflicting pressures, and did his best to steer the NCB through them. He led all the thinking about how to handle the situation in which the NCB found itself and his colleagues were not proactive in suggesting alternative approaches ...'

'A very bad day for the coal industry …'

Peter Jones succeeded Andrew Horsler as PPS in the Chairman's Office "at the beginning of what was to be a particularly tumultuous period for the industry … I remember sitting with the Chairman in the Green Room at the end of the day on which Margaret Thatcher became PM, after the 1979 General Election. He said: 'This is a very bad day for the coal industry'. I ventured to suggest that it might bring a much-needed dose of economic reality and backbone into the Government's relations with the industry after Tony Benn's years as Energy Secretary. 'No, mark my words … Mrs Thatcher thinks we belong to the past'.

"I was able to observe the workings of the relationship between Joe Gormley and Mick McGahey (to a lesser extent) and Sir Derek, as we moved first into two difficult annual wage negotiations and subsequently into what became the 1981 closures dispute. Preparations for each of these negotiations were directed in meticulous detail by the Chairman in a way that probably owed much to his Army Staff training, and involving local communications campaigns that became more detailed with each set of negotiations. Through his direct contacts with Gormley and McGahey, often in meetings in his private room, Sir Derek developed a good feel for what was and was not deliverable having regard to the distribution of militancy in the coalfields, and the continuing vulnerability of a largely coal-fuelled electricity system to even a relatively short national miners' strike … As the driving force behind the 1974 '**Plan for Coal**' – a strong advocate of UK energy diversity and independence – Sir Derek had argued for many years that it was only a matter of time before most of the deep-mined UK industry became viable, given adequate investment. However, overall productivity growth had virtually stagnated; few of the major deep mine capital projects had generated the projected returns …The incoming Government regarded this situation as both politically and financially unsustainable, and there was a growing realisation within certain sectors of the Board's Mining, Marketing and Finance organisations that only a substantial downwards step-change in the size of the deep-mined industry could give any prospect of a viable industry that could sell its output profitably on a 'willing buyer, willing seller' basis. This was not a message that Sir Derek wished to hear, both because it ran counter to everything he had been seeking to promote for much of the past decade and because he did not believe that so substantial a down-sizing of the industry could be achieved without major conflict with the NUM.

"Under increasing pressure from Government, however, Sir Derek eventually agreed to institute a review which led in due course to a plan, agreed with Government, to "bite the bullet" and announce the likely closure, subject to review, of [50] pits … our expectation was that the Government would hold firm. However, the Chairman was asked to meet [David] Howell in private with no other Board representative present. I attended the main meeting at which Howell announced that the Government had decided that it would be appropriate for the Board to 'hold further discussions with the unions on the closure plans, with a view to movement' … the rest of the NCB team felt a profound sense of shock at this. I was not able to gauge Sir Derek's true feelings about this turn of events. On one level, I felt that he was probably relieved to have avoided a bitter strike which would at that stage have had very limited prospects of being brought to a successful conclusion by the Board. On another, he may have felt betrayed by Government, having been persuaded against his better judgment to pursue a course which ran counter to his instincts. He would certainly have felt justified in his initial assessment that the election of Margaret Thatcher's Government was a bad day for the coal industry. Sir Derek came to the end of his term the following year … he was one of the most intellectually acute people with whom I have worked in a career which has subsequently brought me into contact with a wide range of leaders in the public and private sectors.

"Despite his austere intellect and his very private personality, he was able to communicate effectively with union officials, and he had a fine feel for the use of the media and internal channels of communication to get across messages to the workforce. Many of the approaches he pioneered were used to considerable effect by his successors, against a background in which, in contrast to 1981, the Government considered that it was adequately prepared to win in a protracted struggle. To my great regret, he was given no credit for this".

Transitional comparison

A fourth set of observations comes from Simon Kermode, the third of Derek Ezra's three 'Staff Officers' from 1980 to 1982, and then as second in line for the last few weeks of Derek's time, before working under the very different regimes of his two immediate successors, former Deputy Chairman Norman Siddall, and archetypal 'outsider', Ian MacGregor. Derek's three SOs "saw all but the most personal incoming paperwork, and were thus in the privileged confidential position of being able to advise him in advance about looming problems or opportunities. The system was efficient, worked well, and was typical of Ezra's open style of management". The contrast between the Ezra style and what followed highlights the high degree of organisational and person-to-person skills which was a hallmark of his leadership:

"Under Siddall, there was no major re-organisation. The committee structure inherited from Ezra stayed intact; communications remained good – but life in the Chairman's Office changed considerably. The Office still consisted of three SOs but now with one reporting to each of Siddall and his two Deputy Chairmen. It amounted to a sea-change for the SOs who had been so used to the Ezra "inclusivity". Access to paperwork was restricted and the role of the SOs became reactive rather than proactive: the worth of the Office was diminished, the workload was much less varied and with a narrower focus on internal matters. Later, MacGregor decided to create the Office of the Chief Executive, consisting of himself and his closest deputy, Jimmy Cowan, the theory being that this would facilitate rapid decision-making from the top". Compared with the Ezra era, "in practice it did not work well. The committee structure was slimmed down slightly and some committees were renamed, but they became less effective as decision-making bodies because all important decisions had to be referred to the 'OCE' from which final decisions were supposed to emerge. This actually slowed the decision-making process down. Both MacGregor and his immediate Deputy, Jimmy Cowan, " played their cards close to their chests and discussions were very much held on a need-to-know basis – with the inevitable consequence that many who really did need to know simply didn't. The fact that MacGregor emerged from [the 1984/5] strike as the 'winner' should certainly not be attributed to his management, communication or organisational skills – nor to any tactical genius, but rather to the solid political backing he enjoyed throughout, which enabled him to stand firm".

Simon Kermode, like the other young SOs, frequently accompanied Derek on many NCB official or semi-social occasions; the social aspect was always underlain by a serious coal industry communications purpose, and invariably entailed a punishing work schedule, as Simon relates. "One day in either 1981 or '82 we set off early in the NCB's private plane from London for Newcastle, where Derek addressed an internal conference of mining engineers on energy and coal mining issues; we then flew down to Blackpool, where he addressed a Union conference on the same subjects (albeit with different emphases); then on to Manchester where he spoke to a luncheon meeting of local businessmen on the wider economy, energy and coal; then finally over to Brussels for a Consultative Committee of some sort. This exhausting day always seemed to me to epitomise the importance Derek attached to the communication aspects of his job – getting across both internally and externally the objectives of the industry within the wider economic and business environment, and his strategy for achieving them. I well remember the then 'Director of Wages' telling me during the run-up to the fraught annual wage negotiations with the NUM that no one could teach Derek Ezra anything when it came to drafting the NCB's lengthy and carefully constructed opening position statements which formed the basis of the negotiations.

"The Chairman regularly attended union national and area conferences around the country to address delegates. He also made the effort to get up to the annual Mining Festival Weekend in Blackpool. (This was organised by the NCB, with sponsorship from external organisations such as the Co-Op. It was a great 'coal industry family' event, which consisted of all sorts of activities, competitions and shows, for example, performances by colliery brass bands. Anyone connected with the coal industry could attend and very many did, bringing their families). Julie would frequently accompany Derek. At the more social occasions, I was always struck by the respect and affection in which they were held by the majority of Union people – the Ezras did not have to go to these functions, but the fact that they did so clearly went down well. Julie's presence was particularly well received by the 'Union wives' with whom she might have little in common yet to whom she was able to relate without difficulty".

Simon recalls one especial event, which said a great deal about Derek as a person; "Derek was awarded an honorary degree from Leeds University. The occasion was enjoyable – the Duchess of Kent presiding – and we ended up giving Lord Hailsham a lift on the NCB's plane back to London, Hailsham having also collected a doctorate. During the flight, he proceeded to comment on and ask questions about the coal industry in a none-too supportive fashion. Derek was in good form and dealt with him in a very robust while friendly manner! The invitation to the award ceremony had included 'and family'. I remember Derek saying to me that he didn't have any family, and asking me if I would go with him. It struck me at the time that, to some extent, the Chairman's Office *was* his family".

A personal conclusion to this chapter may rest with Andrew Horsler: 'Derek was immensely hard-working, and his office was an exciting place to work. He was intellectually head and shoulders above his Board colleagues and dominated the policy-making agenda. He had a vision of where the industry should be going and was a first-class communicator and proselytiser for coal. He was a private person, not "clubbable" with his colleagues, which led to a certain distrust between the powerful 'mining engineering establishment' and himself. To those few who were close to him, he engendered great loyalty, even though at times his demands might seem unreasonable, and, on occasion, possibly misguided. Working for him taught me more about leadership and management than I could have hoped to learn by any other means at that age'.

These, then, were some of the impressions that Derek made on four of those who worked closest with him as Staff Officers. This privileged family of young men was given very special insights as to 'how' he did what he did. These insights would not have been apparent to those outside the inner circle.

Contributors: Andrew Horsler, Peter Jones, Christopher Pennell, Colin Ambler, Simon Kermode; Mike Parker

CHAPTER 5:
1974 – ONE YEAR IN A CHAIRMAN'S LIFE

Chapter 5 is the final part of the Memoir's account, related uniquely through those closest to him, of the essential qualities whereby one man, backed by his team, was able to do what he had to do. Christopher Pennell was the earliest in the sequence of NCB Staff Officers (after Ron Pyne) to offer his recollections of the 'Ezra era'. He does so from a very special perspective: the diary he kept of one particularly important year – 1974. It is reproduced almost in its entirety. Some of the events described have inevitably also been touched on elsewhere, but they still benefit from being set down here as a single chronological whole. As an overview, Christopher has commented: 'I concentrated on the theme of the extent to which the management of IR disputes and the longer-term negotiation of an effective incentive scheme was often out of Derek's hands – because of the intervention by politicians, the controls exercised by civil servants, the capriciousness of the NUM leadership (where the old guard was being challenged by Scargill) and the occasional disarray on the Board … Derek's 'intellectual rigour and his tendency to treat others as if they were all decent people, who could see the sense of logic, fell short of what was needed with Gormley, Daly, McGahey and others: if he had occasionally and unexpectedly sworn at them, he might have grabbed their attention. I often felt that Gormley took advantage of the constant expectation that Derek would be looking for a way through and a compromise, even when Gormley was ramping up his demands or simply outflanked by his hardliners. I suppose there were two realities at the heart of 1974 and IR: first, that mineworkers had genuinely lost ground in the relativity stakes, and, secondly, that the Yom Kippur War had given the 'headroom' to correct (but not over-correct) that lost ground. Mineworkers became the best-paid industrial workers, but overplayed their muscle when the markets and increasing environmentalism – not to mention Mrs Thatcher – were moving against them.'

Fig.19: Derek Ezra was always on the look-out for signs of morale issues, and the views of young miners entering the workforce, especially in areas where labour relations were delicate. An SO invariably went with him on these visits. Here he listens to a young recruit at Tondu Colliery, S.Wales Area, Nov. 1977

SO Colin Ambler, writing on the basis of Christopher Pennell's observations, also highlighted Derek's 'intellectual strength, tremendous resilience (helped by, rather than despite, the occasional whisky, and the regular *Romeo y Julietta!*), his total commitment to the industry; and his vision and stature way above the others on the Board, who were often poor contributors, and, worse in some instances, disloyal. He deserved better but he was strong enough to paddle his own canoe. One point which emerges very clearly … was the 'IR-heavy' nature of the job. 1974 was perhaps extreme but it was a constant preoccupation, and I often felt that his instinct and judgment on IR issues, and his ability to relate to the NUM top three was surprisingly good and often much sounder than the efforts of the IR professionals.'

Christopher's 'Ezra diary' year, in his own words, "started in the seventh week of an NUM overtime ban, accompanied by the Government's imposed three-day working week, and remained dominated by industrial relations difficulties and traumas. The Union had lodged a wage claim in July 1973 which amounted to increases of 31%. The NCB, operating within Conservative Government counter-inflation guidelines were unable to offer more than a 7% increase in basic wages, with other fringe benefits, and a willingness to discuss the possibility of a productivity scheme. A meaningful incentive scheme remained the ultimate aim of industrial relations and improved productivity for a long time to come.

"It was a deeply disappointing state of affairs given that the industry's performance in 1972/3 had amounted to a remarkable recovery after the 1972 strike and that the Coal Industry Act had provided the industry with substantial Government financial assistance, including writing off accumulated deficits and providing grants for the social costs of the closures. Now the industry was plunged again into an IR crisis.

Political cockpit…

"We are now familiar with captains of industry having freedom to determine the plans and futures of their enterprises and controlling the terms and conditions of their workforces against a background of austerity and counter-inflationary Government policies. These freedoms were not available to Derek Ezra, who headed a huge industry at the vital heart of the UK's energy needs; it operated in a political cockpit from which it constantly but vainly struggled to escape. Politicians of all parties, civil servants, the TUC, the CBI, and others all piled into the dispute between the NCB and the NUM, often serving to make the solution less rather than more likely. Even closer to home, the NUM was no disciplined monolith with whom Derek could easily do business; it was riven with factions and towering egos. The President, Joe Gormley, was a personable, decent man but easily pushed around by his fractious Executive who could force him to do about-turns on negotiating positions adopted with the Board. His deputy, Mick McGahey, was an old-style communist leader who ruled his Scottish miners with a rod of iron; his demands were usually extreme, but he kept his word on a deal. The NUM Secretary, Lawrence Daly was highly intelligent and an impressive orator, one of the few who could give the upstart Arthur Scargill a good hiding; but Lawrence's effectiveness was undermined by alcohol, a problem all-too prevalent amongst union negotiators. Different union leaders from the regions leaned to the hard left or the middle ground or vacillated capriciously between the two. 1974 is the year in which Scargill successfully started to flex his muscles against the 'old guard' leadership of the NUM.

"On the one hand, 1974 was characterised by the heroic and positive efforts of Derek Ezra to develop a vision for the industry which exploited the new headroom provided by soaring oil prices following the October 1973 Yom Kippur War - a vision which would crystallise into '**Plan for Coal**', later to be endorsed through the Labour Government's 'Coal Industry Examination'. On the other hand it was also characterised by a bruising negative industrial dispute, which not only lost the NCB 20m tons of coal production but also led to the fall of the Heath Government, followed by immediate open-ended negotiations to end the dispute and a long tail of further negotiations throughout the year about a productivity bonus scheme.

"The steep rise in oil prices had enabled Derek to envisage a coal industry which could eventually stand on its own feet without Government subsidy, by increasing its prices within the oil headroom (although perhaps insufficient attention was given to the growth of coal imports at very competitive prices from low-cost international producers). However, to meet the demand, which significantly exceeded NCB output, the industry would need to invest in improved productive capacity (for this it would need initial help), drive for much-improved productivity, and gee up all departments to boost their abilities to support these increases. Derek was almost fanatical in his drive to push departments and production areas to gear up for the Plan; indeed, some were amazed and disconcerted by the almost open-cheque book approach which he exhibited to anyone able to claim that their scheme would further the Plan. For example, Peter Tregelles didn't look a gift horse in the mouth when he demonstrated to his Chairman how an enlarged and vastly better equipped Mines Research Establishment at Bretby could contribute to greater face- and road-heading productivity…

Political football

"Before this could take off, the overtime ban needed to be overcome. Already the industry was mired in Pay Board investigations over suggestions from the Secretary of State, Willie Whitelaw, that 'waiting time' might be a device for finding more money. The Pay Board delved deep into custom and practice surrounding the length of a standard working week at a colliery.

"Most industrialists would expect that their unions and management would negotiate their way through a dispute, but coal was ever a political football. On 9 January, Whitelaw met the entire NUM Executive without the NCB being present. Scargill branded the meeting a 'pantomime' and 'a Government PR exercise': probably not far from the truth; the meeting got nowhere. Then the TUC publicly volunteered a view that they would restrain all other workers if the mineworkers could be allowed to settle outside the Government's counter-inflationary policies. Edward Heath, the PM, met the TUC on 10 January to explore this idea, which for a while seemed the only initiative on the table, even though it was highly questionable how the TUC could guarantee the restraint of other unions. In the event Heath became more rather than less implacable, pinning his hopes on sitting it out, on good weather, and on the NUM not escalating the dispute (ignoring the fact that coal stocks were not particularly high, a mistake that Margaret Thatcher would not repeat in the 1980s). On 22 January Derek appeared on ITN to say that he believed that mineworkers had too much sense to strike and jeopardise the industry's future, but two days later the NUM decided to ballot its members on strike action, despite a letter from Heath to Gormley warning the NUM of the implications of a strike for electricity production, and of the likely impact on other workers. Already the overtime ban was losing one third of normal production.

"It was a constant frustration for Derek Ezra, who believed in the essential rationality of his fellow human beings and who expected to be able to do direct business with the NUM leadership, that coal industry disputes quickly escalated to the political stratosphere, often leaving the NCB leadership feeling like bystanders in their own affairs.

The "*New Statesman*" issued a cartoon on 25 January (a day when Derek met Heath) showing Heath at the door of No.10 shouting down the street to retreating TUC leaders: 'And don't you come back until you have something less constructive to suggest'. "By now Mick McGahey was threatening mass picketing of power stations if a strike was called, and Heath was being interviewed on "Panorama" about the developing situation.

'The only NCB initiative was a letter to Whitelaw from Ezra suggesting that the comments of the 1972 Wilberforce Report on the position of mineworkers in national pay structures could provide 'relativity' arguments to justify some movement in the offer to the NUM. This letter was quickly leaked to the press (many thought by a part-time Board Member) and fed a new frenzy of speculation about a way forward. Heath took the idea up, writing to the TUC and the CBI, but he clearly felt that the NUM could be persuaded to call off industrial action until a new relativities review had been carried out. On 4 February the NUM's national ballot gave the NEC an 81% mandate to call a strike, which they duly did for midnight on 9 February. Two days later, Gormley, McGahey and Daly met Ezra and his Deputy Chairs to discuss how the strike would be conducted, but also to sound out whether anything could be paid now in lieu of a further relativities review which could justify calling off the strike. The civil service made it clear later that day to Derek that this was not a runner. Then the Opposition Leader, Wilson, spotting the opportunity for political pressure on Heath, made his own suggestion for a way forward, based on paying mineworkers for meal breaks taken in difficult conditions underground. This proposal was not made to the NCB but in person by Wilson to the NUM leaders at their London Headquarters.

'Who runs this country?'

"Heath then made the momentous decision on 7 February to call a General Election for 28 February in the hope that he could persuade the NUM to call off the strike while the election proceeded. The theme underlying the campaign was: 'Who runs this country?' Sadly for Heath the electorate's reply on 28 February was … 'Not you, since you ask'.

"That fateful Q&A underlay Conservative attitudes towards the industry for the next two decades, and led to Mrs Thatcher being prepared for the 1984 strike with handsome coal stocks and a longer-term intention to privatise it. During the election campaign Wilson and Heath slogged at each other over the coal industry dispute, leaving the NCB as passive onlookers. The Chairman and his team meanwhile had to start work on preparing the huge volumes of evidence required of them on mineworker relativities with other workers for the Pay Board, to whom Heath had referred the relativity issues on 8 February. A committee of Ezra, Vice Chairmen W.V.Sheppard and Siddall, and IR Board Member Shepherd oversaw the work and signed off the evidence at breakneck speed. Then in w/c 18 February each of the players (NUM, NCB, the civil service, NACODS, BACM, APEX, British Railways, Electricity Council and others) gave oral evidence in hearings in the basement of a Piccadilly Hotel, chaired by Sir Frank Figgures. Our 'local' dispute was now the subject of a public enquiry to which all the world and his wife gave evidence as to how far the relativity between mineworkers and other workers had deteriorated against mineworkers, and how the pay of different mineworkers (faceworkers, other underground workers, and surface workers) should relate to each other.

"Derek Ezra and Norman Siddall gave the oral evidence and handled the Pay Board's questions with consummate skill. Here again was evidence of Derek's clear and confident presentation skills in formal proceedings, but later in an impromptu press conference he partially let the cat out of the bag about the level of heavy price increases the NCB was contemplating, both to cover the increased costs of a settlement, and take up some of the 'slack' against oil prices. Handling the press was always more risky than set-piece speeches and formal questioning.

"One incident illustrates how much and bizarrely the dispute had escalated out of the hands of the main players: on 11 February a group of industrialists and merchant bankers offered to pay a daily sum (reputed to be £80,000) sufficient to give the mineworkers a weekly increase of £2.50 or so until settlement was reached, in return for an immediate return to work. Gormley feigned interest but his Executive was now set on its strike path. With the fall of the Heath Government, the Board had to be prepared for its successor. The hawks on the Board (the part-timers led by Jack Wellings, but also W.V.Sheppard, Miron and Clement) were anxious that we were not exposed by the Wilson Government to open-ended negotiations with the NUM, or at least not unless the Government had given prior endorsement to our coal pricing expectations. By 3 March, the day before Heath's resignation, Derek had formulated his four immediate objectives (in part incorporated in a letter to the new Secretary of State):–

- To achieve an early pay settlement without open-ended negotiations;
- To secure a write-off of our likely £150 million deficit in 1973/4 but then to apply substantial price increases so as to cover all our costs in 1974/75;
- To get early Government approval of our 'Plan for Coal' aspirations;
- To establish a rational long-term wages structure.

"While these objectives were in large part achieved, the start was rocky. On 5 March two surprise Labour Cabinet appointments were made – Eric Varley as Secretary of State for Energy and Michael Foot as 'SoS' for Employment. Michael Foot went to kiss the Queen's hand in his duffle coat, met the NUM at 2 pm, then the NCB at 3 pm. The NUM's expectations were high from the nods and winks given to them by Foot. As far as the guidance was given to the NCB (where Ezra and his two Deputy Chairs and his ubiquitous PPS, myself, attended), Foot said we could set aside the complications of the Relativities Review for the time being and instead should immediately re-open negotiations with the NUM on a completely open-ended basis. So much for guidance; we were on our own, with a highly expectant NUM.

"Between 10.30 am on 6 March and 10.00 pm on 7 March the NCB/ NUM Joint National Negotiating Committee sat in session until a settlement was reached. At one stage on the first day of negotiations, Derek rather masterly turned the tables on the NUM by saying that there was no point in the NCB offering anything more if the NUM was not prepared to indicate that they would consider anything less than their full claim. Their Executive went into a nail-biting huddle in Room 16. They then sent their top team to meet our top team in the 'Green Room' … out of which emerged a tentative £45 'face'/ £35 'underground'/ £31 'surface' formula. The NUM returned later hoping for more on the 'surface'. This led to an impromptu Board meeting,

Fig.20: NCB's Staff College, "The Vache", Chalfont St. Giles, Bucks, provided valuable neutral territory for fostering better relations with the Unions. Here a joint conference on Dec.18/19 takes place in the crucial year, 1974, (described in S.O. Christopher Pennell's Diary) with the NACODS Union Executive and NCB managers. (*Std. front row*): (*c.*) Derek Ezra; Norman Siddall, Dep.Ch., NCB (*l.*) and L.Wormald, Pres. NACODS, in between; (*rt.*) G. Simpson, Sec., NACODS. Other NCB Board members present include: C.G.Shepherd, W.Miron; J.Mills; and D.Davies

which haggled over an extra 50p or £1 on the 'surface', and a phone call to the senior civil servant as we inched over our official spending limit. The PPS did a rough Board Member count and advised Ezra that if he took a vote only four hardliners would stick out against the full extra £1. So the vote was taken and a £45/ £36/ £32 offer was formally made to the NUM in the Green Room. The national officials took this offer to the full Executive in Room 16 and it was accepted at 10.00 pm on the second day of negotiations; at which point the drinks cupboard was opened!

Incentives and disasters

"By 11 March the new Government had agreed the first stage of our coal price increases, perhaps to shift the blame in part on the previous Government, to ensure that the link with NUM militancy was plain for all to see, and to show that they understood economic realities. On 20 March Ezra discussed with Varley the format for the long-term review of the industry. Varley wanted it to concentrate on 'Plan for Coal', and leave long-term wages to Michael Foot's discussions with the TUC. This left us with no long-term wages framework which might have limited the ambitions for the NUM's next wages round. By 25 March the industry had recovered to 80% of normal output and the Chairman was turning his attention to longer-term output. He signalled the importance of going flat out for 120m tons per annum by 1974/5. Even with price increases, which the Government had now fully agreed, we could only hope for a small financial surplus if we achieved 120m tons. An optimistic Senior Management Conference was held on 9 April when Area Directors gave enthusiastic support for quickly introducing an incentive scheme which they estimated would lift output by 10%. The early reality was less positive: by mid-May the industry was only getting 2.3m tons production a week when 2.6m were required on a consistent basis to hit the magic 120m tons for the new financial year. At a CINCC meeting on 21 May Derek launched a new Joint Production Drive to get the 120m tons: detailed objectives were set for every level (Area and Colliery) with arrangements for Area and Colliery Consultative Committees to review and discuss progress. In this way he hoped to lock in not only management but also the unions, and he earnestly hoped that an incentive scheme could be superimposed on this to guarantee success. One cannot over-emphasise Derek Ezra's restless energy to devise initiatives to push the industry forward towards more challenging goals.

"By April, Eric Varley's Coal Industry Examination had got into full swing with three working groups on R&D, IR, and Demand and Supply, the first two with Ministers in the chair, and the last with a senior civil servant chairing. The parties represented on the Steering Committee were the Government, the NCB, the NUM, NACODS and BACM. By 18 June, Varley had launched an Interim Report which endorsed the NCB's '**Plan for Coal**' as the industry's broad strategy and added a Government assurance that "short-term fluctuations in the price of competing fuels will not be allowed to interfere with steady progress in the implementation of the Plan".

"It also signalled the need for:–

• Exploiting the Selby coalfield as rapidly as possible;

• Stepping up Opencast production to 15m tons or more;

• Introducing an effective scheme of incentives for increased production;

• Compensation scheme for pneumoconiosis claims, backed by Government.

"Derek Ezra's four objectives of 3 March were now beginning to bear real fruit.

"There is always a price for underground mining. In 1972/73, 80 men had been killed underground, including seven men in a water inrush at Lofthouse. In 1973/4 the figure reduced to 60 but this masked the cruel bunching of major accidents in that year: first at Seafield where five men died in a roof fall, then at Markham where 18 men died in a grisly shaft accident. Derek Ezra had the difficult job of writing to the widow or next-of-kin in every case: it was a task which successive PPSs had no pleasure in helping him carry out. By 1974/5 the number fell to the lowest figure ever, 56, but the safety story shifted from underground and went outside these figures. On 1 June at 4.52 pm the Nypro plant at Flixborough blew up.

"On the following day I accompanied the Chairman to the site of utter devastation. 29 men had been killed in a cyclohexane fireball. Even the fire services were stunned by the impact. Ezra was there because NCB had a significant shareholding in the plant, but the result was that, in doing the decent thing, the recognisable NCB Chairman took the flak in the trial by TV, lifting too much of the limelight off the shoulders of the Dutch majority shareholders. Three days later news reached Ezra in a meeting at Hobart House with an MP that nine men were trapped at Park Hill Colliery. He broke down sobbing when the Area Director rang to say that things looked hopeful (indeed the rescue was totally successful).

"It was an eye-opener that the somewhat cold rational NCB leader could break down under the cumulative pressure of accidents where, as the man in the chair, he must have felt ultimately responsible. Meanwhile the blasé mining engineer, W.V.Sheppard, would speculate about the number of deaths required to constitute a mining disaster. For Derek every death was a cumulative disaster.

"Planning for an incentive scheme was proceeding apace and on 19 June Ezra set up a new Incentives Committee to direct negotiations for its implementation. The Board wanted it to be a national scheme linked to genuine local incentives and easy to understand. Gormley was by then bravely supporting a scheme because it would give his men big increases out of the industry's earnings without rocking the Labour Party boat or being labelled greedy by lower-paid workers elsewhere. Happily at the NUM Annual Conference at Llandudno in early July a militant Yorkshire wages resolution was defeated by 138,000 votes to 134,000, When Norman Siddall met the NUM in the JNNC on 17 July there was little vociferous opposition to incentives (although it has to be admitted that Scargill and South Wales were absent).

Fig.21: Communications opportunities were never far from the NCB Chairman's mind, and the NCB PRO, Derbyshire-born Geoff Kirk (*l.*) often went with him on colliery visits. Also here, Mike Eaton, Area General Manager, N.Yks, and the Colliery Manager

"One of the acute disappointments of July was Varley's chilling news that the Government intended to take over our North Seas gas interests, developed jointly over some years with Conoco. In the event Tony Benn completed this process some time later and created BNOC. It is one of the ironies that Labour rather than the Conservatives took back our gas interests and thereby created for NCB one of its lost opportunities, namely that the NCB could have developed as an energy and chemicals conglomerate with a great future in eventual privatisation.

"Meanwhile the prospects for 120m tons of deep-mined production in 1974/5, and for longer-term expansion, looked poor. Weekly performances were disappointing; there was insufficient evidence that the industry was adequately geared up to drive its future reconstruction, including a lack of acknowledgement of the capacity needed to generate and appraise the capital investment projects at sufficient speed; the introduction of the much-needed incentive scheme still lay far off. Later in August at the Board's GP Committee, where £4m 'pocket money' was sought at Stage 1 for the new Selby Coalfield, the future Stage 2 highly capital-intensive nature of this development was agonizingly laid out; nonetheless this led to a fierce clash on 16 August between Ezra and W.V.Sheppard on Selby, the Chairman saying that for the size of investment we should not regard 10m tons as its maximum potential, and W.V.Sheppard vehemently arguing that it would not be able to do more. Internally the Board was facing the possibility that, given the reducing prospects of getting 120m tons this year we might have to go for large price increases in our industrial markets so soon after last April's 'shocker' increases. This was to become a major issue with the civil servants later in the autumn as the sensitivity of high NCB increases looked like coinciding with another General Election to strengthen Wilson's mandate. During the second half of 1974 Ezra instituted meetings with groups of young NCB executives which provided different and occasionally useful perspectives on the industry's affairs, including the observation that the NCB would never be able to lift its head high until it could say that it was paying its own way, free of Government subsidies - a brave initiative by Ezra to open up a new front of private advice from concerned critical friends.

"Earlier in July, Gormley and McGahey were appalled when they learnt from Ezra how badly South Wales was doing, with withering losses per ton at some collieries. Derek secured a rare one-to-one chat with Daly about incentives and some revelations about how Daly viewed some of the leading NUM and Board figures. The one personal bright spot for Ezra at this time was the receipt of a knighthood on 24 July. One of the key issues for the remainder of 1974 was how successful the NCB would be in persuading mineworkers to vote for an incentive scheme which was meaningful. The barrier was the NUM Executive which was on a knife edge between those who might back a scheme and those who were only prepared to contemplate a scheme if it was based on national performance, which, of course, was far from incentivising the performance of men at their own locations. If the Executive wouldn't support a worthwhile scheme, ordinary miners would never be aware of, or vote on, a good scheme offered by the Board. This would raise the difficult question of how far the Board felt it could appeal over the heads of the NUM directly to the workforce.

"By early September, while Area Directors had done much to prepare the machinery and admin for an incentive scheme, the NUM had done nothing to publicise to its members what was potentially on offer from NCB. When the NUM Executive met on 12 September to consider the NCB's scheme, they decided to refer it to a Special Conference on 26 September to be followed by a general membership ballot. Derek approved IR Department and Geoff Kirk, Director of PR, helping the NUM to draft issues of their newspaper, "*The Miner*", and leaflets to describe the scheme accurately. By 25 September, Scargill was accusing the NCB of "brainwashing" mineworkers over incentives; on the same day a "*Guardian*" story broke that the NCB was organising a large publicity drive, through our own "*Coal News*" and the NUM's leaflets, to ram home the incentives message. The Board remained in hope that the publicity was having some effect with miners themselves, even though some officials refused to allow some of the documentation to be distributed. The NUM Special Conference on 26 September collapsed in disarray when Scargill and his Yorkshire and South.Wales cronies walked out because Gormley refused a vote to be taken on the next pay deal. Immediately the NEC formed and voted for a postponement of the intended ballot and instead for the leadership to meet the Board to secure revision (and presumably watering down) of the incentive scheme on offer. It later became apparent to me that the postponement was engineered by Varley in the interests of avoiding trouble until after the 11th October General Election vote. If that was the wish, it was not fulfilled.

"On 3 October the NUM Executive astonishingly and unanimously rejected our incentive offer and said that they were only prepared to consider a [toothless] national scheme based on national output per manshift! High Moor colliery (North Derbyshire) went on strike in disgust at the Executive decision.

"In September Gormley persuaded Varley of the case for quickening the timetable for preparing the final report of the Coal Industry Examination. Varley saw electoral advantage in early signing off; in fact it waited until the end of October, after the General Election. On 10 September Ezra met Arthur Hawkins of CEGB for another of their acrimonious meetings: their business – but not their personal – relations were difficult. Hawkins was always trying to put Ezra on the back foot with Government. Sometimes Ezra's PPS would be a go-between. Hawkins was determined to demonstrate that, while the NCB was claiming that to be able to meet its contractual tonnage for the CEGB in 1974/5, it would be unable to achieve the annual tonnages that CEGB would require thereafter, and therefore there was a case for new oil-fired power stations, if not for re-opening the nuclear debate. Fortunately he was more muted in a meeting with Varley and Ezra on 18 September where Varley made it clear he wanted agreement between the two organisations (and their chairs!) to avoid their differences over supplies becoming political during an election campaign. This was surprising since on the previous day Varley had agreed, and there had been announced, heavy coal price increases for industrial coals for 1st October and for domestic customers from 1st November.

"On 8 October the Board's negotiating team met the NUM's team with the whole Executive sitting in as observers! NCB stressed the urgent production situation and welcomed the NUM decision to co-operate in the Joint Production Drive with reviews of performance in every Area; it expressed regret at the Executive's rejection of our incentive scheme and rebutted their criticisms of it, making clear that the scheme was still on offer.

"When NCB asked the NUM negotiators to explain what scheme they would suggest, it became apparent that the NUM had as many different schemes in mind as NUM leaders present. NUM decided to set up an eight-man working party on which both the left and the right were represented to hammer out a favoured national scheme. Within two days Labour were re-elected with an overall majority of three.

NATIONAL COAL BOARD
PLAN TO THE YEAR 2000

Fig.22: The optimistic end-product of the revitalised years of the later 1970s, 'Plan 2000' was produced in 1981 with a gold cover, to emphasise the importance attached to the new golden era that then appeared to be looming for Coal. 'It was never formally endorsed by the government' [*Br. Coal Industry* v.5. p364]

"At the full Board meeting on 11 October Derek posed three main questions:

1. Were the Board prepared to consider a national OMS incentive scheme? – to which the answer was a resounding "no", because such a scheme would provide neither significant extra coal nor extra earnings;

2. Did the Board want to stand firm on their offer or modify it? The answer: to modify it, by averaging performance out at the faces and developments at individual pits, and to put the production bonus on a pit basis;

3. What should our tactics be? The answer: to write to the NUM on incentives in the following week and seek an early meeting thereafter where we would reject a national OMS scheme and put forward our modifications to our offer.

"Varley endorsed this approach but wanted to keep his own powder dry. On 15 October, at a Senior

Management Conference, Area Directors strongly endorsed the Board's stance against the backdrop of a pessimistic but realistic presentation from Robert Dunn and Malcolm Edwards showing that we were then under-supplying most of our markets and heading for 112m tons deep-mined output in 1974/5.

"When the same presentation was made to the coal-mining unions on the following day, they were aghast and joined with the Board in an initiative to get each colliery to review its performance against budget and its prospects, involving management and the unions and groups of the workforce; Gormley remained adamant about not seeking a solution through an effective pit-based local incentive scheme. Indeed, on the following day, when the NUM working party met to consider what sort of scheme they wanted, they followed the Scargill route … a toothless national scheme with equal distributions nationally, ignoring the impact of better and worse performances in different locations. Even Varley put private pressure on Gormley and McGahey on 21 October, saying that his serious fears about coal production were tempting him to reconsider his views on nuclear energy and the future of coal-firing at Drax. On 23 October, Norman Siddall led the NCB negotiating team on incentives in a meeting with the NUM. He duly turned down any notion of an ironed-out national scheme and said the Board could not abandon 'face' and 'development' incentives at pit level but were prepared to average out at each pit. The NEC voted whether to continue negotiations and for once sanity prevailed and, by 14 to 11, negotiations were resumed. On 30 October, under pressure from NUM negotiators who wanted the production bonus to be determined nationally, the Board's side conceded that the bonus might be determined at Area level, but before the day was out this had been conceded as being at national level. The NUM then retired to reach a formal Executive decision. To everyone's consternation, Gormley returned, almost in tears, to say that the Executive had rejected the deal by 14 votes to 12. We later learned that Joe Whelan had switched votes contrary to his region's mandate to him, for which he was strongly criticised by the Notts Executive. Varley, who had advised the PM that a deal was in the bag, was shattered. Joe Gormely had seriously lost it, and Arthur Scargill was now riding high, with public talk of a huge wage demand and the £5,000 miner by April.

"The Board resolved to toughen its public campaign for a better incentive scheme. Ezra played his part by visiting Yorkshire on 6 November, taking the argument direct to the militants. He visited Yorkshire Main but gave a gruelling and impressive 75-minute press conference. He got over the need for an effective incentive scheme; some media elements misunderstood him to say that he was willing to contemplate a six-month trial.

"This then became the fresh hare which the press and others pursued for a few days. Other Board Members played their part in other coalfields, but then the whole Board side was spectacularly let down by Wilfred Miron, who appeared in a dinner jacket in front of a red-coated toastmaster making a televised speech to a stuffed-shirt audience denouncing 'latter-day Lenins' and 'saboteurs of the Social Contract'. This gave those we wished to influence, the ordinary mineworkers, the excuse to believe that the NCB was grossly out of touch and itself politically motivated.

"On 7 November the NUM ballot result showed 61.5% had voted against the Board's incentive offer; even in Nottinghamshire only 53.5% were in favour. There were strong allegations of ballot-rigging. Only two days earlier, despite the militancy against the Board's scheme, particularly in South Wales, Ezra and I visited the Area and met the South Wales NUM Executive. It was a good visit conducted with great courtesy by Emlyn Williams and Dai Francis (and I still have the union tie given to me) who were anxious to stress that, notwithstanding their opposition to the Board's incentive scheme, they intended to work hard within the Joint Production Drive to lift Welsh performance. It was also clear by now that Wilfred Miron, the Board representative for South Wales, was *persona non grata* there.

Output, input and setbacks

"The Board's objective of an effective locally-based scheme was lost for the foreseeable future. By the end of 1974/75 a production bonus based on total national output in the final quarter was agreed and paid in the first quarter of 1975/76. but no other bonus was paid in 1975/76 because national output never reached the base level necessary for the rest of the year; where, after all, was the incentive for it to do so?

"However, attention had shifted to the main wage claim which was presaged by Yorkshire and Scottish NUM Area Councils formulating very big claims on 9 December. They had the running. The following day, in Gormley's absence, McGahey chaired the NUM negotiating team, when it voted 6 against 6 in a motion before it. McGahey gave the casting vote in favour of a massive claim. The TUC immediately said they could not support such an ambitious claim. When on 12 December McGahey again chaired the meeting, this time of the NEC, the NEC voted 14 to 12 against the team's recommended huge claim but McGahey ruled against the 6 members who were with the 14 but who had been outvoted in the team meeting, saying that they had to remain mandated by the team vote. At the last minute Gormley rose from his sickbed (and how ill was he) and reversed this all again, squashing the Scottish claim being accepted as the national claim. Ironically Derek's last Area visit of the year (on 23 December) was to Scotland where he met Mick McGahey and the entire Scottish Executive on the Joint Production Drive. McGahey was straight, autocratic on home turf, and spare in humour and emotion. He introduced us to his son, a good amateur boxer, who one could easily believe was his enforcer!

"He said the Scottish NUM was committed to the Coal Industry Examination's endorsement of the industry's deep-mined goal of 120m tons and the Joint Production Drive to produce it. He recognised the union's responsibility to show it could produce. Ezra was very frank in turn: he said that Scotland was our biggest mining problem, development rates were abysmal while the rest of the country was showing some signs of recovery, Scotland was still declining. McGahey had instructed his Executive to hear Ezra out politely. and so they did. There had indeed been some production recovery elsewhere in the country, but 120m tons for 1974/75 was no longer on the cards; 112m tons could be bettered. In the event, and beyond my 1974 perspective, by the end of 1974/75 the Board was able to report (to a new Secretary of State, Anthony Wedgwood Benn) a deep-mined output of 115m tons, and that 10 collieries had closed during the year, and three colliery mergers had taken place, leaving 246 working pits at the end of the financial year. The Board was able to report a £34m operating profit but only £3.5m of that had come from mining as opposed to coal products and ancillaries.

"There was an amusing instance of farce towards the end of 1974, as Derek and the Board prepared for a personal visit by the Duke of Edinburgh to Hobart House to learn about the industry's plans. Never was a simple lunch with the Board so rehearsed, with on occasions Sam Potts and W.V.Sheppard playing the Duke and I even got to play John Mills, a regionally-based Board Member, but I couldn't raise the required pomposity. The lunch was a great success; the

Duke was a live wire and overstayed by 40 minutes; he never knew that his menu changed several times over and every remark had been pre-ordained until natural bonhomie broke through the planning and artifice.

"The pressure of industrial relations emergencies was such at this time that, despite my relatively junior position, I twice had the daunting task of representing Derek abroad at Energy International, a very distinguished advisory board for an important international portfolio of energy stocks. For someone in an early stage of his career, there was nothing quite like being so close to the Chairman of the NCB for living life at the top of a major force in Britain's industrial life. Derek could be infuriating and often blind to the problems of a young father working the same hours as him, but I never regretted what I learnt, both as to how things should be done and how they should not, and I remained loyal to Derek's essential vision for the industry and his personal drive and commitment to bring it about. It pained me that he also had to manage and inspire a factious Board and senior management, some of whom showed him scant loyalty themselves.

"There were times when, despite his enormous talents and intellectual rigour, he lacked the emotional intelligence and was too squeamish to challenge some of the mining big beasts; he failed sometimes to confront opposition and disloyalty head on. He never really understood mining engineers and their egos and, on one occasion, amazed both them and me by saying he didn't know what 'Section 1 Instructions' were [*see Glossary*]. He visited collieries underground wearing wellingtons rather than boots ... but he engaged with the colliery's union leaders with passion at the inevitable surface buffet, demonstrating in discussion his enthusiasm, evident sincerity, and his basic belief that they, like him, cared deeply about their industry being a success.

"**On a visit to Tilmanstone colliery before the year recounted above, I followed directly behind him crawling the length of a very long and low face, where, at 27 or so, I was flagging. I noticed him falter (and who wouldn't at his age and lack of fitness) and I staggered up to him to find him collapsed. We took him out on a stretcher. He had had another minor heart attack; (the first had been in the garden at Brook House, in October 1973). For once, the mining engineers recognized it had been a ridiculous decision to send him along such a difficult long face in such a hot pit. Within a very few weeks he was back at work; his pace had barely slackened and he rarely mentioned his brush with death.**"

This fearsome incident marks the end of Christopher Pennell's remarkable diary account of a momentous year in Derek's, and the industry's life. It is characteristic that little of the difficulty and down-side to that year's events emerged through Derek's own verbal recollections to the Memoir's editorial team. To him they were just part of the job he loved. That positive attitude lay at the very heart of Derek Ezra.

Contributors: Christopher Pennell, Colin Ambler

Fig.23: Derek Ezra's thirty-year involvement with Coal not only reached out to the whole mining community, present and past, but also enabled him to promote the industry to the highest in the land. Here, he and Lady Ezra attend the Festival Dinner of the CTBA, at the Connaught Rooms, London, 16 Nov 1976; HRH Prince Philip, Duke of Edinburgh, President, later Patron, greets Lady Ezra; (*l.*) Rosalind Browne; Mrs Angela Glover & (*rt.*) Mrs Richard Horne, wife of the Dep.Ch., CTBA, PM, The Fuellers

Fig.24: HRH Prince Philip gives his Presidential address. (*Std. l. to rt.*): Sir Derek Ezra, Guest of Honour; President-Elect, Duke of Devonshire; Dr Paul Glover; Ch. CTBA; (*foreground, table sprig*), a guest of the Western Fuel company, sponsors

CHAPTER 6: THE EZRA VISION: MARKETING COAL – INDUSTRIAL, DOMESTIC AND TRADE

It has become clear that Derek Ezra's focus from the outset of his NCB career, fully in the tradition of Robens' own bent for salesmanship, was on the need, and the opportunity, to sell coal in an increasingly competitive world, nationally as well as internationally, not to simply produce and distribute it to a market then appearing to be, however chronically and foreseeably, starved of fuel resources.

To the eye of the present market-driven century this seems like a blinding flash of the obvious; it was not so obvious to either the industry itself, or to its post-war Governments, not least because the bulk market was still to the electric power stations, on a supply and demand footing, not susceptible to any high degree of promotional influence by the NCB. Here is an aspect of the NCB's activity which can be separated out from its political context.

Moreover in the 1950s, coal, in the wake of the other nationalised fuel industries, gas and electricity, was only gradually becoming aware that the very idea of *selling* was fast being subsumed in the wider, more holistic concept of *marketing* – embracing all the disciplines, including of course selling, and – to some, shockingly, *advertising* – although the functional titles which Derek initially occupied were still described purely as 'Sales': the era of NCB Marketing Directors had not yet dawned. The gas industry's pathfinding generic commodity campaigns for "Whizzigas" only hit the astonished British customer by the late 1950s.

There was also another political, and philosophical, impediment: for many ideologues of that time, the basic idea of nationalised industries selling their wares at all, let alone against each other, looked like a misuse of public funds, wrong in principle. Derek knew from early on that he and the small visionary band of brothers who thought like him in the Board, had a mountain – a consumer *un*friendly mountain – to climb. To cap it all, the Nationalisation Act had deliberately precluded its scope from the function of distribution to the ultimate domestic customer: that was still left to the unstandardised private fuel distribution industry. The exception was where the pre-nationalised colliery companies had direct retail operations, e.g. in Lancashire (Manchester Collieries) and West Midlands (the Earl of Dudley's operations). These merchant companies, such as Charringtons and Ricketts, were household names in their own right, with localised, regionally recognised brands of solid fuel to defend and promote. For customers over much of the country, their supplies were in the hands of a multitude of small, often family-run, businesses. The mountain had some formidable foothills to ascend at the start, and lines of communication were too long.

The marketing revolution

In this chapter, a former leading NCB senior manager, and a trade owner, set down their respective perceptions of Derek Ezra's personal impact on this vital aspect of the coal industry's activity, covering his managerial time in the 1950s, and ushering in his role at the top of the Board from the late 1960s onwards, where he was then able to ensure that his marketing revolution was carried forward more comprehensively. This complements the commentary by Paul Glover in Chapter 3. The opening scene is set by the former NCB Head of Domestic and Industrial Sales, Martin Cruttenden, who later worked with Malcolm Edwards (*see Chapter 2*) as Director of Sales. This view is rounded out by that of one of the former owners of an old, family-run distribution operation, which, until rail nationalisation, owned its own fleet of coal rail wagons – Michael Bryer Ash, who describes the huge effort put in by Derek Ezra over many years to bring the coal trade together in a series of highly successful nationwide co-operative marketing schemes, including, as has already been outlined, the Coal Utilisation Council; its role, however, proved to be fairly limited, being steadily overtaken by other NCB initiatives. Martin Cruttendon's account sets the scene:

Organisation

'In the early days of the 1950s, the sales structure was based on the newly-established Divisions, with a small marketing presence in the Production Areas, where Marketing's role was limited to quality issues and the despatch of the product. Under Derek Ezra, HQ's role steadily increased as the importance of promotion and contracting forward users developed. Sales Regions were established in the late '50s, to be followed by nationwide Sales Districts and, decades later, the NCB presence 'in the field' increased under his lead, as the value of customer contact and service was recognised. When I first joined Marketing in the mid-1960s, considerable power was exercised by a formidable group of Regional Marketing Directors, who met monthly at HQ with HQ Marketing Staff, under the Chairmanship of Derek Ezra or his then Deputy, John Menheneott.

'Sales forecasting and targets were subject to regular reviews, and a formal annual cycle established. A paper was prepared for the Board every January, setting out proposals for promotion during the following financial year. Simultaneously, work would have started to put together the various campaigns, although nothing could be firmed up until the actual Budgets had been approved by the Board. Campaigns were usually back-loaded to early Autumn, but often with some lower-level activity for the Spring "home improvement" season. Campaigns were shown to Derek, who sometimes was not completely happy, and suggested changes'; [*anecdotes about this aspect of things are related in Chapter 8*]. When approved, plans would be shown to the NCB Regional and Sales District teams, Trade leaders and domestic appliance makers, and often a team from advertising agencies and HQ Marketing would make presentations round the country. Local Trade contacts and NCB's approved appliance distributors and installers would be involved. Campaigns would normally be supported by local advertising organised at Regional and Sales District level, and by point-of-sale material. Industrial campaigns were somewhat different, being essentially national, but supported by presentations and various events at regional level for actual coal users and potential users'. Martin Cruttenden further comments that 'we were always very conscious that our spending fell miles below that of gas and electricity. Getting agreement to the budgets was achieved despite no great sympathy or understanding from the 'Mining Mafia', but with a grudging acceptance that the industry had to show its face. (It is worth an aside here that the

Mr and Mrs Derek Ezra enjoy the warmth of an open coal fire in the hearth. Picture: ROBERT HOPE

Fig.25: Derek Ezra never lost his early interest in the marketing side of the NCB's activities. Here under the heading "Coal Board chief keeps the home fires burning", he and Julie allow the new solid fuel fire in their sitting room in Belgravia to be photographed as part of a domestic fuel promotion campaign. [Courtesy "*The Daily Telegraph*", 2 Nov 1971]

author of the marketing insights in Chapter 2, Malcolm Edwards, was by 1965 Head of the Industrial Sales branch of the Board. Twenty years on, by 1985, he had moved on from his role as Marketing Director under Derek Ezra, to become overall Commercial Director, British Coal, with additional responsibility for Opencast production; the Coal Products Division; and the Coal Research Establishment at Stoke Orchard, Cheltenham).

(Martin Cruttenden's career path within the Board was predominantly 'marketing-oriented'. Joining the NCB as an Administrative Assistant in 1960 from Cambridge, he became No.3 in Lord Robens' Office, and then in 1964 Staff Officer to Derek Ezra, who was at that stage DG of Marketing. From 1965 he worked for Malcolm Edwards and for the Industrial Sales branch, monitoring the performance of sales contracts, and securing agreement to the terms offered for new contracts. In 1969 he became Head of Industrial Sales, and then in 1971, when the two branches merged, he also became responsible for Domestic Sales. By 1976 he moved out to become Deputy Regional Marketing Director in Yorkshire, and in 1979 to take up the post of Regional Marketing Director in the Midlands. He returned to Hobart House HQ in 1985 as Director of Sales, effectively as deputy to Malcolm Edwards for the years to 1993, when he set up his own consultancy business, advising UK Coal Companies on their diversification plans, and latterly working on energy projects in the newly emerging post-Communist Russian Federation. Thus he has a very special perspective on Derek Ezra's role in marketing for the Board, spanning the eras of both his predecessor and his successors'.)

He writes: 'My first close contact with Derek Ezra was as his Staff Officer after my departure from Lord Robens' office. He had not previously had a Staff Officer, but Robens was at the height of his efforts to diversify into chemicals and building components, and this added to Derek's responsibilities. My initial work was preparing him for his trip to the US to talk to a petrochemical company, Sun Oil. He would be amused nowadays to be reminded how concerned he appeared to be over some of the admin details of the trip – checking how to identify the driver meeting him at the various US stations! However he also revealed a great deal of kindness towards me personally in my being pitchforked into a new job, and also when our first child arrived.

'A view has emerged that whilst Derek always behaved with total propriety as far as his staff could judge, during the mid-1960s Robens seemed to some of them to be coming out with some spectacular outbursts to senior staff, which could be heard by many more junior people, and became the source of much gossip'. Martin continues: 'One suspects that Derek Ezra's progress through the organisation was based not only on his obvious abilities, but also because he was seen as providing something different and vital in an organisation so dominated by the "Mining Mafia" – his rise had not been welcomed by many of the senior mining men.' As related in Chapter 3, the Board had long been headed by non-mining engineer chairmen. Whatever private views they had, Derek's memory is that differences rarely surfaced at Board Meetings; indeed if they had, his recollection is that he would have resolved them there and then. Martin's account resumes: 'much later, when my career took me to Yorkshire, a latent hostility towards Ezra after his retirement was still apparent with some of the senior mining men, who blamed him for weakness with the unions, and who seemed to have completely forgotten the work he did to alert politicians and the media to the possibility of energy shortage, and so making investment in the industry possible.

'When I worked with Malcolm Edwards at HQ, there were a number of occasions when Derek Ezra took part in the final negotiations for large new industrial orders. In particular

I remember the negotiations with Alcan for their new Lynemouth smelter and power station, and with Blue Circle for their new Southfleet works. At the latter in particular, Blue Circle were represented by a very experienced negotiator whose technique was familiar to Derek from previous encounters – interruptions through long silences, when he would leave the table and go and look out of the window for minutes on end. (As a result, Malcolm always wondered whether we conceded more than was necessary!). During his Chairmanship Derek maintained close contact with the Coal Trade leaders, through quarterly meetings over lunch, which were greatly appreciated by the Trade, and often made easier the potentially difficult issues, such as clarification of the often fraught relationship between the NCB as producer, the Trade and the final users, where NCB wanted a long-term contract with industrial trade users, whom the Trade saw as customers. I see too an important part of the Ezra legacy as being his strong support for "R&D" into coal usage, in particular through what was termed "Fluid Bed Combustion", which gave promise of higher efficiencies; the retention of harmful sulphur in the ash and in its various forms offered benefits to both industrial and generating markets, and with "clean coal" developments for the domestic and small industrial and commercial markets. He also did much to ensure that the industry became fully involved in district heating, and this is a field where he later continued his interest. Much later, my main contact was via the National Home Improvement Council [*described fully in Chapter 10 below*]. This body had evolved out of talks between Robens and John Hazel (MD of Sankeys, which NCB then owned) with several large groups supplying the house-building industry, and with the Builders' Merchants' Federation. Through the efforts of George Plucknett, NHIC finally got off the ground.

'When NCB Chairman, Derek Ezra supported our involvement in NHIC, and when he left the coal industry [in 1982] he enthusiastically participated, agreeing to become President, and taking part in many lobbying meetings with politicians, and touring the country, opening demonstration projects. Working with him myself as a Board Member of NHIC and briefly as its Director (for 18 months in 1993/4), I found him a real pleasure to work with. He was always encouraging, enthusiastic and relaxed, giving brilliant impromptu speeches if required'.

Fig.26; All-industry marketing required full co-operation with the Coal Distributive Trade. This was achieved by excellent co-operation between the Coal Board and the trade. Here CMF Past-President, Michael Bryer Ash, uses the opportunity of the Federation's annual lunch, London, 1976, to strengthen this process, in the approving presence of Guest of Honour, new ex-miner Minister for Energy, Eric Varley MP (*l.*) and Sir Derek Ezra [Courtesy, M.Bryer Ash]

The coal trade

Michael Bryer Ash's perceptions of Derek Ezra's impact on the coal industry contrast interestingly with those of this NCB Sales Director. He has written: 'I first met Derek Ezra in 1958 when he was Regional Sales Manager of the London and Southern Sales Region. He was based at Derbyshire House, almost adjacent to King's Cross Station. (My background was as the third generation in a family business, G.Bryer Ash Ltd, my grandfather having retail coal businesses trading in Dorset, Wiltshire, Somerset and parts of Hampshire and Devon – The Wessex Coal Merchants. My grandfather had also owned 360 coal railway wagons, which had been taken over on nationalisation; these were mainly used for transporting bituminous coal from the Northern and Midland coal fields, and Anthracite and Steam Coals from South Wales – all to Merchants and our Industrial customers in the south of England. At the time I met Derek, I had passed through five years of training in London with Hinchcliffes, and four years with Lowell Baldwin, a large firm of Coal Merchants, whose Head Office was based in Bristol; there they later had one of the largest distribution centres in Europe, handling in excess of half a million tons of coal a year. I was subsequently running our retail businesses, and located in Bournemouth). Derek made an immediate impression on me as a quietly spoken man, a good listener, with an enquiring mind, and a keen interest in all aspects of the business. I used to see him at various meetings in Hobart House, when serving on the Central Committee, and as an Executive Member of the Coal Merchants' Federation of Great Britain; I also encountered him when serving on the committee of the Coal Industry Society.

'When he was appointed Chairman of the Coal Board in 1971, I was able to have even more contact with him, due largely to the fact that the Board and the Distributive Trade were working closely together, as a direct result of his policy. He had a skill in bringing people together, making them feel they were an important part of the whole, being fully informed and involved – a policy which proved to be very successful in achieving the best possible outcome to the problems that the Industry faced. I was at the time also aware that he followed the same policy with the NUM. I was privileged on one occasion at a CIS Lunch to sit between him and Joe Gormley, the miners' leader. It was clear to me that there was a special relationship and trust that the two men had for each other. I personally am most grateful for the support I have always received from Lord Ezra in the various offices I held within the Industry, including Chairman of the National Fireplace Council, 1980-82.

'When I was Chairman of CTBA, the industry's national charity, I felt it would be sensible to ask the Duke of Westminster, (the richest man in the country) to be my President; he very generously agreed … Derek Ezra's immediate response was to ask me to invite him to lunch at Hobart House, together with his Senior Trustee, Jimmy James, who happened to be an old friend of mine; (he in turn was President of The Royal Institute of Chartered Surveyors). The Grosvenor Estates were landlords of Hobart House and of course this act duly endorsed and strengthened the link. A further example of Derek Ezra's support was when I was President of the CMF of Great Britain, in the days of 7,500 Coal Merchants across the country.

'Today there are barely 550 and even some of those are running other businesses alongside, handling very small tonnages of coal. Again, I was given his time and support, generously given and greatly appreciated. I also had the good fortune to be at the final farewell party at Hobart House (I understand five were held). Amongst a number of notable figures were Lord Robens, his predecessor as Chairman, and Joe Gormley. Alf Robens paid tribute to Derek, saying – no doubt lightheartedly – that Derek bettered him on every front; serving the Board longer than he had – eleven years, as opposed to Robens' ten; that his "industrial relations" were much better than his (Joe Gormley being present!); and that he had stabilised the market – a glowing reflection on what had been achieved during his spell as Chairman.'

Although the focus on marketing passed predominantly to other hands when Derek Ezra became the Board's Chairman, nevertheless his weighty influence over the earlier years had set the Industry firmly down the selling and marketing path, as indeed its markets demanded.

Contributors: Martin Cruttenden, Michael Bryer Ash

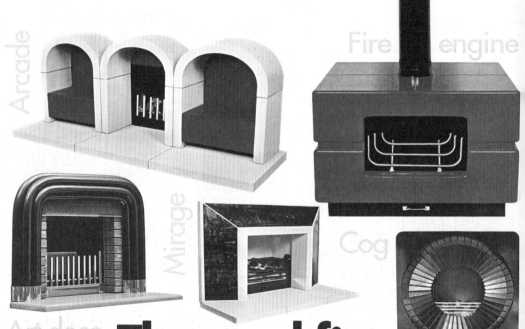

Arcade

Fire engine

Mirage

Cog

Art deco

The coal fire becomes an art form.

War Lord

Egg cup

Heat Wave

The Bannenberg Series of Designs for the National Coal Board

Fig.27: The marketing of coal domestic usage became steadily more sophisticated in the 1970s – with Derek's enthusiastic endorsement. One early project was to commission designer Jo Bannenberg to produce a range of prototype fireplaces in a striking contemporary idiom. A bright, market-aware future seemed to be opening up for coal [Courtesy "*Vogue*", 15 September 1972]

CHAPTER 7:
SIR DEREK EZRA – FOUNDING FUELLER

This chapter focuses primarily on one of the most significant of Sir Derek's involvements, on behalf of the coal industry and the people it employed – the City livery company of which he was not only one of the creators but also the active midwife, bringing it into life, The Worshipful Company of Fuellers.

Before detailing that activity, reference needs to be made briefly to two other fields of endeavour where Derek had a role to play on behalf of the 'world' of coal: the Coal Industry Society; and the Coal Trade Benevolent Association. The CIS had been founded as far back as 1929, essentially as a Coal Trade-dominated organisation. However, following nationalisation, members of the staff of the NCB were welcomed into the Society. Derek Ezra, by then DG of Marketing, became Chairman of the Society in 1961-2, later becoming President after his retirement from the Board in 1982; there was a good precedent - Lord Hyndley, a predecessor as NCB Chairman, had been Chairman of the Society for 20 years, from 1943 to 1962. Following the pattern set by Lord Robens as Chairman, Derek addressed the Society annually. The CIS was yet another area where Derek could extend his policy of trying to achieve informal "togetherness" in the industry, and the Society welcomed the NUM's President, Joe Gormley, three times as speaker. Here was also an opportunity to emphasize the European dimension, and European visitors were invited on a number of occasions, notably to the European luncheon in 1972-3. The Labour PM, the Rt. Hon James Callaghan, also addressed the Society in 1977-8. Although not a quasi-political platform like the CIS, the CTBA was also another of Derek's areas of public commitment to his industry; he was elected President in 1984.

'The Fuellers' was, however, the most salient field for this commitment. Derek had become a Freeman of the company in 1983, two years after the Grant of Ordinances, as the paragraphs below will relate. Initially, as was Derek's intention, most of the members coming forward were of the Coal Trade. Encouragement from Derek followed, and some 15 NCB managers became Freemen. Paul Glover writes: 'As the Company's growth was at that stage limited to coal industry interests, it became clear that broadening the "catchment" area to include other fuel sectors was necessary. As the newly elected Junior Warden in 1990, I was charged, alongside the new Clerk, Wing Commander Henry Squire, with the task of seeing through the necessary changes to the Constitution. Backed by the advice and help of Past Masters Richard Horne and Anthony Cripps, and of my successor, William Pybus, the task was completed, and, incidentally at the same time, I became the new Master'. The full narrative about The Fuellers can best be described in the account of another Fueller Past Master, Edward Wilkinson:

Fig.28: Lord Ezra hosted a reception at the House of Lords for Master Dr Paul Glover and The Fuellers, 9 Feb 1994, to introduce potential members from the wider world of Energy to the Company, on occasion of the amendment to the ordinances

'My recollections of Derek Ezra go back to the days when my father was the NCB's Chief Engineer (Reconstruction) at Hobart House and I was Assistant Marketing Manager in Area 3 of East Midlands Division based at Edwinstowe, a stone's throw from Thoresby Colliery. The Company was where my grandfather and father were both Engineers. In 1956 Derek returned from his appointment in Luxembourg, to become the Deputy Regional Sales Manager of the London and Southern Sales Region, based at the Bolsover Company's previous London office at Derbyshire House. Derek came to the East Midlands Division on a tour of Collieries and Offices and I was delegated to show him around the surface of Mansfield Colliery, later known locally as Crown Farm Colliery. Mansfield was sunk in 1905 on farmland belonging to the Duke of Portland to whom 6d per ton royalties had been paid until nationalisation in 1947. My grandfather, Tom Wakefield, was the Sinking Engineer for the Bolsover Company, having previously sunk Creswell in 1896, and became the Enginewright on completion at Mansfield from 1903 until he retired in April 1929. After World War 1 service in the Royal Engineers, seconded, until the RAF was formed in 1918, to the Royal Flying Corps, my father joined his future father-in-law as an electrician, soon becoming the Colliery Electrician, moving in 1936 to Bolsover's Head Office as the Company's Assistant Chief Engineer. Mansfield Colliery had been substantially reconstructed in my father's "watch", soon after nationalisation, with electric winders and a unique "Chance" coal-washing plant, using sand brought from King's Lynn as the medium to maintain the specific gravity.

'Why the history? Well, I knew the surface like the back of my hand and had worked underground in the High Hazel seam after National Service for long enough to qualify as a coalface worker, so Derek had the full works of a tour with all the background history I could add. History doesn't relate as to whether he enjoyed the occasion as much as I did! In 1967 he was appointed to be Lord Robens' Deputy Chairman, taking over from him in 1971. My next real contact with Derek was in 1969 when I was seconded as General Manager of Associated Heat Services (Central) Limited, an Anglo-French company of which Derek was Chairman, the other shareholders being *Compagnie Générale de Chauffe* and William Cory & Son Limited.

'Colin Cowe was the first MD, followed by B.Chad Smith, their Head Office being across the road from Hobart House in Grosvenor Place. I always remember the Board Meetings in Hobart House with Derek in the Chair, generally conducting the meetings in French with the interpreter there so that the rest of us could follow the proceedings and contribute as required. I was Chairman of The Coal Industry Society in London, which met at the Hyde Park Hotel, during 1969/70, and Derek occupied this post in 1961/62, being its President from 1981 to 1986. My third meeting in December 1969, having previously had the NUM's Laurence Daly and Minister John Eden Bt MP as speakers, was Charles Goodwin representing the Coal Trade. Having made several controversial statements in his speech, he sat down; Derek, sitting on the traditional Past Chairman's Table, got up – before I could reply to thank the speaker as was the custom – to say what Charles Goodwin had said was not the case as he saw it. I remember thanking him for his contribution and then carrying on with my "Thank You" to Charles, with little comment about the NCB Deputy Chairman's intervention! Afterwards I was chastised by some senior members for allowing Derek to speak; my defence was that he was my boss and not theirs, and halting him in full flow wouldn't have been a good move for me! I remember that Derek was not best pleased when I decided in 1971 that the coal industry wasn't going to see me out, and I accepted an offer from Thomas Black Ltd of Sheffield to join the private sector: in hindsight that was the right decision.

'After Derek was created 'Lord Ezra, of Horsham' in 1983, following retirement from the NCB in the previous year, he did invite me on a couple of occasions to lunch in the House of Lords and I remember them for the fact that during the ordering procedure he insisted that whatever he ordered had been nowhere near garlic, which for the Chairman of an Anglo-French company was strange – but it suited me as I can't stand the stuff either!

'Having considerably helped those involved with the formation of the Fuellers' Company – to which this chapter returns below – Derek himself became a Liveryman in 1987, having in 1982 also become an Honorary Liveryman of the Haberdashers' Company, from which vantage point he sponsored the inaugural Fuellers' Lecture in 2005. Finally, in June 2010, I was delighted to accompany The Fuellers' then Master, John Bainbridge, and Past Master Bryer Ash, to greet Derek and Julia at their London house to present them with a Loving Cup to celebrate their Diamond Wedding and

WORSHIPFUL COMPANY OF FUELLERS

Company Year Book & Directory 2012 - 2013

Fig.29: The Fuellers' Coat of Arms incorporated many symbols relevant to aspects of Derek Ezra's own inputs. Here coal is represented as precious "black diamonds", a theme of later coal publicity
[Courtesy, The Fuellers]

to raise a glass of champagne to their great achievement. Some years after I had become closely involved with him over the efforts of various ex-NCB people to try to resuscitate the lapsed City Livery Company, "The Woodmongers", I had to make a recommendation to the Company in 2012 – eventually entitled "The Fuellers" – to sponsor this Memoir. This excerpt sets out something of the early background to that endeavour:

"The company is much indebted to Lord Ezra for the support he gave in the early days – putting forward the names of senior NCB Managers for admission, and personally encouraging their membership. Later, amongst his generous contributions to the success of the Company, he hosted at his own expense receptions at the House of Lords, to which potential members from a wide selection of energy interests were invited. In 2005 he established the Annual "Fuellers' Lecture". The year 2014 will be the 10th anniversary of the inaugural Lecture and it is proposed that the tribute to Lord Ezra be published to mark this occasion." As Edward Wilkinson has written, he had been involved several years previously in the commissioning, with colleagues in the new Fuellers, of an up-to-date Company History. It seems appropriate to reproduce here part of Chapter 4 of that History, which details the origins of the campaign to re-create the ancient medieval Livery. This is preceded by two paragraphs from the Foreword which Derek Ezra wrote for it. These excerpts underline Derek's concern for the well-being of the members of his former world, and his determination to help them achieve Livery status. They also exemplify his skill in finding a path through difficulties, in this case the byways of the City – where his reputation was exemplary – and his capacity for making things happen "on high".

"I gladly give my support to the project for reviving the old Guild … From ancient Woodmonger to modern Fueller has been an arduous and fascinating journey, vividly narrated by the author. Energy has once again become a crucial element in the world economy … The Fuellers are playing an important contributory role in the formulation of energy policy".

A Livery Reborn: the Background ...

The book continued: 'As far back as 1921, Hylton Dale (a director of the Charrington fuel merchants) had bewailed the fact that there was no City Company to represent fuel interests: "It seems a pity that the London Coal Trade does not think sufficient of itself to petition the Lord Mayor and the Court of Aldermen to revive the old Company, whose direct ancestors they are" ... A Minute of The Fuellers' first meeting in the Goring Hotel Drawing Room, to celebrate the formation of the new Company, of 17 February1981, referred to the birth of the project in that same room "eight years ago," i.e. 1973!

'Motivation must here be distinguished from effect. One of the Company's progenitors, Lord Ezra, explained to the author and to former Fueller, John Josling, at a private meeting on 3 November 2006, that the broad idea in the minds of coal trade leaders had been to develop the community of the UK solid fuel trade at a time when it was still riding as high, in commercial terms, as in morale ... When [he] wrote to George McGeechan on 25 April 1979, after having presented the SCM [Society of Coal Merchants] Chairman's first chain of office, he added: "I hope we may have a chat before long about the Livery Company aspect". The idea was boosted when the NCB Chairman invited the Lord Mayor Sir Peter Gadsden, with NCB Finance Director and future Fueller Master, Brian Harrison, to the customary lunch at Hobart House, in his year of office, 1979/80. Pursuing one of his traditional mayoral duties – the promotion of the City Livery idea – the Lord Mayor asked why there was no Livery Company for the UK coal industry?

'Its eventual effect at a subsequent time when the industry's fortunes had started to wane, was as a mechanism for binding the threatened solid fuel community together in a way that existing structures were not positioned to do. Like any other group of citizens seeking to be a Livery Company in the City of London, all concerned needed to be aware of the delicate conventions implicit in the process ... Moreover, many of the potential Members of the proposed Company would bring experience as Liverymen of other Companies, mostly the outcome of long-standing connections, for example the Horne family through the Clothworkers, or Lord Ezra's educational involvement with the Haberdashers ... The evident interest of the NCB, manifested through Sir Derek Ezra as its Chairman, would soon unintentionally highlight the first two of three hurdles across the [organising] Committee's path. The suspicion surfaced that Aldermen – traditionally "apolitical" – might have reservations about this form of involvement with a nationalised industry, at a time when nationalisation was still a *bête noire*, quite apart from the question as to whether such a corporation might be precluded by its statutes from such activity. This would in no way reflect on Sir Derek himself, who, as Sir Bernard Waley-Cohen would later confirm, "was held in the highest regard by the City".

'The NCB had had a long-standing interest in the marketing of its products, and Sir Derek Ezra was particularly involved in this aspect. Nevertheless, an early casualty would prove to be the impossibility of realising his dream of a Livery explicitly open to the entire coal industry; these aspects of future membership would have to stand over for subsequent resolution ... As to advocacy to the City, the original meeting on 22 May had taken the view that this might be secured by contacts with the Clothworkers. Despite those valuable links, the Committee again decided to ask for the help of Sir Derek Ezra, as the person best placed to approach the Lord Mayor, Sir Peter Gadsden. The purpose had been to sound out his informal reaction to the idea of a new City Company incorporating the name "Woodmongers". The Lord Mayor's office, with its necessarily special overview of wider Livery interests and backgrounds, had in fact predicated that there might be one Livery, the Company of Carmen, who would object. Their reasoning was surmised to lie in the events of four hundred years earlier … when the Company of Woodmongers had had to yield its Grant of Arms and Charter back to the Crown.

'Sir Derek Ezra now advised the coal trade leaders to think again, with as much dexterity as they could muster … A subsequent meeting between Charles Stephenson Clarke and the Carmen's Master, Lt Col Geoffrey Clarkson, on 16 May 1981, made it clear that the Carmen would indeed cross-petition to challenge the use of the title "Woodmongers" ("part of their history") unless Sir Derek's idea for a Company of "Fuellers" was substituted … What started ominously quickly ended. "The [Carmen] extended the hand of friendship to the coalmen [sic], and helped them progress – as the Worshipful Company of Fuellers. The last spark from the embers of the past flickered and died". Unknowingly, the Carmen had in fact done The Fuellers a great service: the new title would position them to take a more comprehensive view of what would turn out to be a unique role within the whole field of global energy…

'On 29 June 1982, the new Master, Wardens and Court of Assistants petitioned the Lord Mayor and Court of Aldermen for recognition as a City Company without Livery. On 13 October the City and Aldermen agreed that the Company Ordinances should be enrolled in the City of London records. A letter from the City offices of 21 October recognised "The Company of Fuellers" as a "City Company". By the meeting of 26 November 1982, membership had reached 100 – with the election of Lord Ezra. By 20 October 1983, the formal Ordinances and Objects had been documented. Thanks to good steerage, and powerful advocacy within the City, the formal steps had only taken an impressive four years. As the concluding Minutes of the extant Society of Coal Merchants would rightly record, given that such a process might well last the emerging norm of "four years plus four", or even the earlier traditional apprenticeship of "seven plus seven" years, "The Company of Fuellers" was now well under way – a major achievement in such a short time. The final post-hoc rationalisation of the Livery was for it to petition that it should widen its Ordinances beyond "coal", and indeed the implicit distribution of all fuels, and thus appeal to all those associated with every aspect of the energy market. There were precedents for such extensions and it was later agreed by the City authorities on 16 March 1993, twenty years after the first "gleam" in anyone's eye. As NCB Director of Staff and future Fueller Master, Dr Paul Glover, expressed it, no doubt with unconscious irony, in "The Fueller" newsletter, in the opening Autumn issue of the same year: "What foresight our forebears had in their selection of the title "The Fuellers" instead of the more restrictive, if earlier, "Woodmongers and Coal Sellers". The Worshipful Company of Fuellers now has the *entrée* to all the energy industries of the nation".'

These brief excerpts from The Fueller's Tale, which Edward Wilkinson, together with Mac McCombe, John Bainbridge and their colleagues, helped to bring about, prefaced by the references to his involvement with two other coal industry-related bodies, the CIS, and the CTBA, serve as a further reminder of Derek Ezra's deep commitment to the people he worked with, illustrated above all in his career in the unique, legendary and still very closed world of the British coal industry.

Contributors; Edward Wilkinson; Paul Glover; John Bainbridge, Editor, "The Fueller"

CHAPTER 8:
MANY FACETS – THE EZRAS AND COAL

If the main purpose of this Memoir had been to introduce the personality of Derek Ezra for those who did not know him, this chapter would have come first in the sequence. Although glimpses of his elusive *persona* have surfaced at various points so far, including the section in the Introduction, 'The Man in Context', most of the emphasis has necessarily been on the outward man, on his own, seen moreover, in the setting of his later, established working life. Here at last, we can redress that balance, and also reflect a little more of the central role that his wife, Julie, played in his work. Not many people were privileged to encounter the informal Derek Ezra of the lighter touch, or as someone put it, "the man behind the mask". Here are a variety of such insights, from the wider world of people whose lives he touched informally at various times, but also including stories that Derek told against himself. For a start it should be said that Derek Ezra has always been a strikingly handsome man: a high domed forehead, a strong aquiline nose, a sallow complexion, as if born under sun-drenched skies – which indeed he actually had been – piercing blue-grey eyes, but with a discernible twinkle of humour in them if you were observant, although laughter rarely broke the line of his firm mouth; all crowned by a good head of dark brown wavy hair, albeit grey and receding in later years. Interestingly, not merely men, but, as the chapter on the House of Lords era will reveal, even more so women, found him to be a delightful person to meet and talk with socially, with a deep, gravelly, sonorous voice that some could listen to for its own sake. He should not be labelled as a 'ladies' man' – that would imply an intent to appeal, which was not part of his make-up – but certainly the women in his circle of friends found him attractive and likeable – in a word, from his beloved second language – *sympathique*.

Fig.30: Despite the continuous pressures of public life, the Ezras still needed to make time for their private life, with occasional week-ends spent at Brook House, near Horsham, in Sussex. Horsham would be the natural choice for his title, when he was created baron in 1982

The very idea of there being a peak, as well as a nadir, in his life was itself the subject of one of his many humorous anecdotes, this one with an amusing equine flavour. Someone told him that a horse running well in races in the North was called "Captain Ezra". People who knew him, including miners, rushed to back it, and as long as it continued to win, Derek's own stock ran high with it. As he commented: "There was a time when I was popular with everyone!" Neither phenomenon could last for ever, nor indeed did they. Equally tangential to the main thrust of his being – and typically self-deprecating – was a story he would tell of the abuse he received in the post, relating to the allocation of homes for retired pit ponies. "Ponies had been employed in the pits to move equipment. They were always treated very fondly by the miners in charge of them, but with increasing mechanisation the services of the ponies were no longer required. The Coal Board therefore decided to find homes for them where they could be treated as well as they had been underground. Advertisements were put out about this and many more applications were received than the number of ponies. The Board employed animal welfare organisations to select the most suitable homes". The trouble arose in having to advise those who had not been selected. Derek received some very angry letters from them.

Another minor aspect of his life was also part of his store of stories, rolled out effortlessly and spontaneously at social gatherings. This was the fact, as detailed in the 'Time-Lines' section in the Introduction, that he had been born in Hobart, Tasmania but fate had decreed that he would be unable to escape his origins, finding himself finishing up his NCB time by working in a building of the same name, the second NCB HQ, Hobart House.

In his final days at the Board, he was alerted to the existence of a coal merchant in Durham, with the name of Ezra Scargill! At appropriate lighter moments, when an intrusive press was not present, he would bring in this wry coincidence. Inevitably, as on an occasion in the editor's memory – a meeting of the Institute of Public Relations – the chairman, James Derriman of the City communications consultancy, Charles Barker, would make the same amusing biblical allusion as others would adopt, by way of introducing Derek as the evening's guest speaker, attributing his public utterances to the Book of Ezra.

Derbyshire House man

It is, however, right to introduce, early on, the recollections of NCB's Geoff Ashmore, who later became director of the Board's successful export coal sales branch in 1974. Only two of the contributors to this Memoir can now bear witness to the existence of the Coal Board's London sales office, at Derbyshire House, near King's Cross. Geoff Ashmore, however, is the only former NCB manager who can now write of Derek's time in his first post "at the sharp end" of direct contact with the customer. This was in the London and Southern Sales Region, which stretched diagonally from the Wash to Dorset, taking in the whole of the South-East. Geoff is the oldest former coal industry employee to offer memories of the industry before 'DJE' (as his first nickname went) arrived on the scene at all. (Born in 1926, Geoff had grown up in Chesterfield, left school at 16 with his 'Matric', and had the good fortune to be "taken on", at the largest coal selling agency in the Notts and Derby coalfields. Called up into the Royal Navy in May 1944, significantly for his future, he rose to become a Petty Officer on the supply side of the Navy's business. When his "demob group" came up in December, although he could have stayed on for a commission, Geoff already knew that his "old firm" would take him back, having heard that with so many men coming back from the forces, jobs were hard to come by. Geoff chose the safer course and accepted the offer. In October 1955, Geoff applied for and secured the second position in the Public Utilities branch of the London and South Office at Derbyshire House).

"No shop egg"

There the "Derbyshire lad", by now entrenched in the traditional coal industry, first encountered the very different presence of the non-mining "new boy", Mr Derek Ezra, on his arrival two or three years later, to be 2ic to Frank Wilkinson, the MD. Wilkinson then became DG of Marketing at Hobart House, and Derek was promoted to fill the MD vacancy. Geoff felt that here was a man for whom a typical piece of Midlands vernacular applied. Although he was still fairly new to the British coal business, Derek was clearly "no shop egg" from the shelf, but a lively quick-minded man with significant experience: he was a new force to be reckoned with as the industry slowly started to recover from its wartime limitations. Geoff's memories become more vivid after he was promoted from the Marketing Department of the East Midlands Division, while Derek was now working at Hobart House: "I remember what to me are notable contacts with DJE. He never raised his voice in anger … I recall that he always listened to what one had to say, That is not to say that he always said what we thought he should say!

"In 1960 DJE asked me if I would mind moving over to act as the No. 2 in the Industrial Branch; where the No.1 needed extra help. Many of Derek's journeyings were by no means reported, red-carpet affairs, and they were often unsocial and strenuous. A year or so after the move, DJE told me he had arranged a visit to the Northumberland Division's Marketing Department in Newcastle-upon-Tyne, and would I go with him? He had invited the Manager of the Marketing Office for the South West, situated in Bristol, to join us. It was in February and freezingly cold yet DJE wanted to see the opencast site, reputed to be 'the biggest man-made hole in Western Europe'. We journeyed north by a late-afternoon train ready for the tour next morning, going straight to the hotel booked for us. Next morning we awoke to a room temperature near zero – bedrooms and public rooms alike: the heating system had broken down! The man from Bristol was in the breakfast room when I appeared and it was some time before DJE came in; he had got himself dressed in a thick overcoat buttoned right up to the chin, grumbling about the inadequate arrangements made for us. It didn't help much to have a cold breakfast, and the prospects for the day seemed as bleak as the weather itself.

"The transport arrived on time but the cheerful driver seemed not to notice the bad weather. DJE was not in a talkative mood. Prospects on site were no better, as there had been snow. Throughout the tour DJE asked questions of the guide, whose answers seemed to satisfy him, but on the whole the cold weather caused a lack of interest. Back at HQ, despite the discomforts of the morning, we had a good lunch and prepared for a general discussion in the Divisional Director's room, with the Deputy Director seated behind the great desk but the rest of the party fanned out around the front of the desk, with DJE left to lean up against a wall. Nevertheless, he dominated the discussions from that unsuitable position, summing up, and asking a number of questions about current affairs affecting the Northumberland Division. I was very impressed by his handling of the whole interview and by the way he marshalled the facts.

"On the train back, DJE asked me to let him have a report on the visit for next day; I wrote a report but was so dissatisfied with it that I put it in my bottom drawer, hoping he would never ask for it! It stayed there for several years before I scrapped it. Later, in 1970, when I was appointed General Manager of the New Immingham Terminal for coal exports, built for the NCB at the instigation of Chairman Alf Robens, DJE's secretary phoned me that he wanted to make a visit there … could I meet him at Lincoln Station? It was another tiring day, walking round the land works and coal stacks onshore and down to the jetty offshore. He always drove himself hard; on the way back he fell asleep beside me in the car whilst I was racing furiously in order to make sure he didn't miss his train. Quite a responsibility!

"In 1974 I returned to HQ Marketing to head up the Branch for the sales of coal and coke overseas. I was asked to join DJE on a visit to Lisbon, where he was due to give a speech on behalf of the British National Chamber of Commerce to the Portuguese equivalent. This was one of the many 'PR' jobs that he believed he should undertake as a leader of British industry and representing the Board. We had a number of export customers there. To my surprise, on the plane out he seemed to be worried about what he should say! All I could think of was to offer him something the Head of the Portugal Chamber had written about themselves, and that he might comment on some of the content. When it came to his turn to speak, I was amazed to hear him firmly and fluently give his message in terms the audience understood; the Portuguese hosts had English as a second language. From the applause, his message was greatly appreciated, although he didn't tell them much about the NCB!

"We understood that Alf Robens wanted Derek to succeed him, and was behind his appointment as his Deputy … I saw much less of him in those later years, although they were my own best years, when Export sales rose to their highest ever level.

"Nevertheless, I recall that one day in 1982, nearing the end of his third term as Chairman, with plenty of other matters on his mind, I was waiting for the lift in Hobart House when the doors opened and out stepped Sir Derek. Instantly, he recognized me and said: 'Ah, Geoff, I need to know something about (so and so – I can't recall what)'. The recognition was not unusual, but remembering what the item was among the many threads going through his mind in the split second it takes to pass out of a lift is pretty remarkable. I duly obliged." Geoff Ashmore's interface with his 'DJE' was understandably more informal than social, and not necessarily in the lighter, humorous vein which others experienced.

The lighter vein

Close friends echoed this lighter vein. John Josling and his wife Liz have already been mentioned, as friends of long standing of both Derek and Julie. They were among a select few invited to join Derek at a gathering in London to remember Julie, after her death in 2011. They would come down to London periodically to have dinner with the Ezras, or go to Covent Garden Opera with them. John kept in regular contact with Derek, and was one of the first to visit him in Chelsea and Westminster Hospital, after his fall outside his home in 2011, which resulted in a broken hip and three agonised weeks away from looking after Julie. Liz Josling thinks of Derek with great affection: "he is a lovely man, extremely kind; I am very fond of him, and we very much enjoyed our get-togethers with them both". The Joslings got to know them so well, that John felt enabled to ask Derek a personal favour at one stage in the 1970s, after Derek had taken over the chair at NCB. "When I was President of the Old Albanian Club [the Old Boys' association of St Albans School] I invited Derek to be the principal speaker at the annual club dinner. He duly arrived and in due course got up to speak. He started to talk about dealing with Joe Gormley and you could see interest fading around the room (these dinners were meant to be fun).

"However, it soon turned out that he was talking about the annual election of the Coal Queen, Ezra and Gormley being jointly responsible for electing her [*see below*]! Ezra at his amusing and articulate best – and a great reception to him at the end." Another Josling memory of Derek's humour, and humanity, but on the business front, was in his capacity as MD of Interlink Advertising. As outlined above in Chapter 6, they were the Coal Board's main advertising agency, appointed in 1968, for the domestic fuel 'home heating' campaigns in the 1960s/70s, around the concept of the then still effective, emotional appeal of solid fuel as the only real 'Living Fire'. Following in the tradition set by Lord Robens, but mainly because the marketing side was always near the top of Derek's priorities, he would interest himself in all the campaign proposals, and was seen by everyone as the final arbiter of what appeared in the media. His in-house NCB marketing team, including at that time Malcolm Edwards, Martin Cruttenden and Laurie Penser, would endeavour to double guess in advance what he might be prepared to sanction, and the hard-working Agency creative team would go to great lengths to put forward ideas that Derek might ultimately be able to approve, a process which Derek, as the ideal client, understood and sympathised with. However, "they couldn't always get that calculation right"! John recalls one of the Agency's annual advertising presentations, "where we were putting forward a very amusing campaign based on '**Set Your House on Fire!**' [the repetitive strapline, running under each advertisement]. Although Derek readily acknowledged that it was very creative, he perceived, as others had not, that in a wider context it presented some dangers [of misinterpretation and adverse "PR"], so he, on behalf of the Board, turned it down, with some reluctance, and asked the Agency to re-think that aspect of what was accepted as an otherwise good campaign. As Ezra left the room, he murmured to me: 'Sorry to pour cold water on your fire'!"

Another with fond memories of Derek in a purely social context is Thérèse Clarke, whose husband, Charles Clarke (Chairman of traditional fuel merchants, Stephenson Clarke), was one of the three founders of The Fuellers (*see* Chapter 7). Thérèse recalls going to many social events with the Ezras, notably Glyndebourne Opera in Sussex, – although she was not sure how much Derek actually liked opera as such! – at least "he always showed great enjoyment of the occasion".

Thérèse saw him as "a good, strong friend and ally" to her husband during the many interactions that took place with him as one of the senior figures in the coal trade, at the period in the 1960s when the NCB was being steered by Derek into ever closer co-operation. Thérèse, perhaps with a Frenchwoman's natural insight into the *condition humaine*, recognises in Derek certain qualities which might well be said to have also characterised his business *persona*; he is "extremely tactful", "generous and kind", "tolerant without being soft-hearted", and "ready to adapt to new ideas and make them work". In particular she perceives "a strong sense of pulling out the non-obvious and bringing it to the surface", and a capacity for "discussing rather than arguing". She offers a perspective which could well serve as an apt summing-up all round: "he was liberal in every sense of the word".

Many of the personal recollections in this Memoir have been of Derek in a quasi-official capacity, including those of his Assistant at the House of Lords, Jill Clements. His personal network, as evidenced over the years in his Christmas card collection, was vast – ranging from the Duke and Duchess of Kent, to Henry Kissinger, and of course including the major political figures of his day.

With the miners

It is an astonishing fact that this austere, shy, well-educated and self-evidently "middle-class southerner" did succeed at all, as Deputy Chairman and then as Chairman, in becoming

accepted by the vast majority of the mining workforce as "one of us". That had been no problem for his school-leaver-at-15 predecessor, Robens, himself egregiously of "working-class" origins, and, as Derek recalled, "a salesman to his finger-tips". For the highly intellectual Derek Ezra – and in no small degree for his wife, Julie, as well (for she, as the array of photographs demonstrate, invariably enhanced his presence at his many colliery visits, to which she brought her nice down-to-earth touch, and which she greatly enjoyed) – it was simply a triumph: a triumph of mind over image, an overcoming by force of sincere conviction, disarming the deep-seated, historical prejudice of miner against "boss".

Fig.31: Lady Ezra, photoportrait, 1980s

Most famously, this perception of Derek as a committed friend of the miners would later be recorded in print by their leader, Joe Gormley, a traditional miner, with whom Derek forged a warm, even affectionate, friendship, through and beyond their necessary working dealings. This amazing achievement had of course its dangers, as related earlier, both within and outside the industry. No one – possibly not even Derek himself – could be quite sure if their wage compromises were 50:50 or slightly in the union's favour, when Joe would intimate to Derek "the feeling of the lads". Opponents would no doubt have conjured up metaphors of "supping with a long spoon", but the basic truth is that for most of the Ezra decade in high office, the sometimes maligned "Derek and Joe show" kept the peace, and kept the mines open and producing.

Derek recalled one minor instance of the informal relationship which he and Joe Gormley came to enjoy. The occasion was the annual "Coal Queen" competition at which the two leaders were joint judges – as recounted by John Josling. The bevy of attractive young finalists from the different coalfields all looked equally deserving to both, but Joe got them out of the dilemma by saying: "Look, Derek let's give it this year to one of the smaller coal fields (no question of awarding it in terms of pulchritude) – let's give it to Lancashire!": (nothing to do with the fact that Joe himself was an ex-Lancashire miner!).

It was impossible to find miners still able to recall personal encounters with their former Chairman at his colliery visits, but one ex-miner, later CMF official, Rex Rose, was sufficiently impressed by one such visit to Leicestershire, as to put into poetic form an appreciation of the welcome offered to the NCB Chairman by him and his fellow-miners on the day. This is a brief, respectful, if slightly McGonagle-esque, excerpt from his poem!

> "Bentinck colliery, the choice they say, For the Chairman's visit starting today; …
> Arrived on time as we planned he would; Welcome words from Manager Wood;
> "Manager Caunt, guide for the day, quickly put Derek Ezra well on his way.
> A four-mile journey to the coalface; Man-rider transport all the way to the place …
> "Conveyed to the surface, the pithead showers; more staff to meet to discuss the last hours;
> Pint and a sandwich, an enlightening day, then off to t' next meeting with no more delay!"

Derek's inner *persona* was not reserved for the major characters in his life, but could become equally accessible to the people at all levels whom he got to know well within the coal industry, wherever possible within the limitations of time and opportunity. Although South Wales mining engineer, Ron Price, was a part of the so-called 'Mining Mafia' – reputed to bear antipathy to this non-engineer at their helm – he was another of those engineers who manifestly carried with him no such feelings. He witnessed at first hand Derek Ezra's constant preoccupation with the men and women in his care in the NCB, without regard to his own comfort or diary pressures: "I met him in the mid-1970s when he visited a mine in the Potteries Florence Colliery, in the Group for which I was responsible as Production Manager. I was then Area Chief Mining Engineer in the South Notts Area until I moved to London HQ as Director of Planning and Major Projects, later Head of Mining. My only close contact with him was in early 1981, when there was an explosion at a Scottish colliery in which six men were injured, with burns. He contacted me in the early morning to tell me that he intended to fly from Watford to Glasgow where the men were in hospital so that he could visit them – I was to accompany him. We went to see the men in hospital, then flew back to London the same day. He thus demonstrated for me the real concern he always had for the people working in the Industry."

Fig.32: Notwithstanding the ceaseless demands on his diary, Sir Derek's presence was continually invoked for a wide spectrum of public organisations. Here the Ezras plant a tree for the Keep Britain Tidy group, of which he was President

Another insight, from the ground, comes from one of the young NCB Staff Managers, Tim Burton: "The first time I saw Derek he was DG of Marketing. I was a lowly clerk and his PA needed some help getting up to date with a huge pile of filing. I was in his PA's office trying to sort out all the papers. The easiest way was to put them into piles on the floor; there I was, sitting in a corner, cross-legged, dealing the papers into piles, when he came back from lunch. 'He looked at me and then walked into his office without saying a word!

"In the early 1970s, in Coal Products Division, I put together a team that got to the finals of the National Management Game. In previous years we had asked departments to nominate people; that year I handpicked the members. After our success, we were invited to an evening with Derek (then Chairman) in his office; (Colin Ambler was his Staff Officer at the time). I hadn't realised how shy a man he could sometimes seem. We were a bit nervous; as he appeared so shy, conversation was hardly scintillating".

"The Battered Cherub"

Perhaps it would be appropriate for the conclusion to these personal views of the Ezras to come from the ex-miner who had to oppose him across the industrial divide, and yet who always respected his NCB protagonist – Joe Gormley. Writing in 1982, in his autobiography, **Battered Cherub**, about the time when astonishingly Tony Benn had been minded to ask Joe, not Derek, to be the next NCB Chairman – a would-be throwback to the days of ex-NUM President James Bowman as Chairman – the future Lord Gormley had made clear to the Minister his firm view that Derek was the right man for the job: "Even though he may not be a great extrovert, [he] understands the industry. It has been his life … I've had enough fights with Derek in my time, but in my view there wasn't a fellow in the country who fought harder for the coal industry than he. His heart was totally in it, and unlike some Chairmen of Boards there was never any suspicion of personal ambition about him, no feeling that he was using the job towards other things … He takes his job very seriously, and in all our arguments I have never seen him lose his temper – in fact, I've told him many times that it would have been better if he had stood up and shaken his hands around a bit and shown emotion. But he's not that kind of man.

"Above all, he's a man you would call 'dedicated'. Joe bestows the final accolade: "To me, Derek Ezra is a worker …"

Contributors : Ron Price, Thérèse Clarke, John & Liz Josling, Geoff Ashmore, Jill Clements, Rex Rose, Tim Burton – and, in print, Joe Gormley

CHAPTER 9: A TRUE LIBERAL VOICE – LORD EZRA IN THE UPPER HOUSE

One interesting fact about Derek is his life-long, though *sotto voce*, Liberalism. Although Alf Robens' own background had been a factor earlier in Macmillan's appointment of him, at this later time a chairman's political convictions did not interfere with his successor's task at the NCB.

Cambridge Liberalism

A pamphlet compiled by Derek at Cambridge is perhaps a first clue to this conviction. Derek had been elected the Meetings Secretary of the University Liberal Club. **Politics in Paris** was produced in 1938 by Derek and by a group of second-year undergraduates across the University, and from the whole range of University politics – a nice example of an early 'cross-bench' approach to things. These were the days prior to 'Munich'. Anthony Eden had earlier resigned from the British Cabinet under Chamberlain; France was purportedly being led by some sadly doomed politicians of that dubious era: Herriot, Blum, Reynaud. It was Derek's characteristic idea to go out and see for himself, 'on the ground', what the situation really was, unbiased by the media. In this case, to find out, through a University delegation, how France was coping with the European fascist threat.

Derek was Secretary of this delegation, and it had just visited Paris to report on that strangely unreal, self-deluding period leading up eventually to the Second World War. As he recorded in 'General Impressions', the Introduction to the report, 'we were in Paris at a time of crisis'. It was also a time of absurd over-confidence, acutely and ironically observed by Derek himself: 'An ex-Minister told us that the French General Staff were never in a more efficient state of organisation; and throughout the armed forces there is clearly great competence and discipline. The spectacular antics [sic] of the totalitarian states should not obscure the fact that the democratic nations too have armies and air forces.' Even at that early stage in his life, Derek was quietly manifesting that sharp but balanced interest in the political scene which would surface again, unforeseeably, in his later NCB days; 'M.Reynaud told us that he expected a government of all the parties under the leadership of M.Herriot. The events, so far, have proved him wrong; but the differences that have prevented the formation of a national government must not be exaggerated … The French, as has been stressed, are a nation of politicians.' Among the other students that Derek brought together were a number of future Liberal MPs, as well as Abba Eban – then 'up' at Queens' College – the eventual Foreign Minister of the as yet almost undreamed-of State of Israel. Already, Derek seemed to have the knack of mixing in interesting company. He maintained his interest in the Liberal viewpoint, but it was only when he retired from the NCB that he was able at last to speak out as an individual citizen – and, incidentally, to talk for the first time of the coal industry in the past tense!

The role of the British Bi-cameral System

For some, even close politics-watchers, the 'Upper Chamber' of Parliament might seem to embody the nature of the tradition-laden words themselves – away from real life, and secreted behind walls of anonymity, an historical overhang with no visible impact on daily events. However, its importance is never to be assessed in direct terms, nor certainly do Derek Ezra or his fellow-peers so assess it.

Fig.33: Now enobled member of the House of Lords, and new Lib.Dem. peer, duly attending annual Liberal Assembly, 1986. Lord Ezra became a committed and valued member of the party from his very first days in the House

Its ongoing role must be seen in what is proclaimed as its four-fold influence, in a sign at Black Rod's Garden Entrance: making laws, investigating issues, and questioning and debating policy – but, most relevantly for Derek, its independence of thought: 'bringing experience and specialist knowledge from wide-ranging backgrounds'. Therein lies its special value. It can change and modify thinking and actions in the Lower, 'people's' House, the Commons, through quietly reasoned, often non-party discussion, and the scrutiny of ideas going through the "Committee Stages". In the second half of his public career, Derek Ezra's *forté* has manifestly emerged in this area of the persistent, longer-term moulding of opinion, both inner-political, and among the wider, informed public, as spokesman for the Lib.Dems. on 'Economic Affairs' but predominantly on his preferred theme – Energy and the Environment.

Peer group assessment

This capability on Derek's part has certainly been appreciated by his fellow-Peers of all persuasions as well as by those who have worked closely with him in the House. Perhaps one of the most eloquent is fellow-Lib.Dem., Lady Celia Thomas of Winchester: "I am a huge fan of Derek's … Basically we were thrilled that someone of Derek's stature should have decided to take the Liberal whip, and we learned that he had been a Liberal, albeit a covert one, since Richard Wainwright persuaded him when they met at university … It must not be forgotten how well known Derek was when he was at the top of the Coal Board. He was always on the News, and everyone had heard of him. He knew so many people; he gave Lib.Dems. a lot of credibility. People listened to him, particularly on energy conservation and renewables, long before that topic became fashionable … He really was a 'big cheese'.

"Derek's speeches were beautifully constructed. He said what he was going to say; he said it; and then he summed up. Part of my job was to report what our Peers said. Derek's speeches were so clear – it only took a minute to report what he said. He had a very good manner in the Lords: he had a lightness of touch; he could think quickly on his feet; he had picked up the whole conventional way of speaking, and he knew the time limits – so much of our work is now time-limited." These views were echoed by a Peer from across the benches, former Minister Lord Quentin Davies of Stamford, who had in fact crossed the floor himself when he migrated to the New Labour benches from the Conservatives. He had also been a colleague of Derek's at merchant bankers, Morgan Grenfell (now part of *Deutsche Bank – see also Chapter 10*). "Derek was always professional in all he did, whether as a spokesman in the House, or round a Board table, always well informed, and an excellent listener to others' views." Another viewpoint was that of one of the hereditary Peers, cross-bencher Viscount Falkland, who described his perception of Derek with three words: "integrity, clarity, relevance".

They worked together on a whole range of issues, with Lucius Falkland, then a Lib. Dem., who had entered the House after Derek's elevation, often backing him up on a given Motion. "He was good to work with and always very open to differing ideas". In particular they co-operated in the Select Committee on Overseas Trade in 1984/5, whose Report had a considerable influence on government policy at that time.

A particularly evocative comment on Derek's emergence into the House of Lords' arena has come from someone who had nothing directly to do with that Upper Chamber, Edward Wilkinson, ex-NCB colleague, fellow-Fueller, and fellow Director of AHS Ltd: "Derek took to the Lords like a duck to water – he entered into its life and its role quite naturally".

Someone who worked closely with Derek – as well as several other peers day-to-day – is his Assistant, Jill Clements. In later times she had been a frequent visitor to the Ezras' home, bringing him papers or other documents, and he was still until quite recently, prior to his fall and broken hip, a pretty regular attender at the House itself, "always turning up dressed immaculately. He always appeared utterly competent, and well organised. He might sometimes express urgency, in addition to his normal insistence on accuracy, but he was never unreasonably demanding … he was never impatient, and always courteous, although ever a private individual, yet if he knew of someone's particular problem, he was truly solicitous and sympathetic." … Jill recalled how another peer, Lord Shutt of Greetland, had once remarked to her, on the topic of Derek's ability to phrase good Questions for a debate: "Derek ought to give lessons to the rest of us on how to put down Questions in the House". Jill also recalled how Julie, faithfully accompanying Derek on his public occasions, also retained a characteristic directness and impartiality about current events. Once when asked her views about an impending miners' dispute, she is reported to have remarked privately, without any pretention to take an NCB party line or to political *nous* or correctness: "Well, they do have a point, don't they!"

Of especial interest, given the highly politicised era of the Coal Board time, Derek's standing during the calmer years of the Lords has been happily objective, not least among Conservative peers. One peer whose path only crossed with his after that time is Baroness Shirley Williams, one of the four founder-members of the SDP, and later a leading figure in the subsequent Liberal "Alliance", albeit that her own Ministerial field was Home Affairs and education, not the world of industry and Energy. "He has been much respected by other parties. He is seen as very focussed and committed". Borrowing Churchillian phraseology, she added: "With his scalpel-like brain, once he had some issue between his teeth, *he never gave up*". Baroness Harris of Richmond, currently a Deputy Speaker in the House, speaks of Derek as "one of my greatest heroes … a wonderful inspiration to so many of us Lib.Dems., deeply respected not only on our benches but across the entire House. He was one of those rare phenomena, a few in each generation, who are listened to with total respect by everyone and without interruption: I think of Jack Ashley, or Lord Selkirk or more recently Baroness Tanni-Grey Thompson.

"I first met him in the early 1980s, at a Party Conference; I was already a Lib.Dem. Member, having previously worked in local politics in Yorkshire. We were thrilled when we learned that he had elected to join the Lib.Dem. cause, rather than speak just as a cross-bencher – thrilled, because he was so well known throughout the country for his management of a difficult industry during such testing times, and such a frequent face on TV programmes too. In his career at the NCB, he was always the natural conciliator, it was a fundamental part of him, and he strove to follow that path with amazing tenacity. His skill in achieving a precision of language was, of course, essential for the daily work of the House, making the clauses of proposed legislation clearer and thus better. During his time, with the sidelining of the hereditary peers, we have been becoming steadily a different kind of Chamber, a really hard-working House, and that evolving analytical, critical role has suited Derek well.

Excoriating

"If I had to select the salient points about him, I would say above all he was the perfect gentlemen" [a recurring metaphor in this Memoir] – "immensely generous, kind, and thoughtful. He was himself a good listener, very far-seeing, and 'liberal' in every sense as well as being by conviction a Liberal. I have known both him and Julie throughout my thirteen years as a Member of the House, and I fell in love with both of them. My husband and I met them both socially, and they were a delight to be with. Derek absolutely adored Julie, and she was a wonderful support to him throughout his career." Later Lady Harris went on to recall one of the many occasions when Derek spoke in the House on 'Energy':

"The whole House was hushed as everyone listened intently to what Derek had to say. He could be excoriating, in a quiet, determined way, about what the Labour government was proposing – or rather not proposing – to do about future Energy provision for the country. A rather white-visaged Minister had to reply to him – not an easy job when faced with the great knowledge and clarity of thought that Derek had just shown! He did so on so many occasions that I felt the civil servants ought to ask Derek for a Master Class in how to present arguments on Energy matters when confronted with the supreme expert!" Lord David Steel's summary, as Party Leader, of Derek's input was that "he added greatly to the prestige of our benches, and even lately his questions in the energy field were always regarded as pertinent and wise".

The Lib.Dem. viewpoint

The viewpoint that Derek put forward in the Upper House can best be gleaned from a retrospective pamphlet which he wrote for the Liberal Democrats in the early 1990s: 'in 1983 David Steel recommended me for a peerage in order to introduce industrial experience onto the Liberal benches in the House of Lords … For a number of years I was Chairman of Sub-Committee F of the European Select Committee and during that time we issued a number of reports on energy policy … I worked closely with [Lady] Nancy Seear in the period when she led the Liberal Democrats in the Lords, and was pleased to support her in many debates on the economy and on Europe. After Roy Jenkins became leader in 1988 he asked me to speak for the party on economic affairs generally. This meant taking part in a wide range of Treasury and industrial debates. The main theme which I sought to hammer home was the need for more investment in industry and infrastructure, and in a series of debates I drew attention to the plight of the manufacturing sector.

'When Bill Rodgers [Baron Rodgers of Quarry Bank] took over from Roy Jenkins in 1997, I suggested to him that in view of the large number of new and very able Liberal Democrat Peers I should give up my wide portfolio and restrict myself to the subject of energy. I am now [1990] concentrating on what I consider to be one of the overriding issues of our time, namely how to deal with the impact of energy on the environment. In this I have not forgotten my old association with the coal industry which I believe would have an important role in the future as long as more effort was put into the development of clean coal technology …'

During his most active decade in the House, the 1980s, Derek spoke well over 100 times, either putting down Amendments, or declaring his interest for the National Home Improvement Council of which he became President (*see* Chapter 10), or posing formal, critical, probing

Questions. Derek lived up to a personal commitment to speak as often as he could – always with insight, and invariably wittily – across the whole industrial portfolio, drawing cogently from an unequalled historical perspective on the public sector.

Introduction speech: the railways

Reproduced here are excerpts from three contrasted speeches: first, his 'Introduction' speech on 9 February 1983, which he chose to make on the occasion of a railway debate, led by the former Labour MP, Dick Marsh. The second is on electricity and a favourite theme – transparency. The last relates – with a nice anecdote – to his declared 'interest' as spokesman for the National Home Improvement Council.

"My Lords, it gives me particular pleasure today to be speaking in a debate on the railways which has been introduced by the noble Lord, Lord Marsh. He and I have worked closely together in a variety of ways since 1966 when he was Minister of Power in a previous government and subsequently when he was Chairman of British Rail … Having been in the coal industry since it was nationalised in 1947 until last year, 1982, I was able to develop a very close and continuous connection with the railway. This began in 1940s when it was my task to sell them coal to run the locomotives, something which does not occur (some would say with regret) these days. They were then very big users, but they also negotiated very hard. I remember visiting the railways buyers, two gentlemen of sombre mien, who received me in a stark office near King's Cross and conditioned me by showing me charts which demonstrated conclusively that all rail delays were due to poor quality coal. I am not quite sure what they would say today …

"I happen to know most about a certain aspect of the railway system, as someone from the outside: that aspect is the freight side of the operation. I have been in an industry which represents the largest element of the railways' freight traffic. If your Lordships will address yourselves to the table on page 21 of the report, you will see that the vast proportion of freight traffic moved on the railways is bulk traffic – 90 per cent, as the report states, of which 60 per cent is coal, a large proportion iron and steel, with petroleum and chemical products representing another proportion, and aggregates and building materials representing yet another. Over the years, the railways have developed a most efficient way of moving bulk traffic … This started in the days of the chairmanship of the noble Lord, Lord Beeching … I myself, as chairman of the National Coal Board, working with the railways, have been party to it … bulk loading at the colliery; rapid transport to the power station, steel works, cement works or port; the rapid discharge; and excellent economy and handling throughout. It is a great pity that … this great achievement … was not recognised. I do not know why we in this country seem to ignore that which we achieve, and concentrate unduly on that which remains to be done …

"I cannot conceive of a reason why, in this country's present predicament, we should even be contemplating the possibility of cutting off from the railways a form of freight transport in which they have excelled themselves. So I suggest that when we have the yet further enquiry into the railways which I am afraid the present report leads one to holding, these factors should be taken into account." Derek ended this first speech, which was not without its party-political nuances, on a note of would-be cross-party optimism – managing as ever to peer with his peers into the future and with a global perspective – even though Britain was then in the grip of an economic downturn almost comparable with the Eurozone crisis of this past decade: "There are signs at the present time – particularly in the United States, and this ought to be spreading to other countries - that the [current] world recession may be nearing its end. No doubt recovery will be slow, but it looks as if [it] will be coming in the course of the next year or so. Our objective in Britain must surely be to prepare for that eventuality and obtain a major share of it. We must create the circumstances in which our manufacturing enterprises can expand on a competitive basis. We must ensure that they are served by an adequate and efficient infrastructure. My Lords, there is no doubt that in that infrastructure the railway plays a crucial role."

[*Hansard adds, appropriately (col.1169): 'Several noble Lords: Hear, hear!'*]

The second excerpt is from two short speeches on May 1983 which, losing no time, followed on the heels of that Introduction, on an aspect of the Energy Bill then before the House, but speaking to a key technical point, not about coal, but electricity.

Electricity and transparency

"My Lords, I beg to move Amendment No.1 [which] proposes that the words 'other than the Central Electricity Generating Board' should be omitted from Clause 7 of the Bill. The reason for putting forward this amendment (which was also put forward at the Committee stage) is because we [the Lib. Dems.] consider that if the object of the clause is to introduce transparency in regard to the basis on which the electricity authorities purchase electricity produced by other bodies, there should be total transparency. What we are complaining about from these Benches is that there seem to be two systems. The electricity boards have to publish tariffs so that the prices are transparent and known to everybody, but the CEGB, which on occasion might have to purchase privately- or otherwise-generated electricity, can apparently negotiate terms which it considers desirable. In my opinion, based on my experience, it is possible that the amount of electricity which the CEGB might have to purchase will grow.

"If there are organisations which generate electricity throughout the country, due to the fact that they have branches in various parts of the country, I see no reason why they should not be in a position to negotiate centrally for the sale of that electricity.

"On these Benches we understand that the [conservative] Government believe in the market philosophy, which implies the exercise of options by those who want to dispose of a product, and we believe that this philosophy should be carried through in this clause. I therefore wish very strongly to press the amendment. I beg to move". This debate was notable for an intervention by the venerable architect of the Coal Nationalisation Act of 1946, Lord Shinwell, correcting a misapprehension about the history of local authorities generating electricity (His short speech also served to underline that nationalisation had never been a one-party issue); "The first step was taken, not by a Labour Government but I believe by the Baldwin Government in creating the Central Electricity Generating Board. That was the situation. That is the story … I should like to remind noble Lords of what happened in 1946-7 … There was an occasion when electricity was in short supply … Why were we assailed by a crisis? It was not a coal crisis … it was because of transport. There was plenty of coal at the sidings. We could not get it to the power stations where we required it. That was all. What is the objection to this proposition? Why not use the local authorities?"

As the debate proceeded, Derek Ezra agreed formally to withdraw his own amendment after receiving various assurances about how the CEGB would proceed in practice. There was then a second Amendment on a topic dear to Derek's heart – the use of waste as an extra energy source – by a former Labour Minister, the late Lord Strabolgi, (*and, as it happens, a longstanding friend of the editor of this volume*), who was a firm admirer of Lord Ezra across the party divide.

Derek came back with considerable conviction to lend his weight to this amendment: "I support the amendment moved by the noble Lord, Lord Strabolgi, and supported by … Lord Balogh. This is a very moderate amendment and entirely in keeping with the sense of this Bill. We from these Benches request that the Government think yet again about giving local authorities the same degree of incentive for the promotion of energy efficiency as is provided in this Bill for private enterprise. I should like to press very strongly that the Government concede this point".

Speaking on NHIC matters

A further short excerpt may be taken from a later speech which Derek made on the 'Inner Cities' debate on October 20 1987, in relation to – whilst always declaring his interest in – the National Home Improvement Council. Implicit throughout the speech is the care with which Derek had sought briefing from Ernest Cantle, DG of the NHIC, but above all the evidently detailed mastery that he demonstrated over a field on which he had been only indirectly involved in the NCB. It exemplifies once again three characteristic Ezra concepts – the need to invest in the infrastructure; the need to take a long view of politico-social problems; and the importance of always looking outward at other countries' examples. It also further underlines his ability to analyse and focus rigorously – and perhaps sometimes uncomfortably for his inner-political audience – on the real nature of a problem:

"We are much indebted to the noble lord, Lord Windlesham, for introducing this subject because it enables us, on a matter on which there is great national awareness, to take stock and to see whether, out of all this array of initiatives, reports and legislation, we are moving in the right direction; and whether, as a result of this great effort, that achievement is within sight, and this problem, which will clearly take some time yet to be resolved, is on the way to solution. Perhaps the most graphic description of the so-called 'inner city' problem was contained in the 1986 White Paper on public spending which said that '*since the mid-1960s the central problem of inner city areas has been economic decline. This has led to a loss of population, employment and of the more skilled and mobile. It has also led to poor housing, decayed infrastructure, derelict environment, lack of private investment and increasing dependence on the state*'.

"I think that is about as clear a definition of the problem as one is likely to have and of course, stated in those terms, it is very stark and very serious, wherever it arises. The first question I would like to pose is this: is the definition of the problem right?

"The term 'inner cities' is a graphic one and it has stuck. But, geographically, many of the areas affected by urban blight are not located in the inner part of cities. The term must be seen as covering all areas of serious urban decay wherever they are located. What we are facing is an urgent need for urban renewal – a more appropriate term, I believe, for that is what this is all about.

"Secondly, are we entirely clear on our objectives? Obviously, what we are attempting to do is to bring back economic activity into areas from which it has disappeared. But experience has shown that the ways in which this has been done in some cases do not necessarily lead to [the] increased employment of those living in those areas. What we need to define, therefore, is whether that is one of the prime objectives or not. If it is one of the prime objectives, then we need to consider whether we are tackling it in the right way. Thirdly, are the methods right? This is the area which has attracted the greatest degree of controversy. There was an article in the *Financial Times* of 12th August which puts the problem fairly graphically. The heading of that article was: 'Too Many Fingers in the Urban Pie'. No doubt many noble Lords have read the article. I would like to quote briefly from it:

'While Minsters have a lot to say about the inner cities, no coherent policy exists to tackle their problems. What the government does have is a series of programmes owing their existence to a variety of ad hoc ministerial initiatives over the past decade'.

"Is this a fair statement of the situation? This is what we need to discuss. My next question is on the subject of resources. The resources which I understand will be available from the Government for these initiatives will amount to something over £500 million in the year 1987-88. This is a very large sum of money. But the question we are bound to ask is: is it adequate? What steps have been taken to decide whether this is the right sum of money or not? Have the Government conducted enquiries into this, or has this sum been arrived at by some other means? I think we are entitled to ask that question. Of course, it is a prime requirement in all this that a large part of the funding should be stimulated from the private sector. Have the Government considered at all, following the experience in the United States, tax-exempt bonds to stimulate private sector investment in desirable infrastructure projects? This seems to have worked very well over there. Is it something that can be tried over here?

"Finally, I should like to ask whether the right environment is being created in those areas of urban decay to bring back activity and employment. Delapidation and a poor built environment are the outward signs of urban decline, and it seems to me that that is the first job that has to be tackled, to bring back economic activity and employment in these areas. There is the question in particular of the state of the housing stock in these areas referred to by both the noble Lord, Lord Windlesham, and by the noble Baroness, Lady David. This matter requires urgent action. No doubt action is being taken in some cases, but I venture to suggest that this matter requires prime consideration in trying to renew the delapidated urban areas.

"Let me quote certain measures which might be taken. There is a strong case for the relaxation of local authority spending controls so as to permit the funding of more work through the sale of assets, at least in the deprived areas. There is need for a joint promotion campaign to alert householders to the importance of regular maintenance and occasional major improvement, including publicity for warranty schemes. I happen to be personally involved in an initiative of this kind through the National Home Improvement Council. I am glad to say that the Government have given us a degree of support and this needs to be extended. There should be a clear commitment by Government to provide a sufficient and stable flow of funds to tackle the worst problem areas. There should be a concentration of resources on areas of serious housing decay and a co-ordinated approach toward tackling their problems. I have highlighted the housing problem because that is one of the most outward and visible signs of urban decay. Until it is corrected it is difficult to see how anything else can be achieved."

A minor rider to this reference to the NHIC relates to an attempt by them, through Derek, to get an Amendment to the 1985 Housing Act which would enable Agency Schemes to be set up. It had reached the third reading and Derek and Ernest Cantle had almost given up hope of getting it through. A confidential last-minute phone call came through from a senior mandarin, indicating that they ought nevertheless to table the Amendment and this would be well received and in due course adopted! For Derek and the NHIC to get this Amendment accepted was quite a rare achievement.

Many other speeches could illustrate the standing that Derek achieved in the significant but, to some, rather rarified context of the Lords. His role there, over more than thirty years, forms an essential part of the overall picture of Derek Ezra as a forceful, farsighted public servant, familiar both with the corridors of power and the workings of the civil service that peopled those corridors.

On a concluding note, and as a complementary activity to his actual presence on the public stage, Lord Ezra's unflagging correspondence in *"The Times"* must not be forgotten: if his voice might not later be heard in the House itself, it would still register through the national press. The measured tones of this excerpt from one of his most recent letters, belie the real anger he would express yet again in private conversation, over the apparent inaction of Government, then the Coalition, with regard to the UK economic situation.

Letters to *"The Times"*

As currently as June 2012, when attendance at the House was increasingly difficult – (although he was still putting down Questions in October 2012!) Derek was ever grasping the need, and opportunity, to influence public opinion. This was in his letter of 19 June, following immediately, while the iron was hot, on an article of the week before:

'Sir, Tim Montgomerie (Opinion, June 18) has listed the possible economic reforms being advocated at the present time. Among these is investment in the infrastructure. I am a strong supporter of this and believe that, in addition to the measures recently announced to stimulate bank lending, the Government should take advantage of the very low interest rates to launch into much-needed refurbishment schemes for the roads, railways, and airports, and also in the construction of more affordable housing, (referred to by Bill Emmott in his very perceptive article, June 11). To those who argue that direct government investment of this sort would simply add to public indebtedness, it could be answered that the bulk of the work would be carried out by private contractors who would employ more, adding to the tax take, and so reducing unemployment benefits. There would also be stimulus to other sectors such as retail, through increased spending power. Now is the time for bold measures instead of just blaming factors outside our control'.

Lord Ezra, House of Lords

In this as in so many other ways, the capacity of Baron Ezra for communication, a skill learned – and well-honed – at the NCB, had not been wasted.

Contributors: Viscount Falkland, Baronesses Thomas, Harris, Williams;
Barons Shutt, Steel, Quentin Davies; Edward Wilkinson, Jill Clements

CHAPTER 10:
THE SECOND CAREER – ADVISER TO INDUSTRY

One of the NCB Staff Officers, Andrew Horsler, has written about Derek's longstanding involvements beyond but coexistent with his pure Coal Board remit: 'Derek Ezra was undoubtedly a leading name in British business and public life, a status he maintained after he left the NCB. Some of his roles arose from that position, others reflected his own interests, especially in international and European affairs. He furthered relations with many major personalities in the private sector – independent entities such as Warburgs, Hlll Samuel and Kleinwort Benson. He was a person who wished to keep in touch with thinking outside the rather narrow, introverted confines of the NCB, and also one whom others wished to meet. He had been a Member of the British Overseas Trade Board (BOTB) for many years and Chairman of its European Trade Committee (ETC). an active member of the CBI Council, and of the CBI Europe Committee. For a period he was Chairman of the British Institute of Management (BIM). For him, none of these appointments was something which simply involved going along to a few meetings a year: all of them were important, requiring thought, study, the development of a strategy and. in particular, action. While at the BIM, he transformed its organisation through a series of high-profile initiatives.

'The NCB Private Office helped with all these areas, providing briefing … and liaising with officials of other organisations, some of whom were unaccustomed to the demands which Derek would place on them! For some years I was particularly involved in the BOTB and ETC activities … Derek's desire for "facts" on which to base action led the DTI to produce a quarterly publication known, because of its colour, as the "Yellow Book": this enumerated in enormous detail the level of exports and imports between the UK and each of the western European countries. Information was the spur to action … Derek travelled frequently in the pursuit of promoting British trade, usually accompanied by a member of the Private Office, by a civil servant and sometimes with other industrialists. Not every trip was of unalloyed pleasure: on one occasion he was invited to a fashion show at the British Embassy in Paris – he returned the following day, muttering! … Wherever appropriate, these visits were used to promote the exports of coal and technology from the UK. I recall one memorable visit in 1978, where Derek and Julie accompanied Michael Sieff, of M&S, Chairman of the British Overseas Trade Group of Israel. who at that time were building a new coal-fired power station which was commissioned in the 1980s and in fact purchased some coal from Britain. A packed six-day programme was arranged by Michael Sieff together with the British Ambassador in Tel Aviv, but the range and seniority of the people met demonstrates the "drawing power" which someone like Derek was able to exert. The visit was concluded with a Memorandum of Understanding between the Government of Israel and the NCB, covering future co-operation – typical of Derek's approach: every series of meetings must be capable of being followed up in tangible ways. Derek and Julie made annual visits to the USA, including meetings with *inter alia* the National Coal Association. Leisure trips these were not!'

By the start of the 1980s, Derek was looking ahead and he welcomed, as an opportunity, the approaching conclusion to his third, and record, term at the NCB. His active mind, as well as those of others who knew him well – not to mention the data bank compilers of the "head-hunters" – had already begun to identify the prospect opening up before him: what was to be the new career of Sir Derek Ezra after Coal?

As will be clear from the preceding chapter, his friends in the Lib.Dems. had placed him firmly in their sights for some time as a potential recruit for their whip in the Lords, and that opportunity translated itself into a recommendation by the Party Leader very soon after his official retirement date.

However there were many admirers within his extensive world of contacts in financial circles and industry, in mainland Britain as well as in continental Europe, who quickly realised that here was a rare talent and depth of experience, and a peerless reputation for integrity, about to "come onto the market". The Career summary in the 'Time-Lines' section illustrates vividly just how wide and indeed demanding that field of activity was to become.

Morgan Grenfell

In some cases these areas of influence – or rather, sources of competition for his time – would in due course overlap. So for example, at the merchant bankers, Morgan, Grenfell, (later taken over by *Deutsche Bank*) one of the earliest City organisations to approach him in 1982, he found himself in working contact with the then Conservative MP and full-time Director, Quentin Davies, who headed up one of the main Divisions. Lord Davies, as he later became, explained in discussion in June 2012, how the bank was then, under its ambitious Chief Executive, Christopher Reeve, seeking to develop its contacts, and its portfolio of corporate clients to be financed, in the profitable field of international energy providers. Derek's unrivalled knowledge of the coal industry worldwide offered them a chance to 'exploit' in a positive and creative way this new potential, and Derek was duly appointed as their Industrial Adviser. Derek was with the bank for five years in this capacity, and Lord Davies got to know him well, both as a colleague to be brought into the bank's various deliberations and sub-committees, on Energy and on Europe, as well as in the Upper House – albeit "across the benches", Quentin Davies by now having decided to cross the floor to take the 'New' Labour whip. Derek's hands-on participation in the bank's decisions contrasted with their somewhat muted experience of another Lib. Dem. recruit to their Non-Executor ranks at this period, Lord (Roy) Jenkins.

"He showed evident pleasure and interest in learning new tricks and working with people 30 years younger than him, at a time when he had retired with great distinction from the chairmanship of a major national organisation. His intellectual curiosity, his interest in people, and complete absence of pomposity were much remarked on. I recall with great enjoyment our business trips together on the Continent (and I adopted his routine of always buying coffee in Belgium!). He knew the Italian statesman and pro-European, Signor Ortoli, who clearly liked and valued him." Lord Davies added a perceptive comment which applies across the whole field of Derek's work: "There are two ways of dealing with difficult human conflicts including social problems: confrontation, and conciliation. They do not both work well in every situation, and sometimes, of course, there is no solution at all. But Derek believed in reasoned argument, quiet persistence, and tact. I think he made extraordinary progress at the Coal Board on that basis; these qualities made him a very agreeable and also effective colleague. He was always listened to with great respect, and his advice was invariably sound. He would cross London to the City on a daily basis if required, to take a full and proactive part in our affairs. We benefitted greatly from his distinguished presence, and I believe he too got a lot out of his time with us. We were sorry when time pressures forced him to concentrate his undoubted energies on other interests".

Associated Heat Services

However, Derek's involvement with other interests outside the NCB had really seen its first fruits in his joint creation on 8 July 1966, with French counterparts, of a company to develop business in the field of contract energy management, Associated Heat Services Ltd (AHS), later called Dalkia. This was a venture which has already been mentioned in this Memoir by Edward Wilkinson. Here Derek's role was very much central and hands-on as Chairman, and on some occasions conducting part of the Board Meeting in his impeccable French. Rod Castle, who joined the company as Company Secretary in January 1981, and attended some 250 Board Meetings under Derek's by now well-polished chairmanship, has written this account of his inputs to their Board table, much of his comment echoing the experience of others from his NCB chairmanship days:

'Derek was always very approachable – the best chairman I had the privilege of serving, excellent for a Secretary as he was a superb summariser of discussions. He only missed one Board Meeting during my time, and asked that the Minutes stated that fact. He was a stickler for time, meetings started and ended at the right point on the clock. Papers for Meetings had to be circulated a week beforehand, and he required to be well briefed in advance; draft Minutes had to be prepared quickly. When AHS went public in May 1982 (the original floating date had to be deferred due to the Falklands conflict – whose impact could have adversely affected a successful flotation), his Chairman's Statement in the briefing papers for AGMs had to be prepared in full so that no market-sensitive information was given away.

"Ezraisms"

'In December 2002 I gave the farewell speech to celebrate his retirement from a subsidiary of AHS. I mentioned that on the Saturday before the "do" I had been watching an adaptation of George Eliot's Ezra Cohen, useful because Ralph Cohen was also a director and would be attending the function. I addressed him now as Derek, not as Chairman, and threatened to stop speaking if he did not agree, and dwelt not on his achievements, but on what I called his "Ezraisms", some of which follow. Derek retired from NCB in 1982. That retirement and so many others followed; he should have his name entered in the Guinness Book of Records – I went to at least five – better than Sinatra and his final world tours! Derek also appreciated some of the finer things in life, but with particular tastes – a topic already encountered. A lunch had been arranged at Mossimans to mark another director's retirement, not his own. I was told; "Rod, make sure that the lamb is not cooked with garlic". However, I decided that I would rather face his wrath, than that of Anton Mossiman, and so did not do as I was told. My fingers were crossed as I watched his face as he ate the meal, but to my relief garlic was not used – no adverse reaction, so 'OK'. There was one occasion when we held a Board Meeting in a very hot French village. Over breakfast Derek agreed that it would be acceptable not to wear ties – in the days when ties were still *de rigueur*. He was as good as his word. When the meeting started, there was Derek at the head of the table, with no jacket, no tie, and wearing sandals! The first time I saw him without a jacket on.'

These memories are complemented by those of Ralph Cohen, who was a Director of AHS and its sister company, ALEC (Associated Electricity Supplies Ltd), from 1981 to 2001. Recollecting in July 2012, he has written: 'I remember all too clearly my first encounter with the then "Sir Derek Ezra". I had been invited by AHS's Managing Director to join its Board as Finance Director. This was an outside appointment in the run-up to the flotation of the company.

Everything had been agreed and my appointment was subject only to rubber-stamping by the chairman (at that stage still Chairman of NCB). At the appointed hour I was duly ushered into the "presence", to find Derek chatting fluently in French with the Paris-based directors of AHS. I was waved genially into a chair and his first words to me were: "Now, you speak French, of course". It was not a question! His response to my denial was: "Oh dear, Oh I see, Hmm – oh dear me". This bad start was the beginning of a good working relationship lasting nearly 25 years and a personal relationship that continues today. I have cherished both enormously.

'Derek's impact on the affairs of AHS was considerable. He was the driving force behind its creation (before my time with the company) and kept the ship precisely on course throughout and beyond its period of corporate independence. This covered its tripartite shareholder arrangements, which he ensured were always managed in a cordial and constructive way; its flotation and its life as a public company; and, finally, its full take-over by the French shareholders. During this time, his stature in the community, his profound knowledge of the energy sector, and his incisive views on the wider industrial scene provided a highly effective weapon in promoting the company's business and, much to his satisfaction, in promoting energy efficiency in a truly practical and measurable way.

The Micropower Council

'In the same vein, the founding of the Micropower Council in 2000 was entirely Derek's initiative. This organisation was dedicated to collegiate lobbying by the energy sector in support of the development of small-scale and efficient energy generation; it can boast the successful advancement of legislation (*) that it played no small part in promoting'. (*This legislation included the Climate Change & Sustainable Energy Act of 2006, which set out to control the emission of greenhouse gases, and the promotion of microgeneration).

The consummate communicator

'Derek was and remains to this day a consummate communicator. I recall attending the inaugural Energy Lecture to the Worshipful Company of Fuellers in 2005. He began his address by announcing that he wished to reminisce, prompting the lady sitting to my right to whisper that this threatened to be "heavy going". She needn't have worried, as I could have told her. Derek enthralled the assembled company with a lucid, highly informed and wide-ranging review of the world energy position, summarising and concluding precisely on time, as always. His address was greeted with great enthusiasm, not least by the lady on my right! I am reminded of the party he gave when he relinquished his Chairmanship of AHS. This was held at the House of Lords and he delighted in telling us that Lord X had replied to his invitation by saying: "Of course I shall come to your retirement party. I come to all your retirement parties!" Needless to say, this reflected both the exceptionally broad portfolio of interests that Derek pursued, and, I think it is fair to say, his willingness to party!'

Symonds

The comments by Rod Castle and Ralph Cohen are complemented by those of Dr Norman Biddle, another AHS Director, whose consulting company, specialising in construction, consultancy and facilities management, had been taken over in the early 1990s by the eventual French owners. He wrote: 'I can best sum up my personal views of Derek by recalling two instances in the seven years that I worked with him. A few months after I had sold my consulting business, Symonds, to the French company chaired by Lord Ezra, he asked me, with a twinkle in his eye, how I thought I would settle and operate within a major corporate structure after having run my own business for more than 35 years. My response was "with difficulty". He responded that life was all about people, and he thought he and I would work well together. This proved to be so. He was a truly excellent chairman - perceptive, loyal, kind, but determined, with an understanding and fair nature: he was good at giving encouragement to younger persons. The French were very fortunate in having him to look after their UK business interests, which he did so well, and which he developed to be very successful and profitable. My company, Symonds, through one of our subsidiaries, Symonds Travers Morgan, were responsible for the design and management of the Oresund Tunnel that was part of the infrastructure that linked Norway and Sweden – a major civil engineering project. This fascinated Lord Ezra, and he joined me for a site visit that included having to take in a full description and tour of the project, including the offsite manufacturing plant. The quick and ready way that he understood the intricacies of this major development, and his questions to the design team and contractors, were memorable, as was his sprightly and fast tour of the various locations. He showed much enthusiasm for the site people – as we all know, he is a real 'people person' – he inspired those younger than he – "Firm but Fair". I still visit Derek at his home and also keep in touch by telephone and e-mail. He is always interested in others … he is a great friend and an outstanding leader, who was supported unstintingly by his wonderful, loyal wife, Julie, whom he adored'.

"The perfect English Gentleman"

These recollections were enhanced by the comments of the two French directors involved in this complex structure. Bernard Forterre was deputy president of *Compagnie Générale des Eaux*, the French parent company, before the name was changed to Vivendi, and before the new president, Jean Marie Messier, was appointed. Bernard St.André was MD of international development, reporting to Bernard Forterre, and also on Derek's UK Board.

M.Saint-André's comments reflect the esteem in which Derek was held by the Frenchmen with whom he came in contact: 'My collaboration with Lord Ezra for close on ten years has probably been the most memorable and rewarding period of my business life. I joined *Compagnie Générale des Eaux* in 1989 as head of international development in energy, and therefore took up responsibility for the UK business. At the time it consisted of a heating management company, 'AHS', and a lighting company, Parkersell. Lord Ezra was the Chairman. 'My first meeting with him made a deep impression on me I had spent a few years in the US and was used to the hectic way of doing business there. I was welcomed by a very calm man, very dignified and somewhat imposing, but who gave out immediately at the same time a warm feeling of friendliness. What a contrast! You could sense his strong, natural and quiet authority, along with his outstanding vital energy, and you were fascinated by his acute analysis. And what enthusiasm about growing the business! Indeed, the Group's growth went like a dream, precisely because he formed under his authority a dream team … No useless committees, open team work, and a short communication line with the mother company's boss, Bernard Forterre – an effective recipe for success! Board Meetings were sacred, everyone attended religiously, and Lord Ezra conducted them with a rod of iron … not the least question was missed! After five years, the Group had become, through acquisitions and project development, a very diversified energy concern in the core activities – heating and energy management, hospital and industrial utilities, facility management – but above all in pioneering sectors related to waste incineration, co-generation, and energy markets liberalisation: ALEC was trading electricity; AGAS was one of the first successful natural gas suppliers; and the Group was a leader in developing the IPP combined cycle project at Sutton Bridge. None of these new-frontier endeavours could have succeeded, had not Lord Ezra been directly involved, with his deep knowledge of markets and government circles, and his extensive business network. He was a very respected man, everywhere, and that was invaluable. Despite the years when we did not work together any more, my deep respect for him has not faded. In spite of his advanced age, he strives to remain active not only at the Lords, but also in business: he even launched a new company promoting small-scale electricity generation. He does not do it for money; he never was a money man. He does it because he deeply believes, through his long experience, that mankind must build – urgently - a sustainable energy future. He is ever at the 'frontier'. This is still his mission, as it has been all along his outstanding career. Summarizing in a few words Derek Ezra's character: he is and always has been a man of great vision. His whole life is devoted to the common good. To my French eyes, he will for ever personify "the perfect English Gentleman". I am glad that I was given the opportunity to work with him, and be, modestly, his friend.'

Bernard Forterre's comments - his *témoignages* – present Derek as *un homme sérieux,* as does Bernard Saint-André. His concluding sentiments, of October 5 2012, describe the developments that M. Saint-André mentions, in his eloquent French (*a translation follows*):

['*Je me souviendrai toujours du jour où, arrivant au petit matin à Londres, pour voir Lord Ezra, je lui ai fait part de mon projet d'acquérir la totalité du capitale de AHS. Lord Ezra, qui avait le grand avantage de parler français, m'a écouté tranquillement, sans marquer sa surprise, puis m'a dit: "Bernard, un Président est garant des intérêts de tous les actionnaires et il convient que ce projet d'OPA soit muri avec l'aide d'un Conseil indépendant extérieur" … l'OPA fut ensuite réalisée et réussie. AHS, sous l'impulsion de Lord Ezra, et avec l'appui de la CGC s'est fortement développée par croissance externe et interne avec, notamment, quelques étapes marquantes: acquisition de Parkersell, société spécialisée dans la gestion de l'éclairage et des économies d'énergie; création d'ALEC pour la vente d'électricité provenant du cable trans-manche de puissance 2,000 Mw; acquisition du groupe de 'facility management', Symonds; création de SELCHP, société concessionaire pour la réalisation et l'exploitation de la première grande usine d'incinération des ordures ménagères de Grande-Bretagne dans la banlieue de Londres … Lord Ezra aura toujours été un partenaire entreprenant, dont on oubliait l'âge, ouvert à toutes les potentialités qui pouvaient s'offrir, et très au fait du contexte économique européen. Le temps passe, malheureusement, mais j'ai été toujours très fier de l'amitié de Lord Ezra, car j'ai infiniment d'estime et de respect pour l'homme qu'il est et pour le parcours de la vie qui est le sien.'*]

'I will always remember the day when on arrival at crack of dawn in London to see Lord Ezra, I made him privy to my plan to acquire all the capital of AHS. Lord Ezra, who had the great advantage of speaking French, listened to me quietly, without showing any surprise and then said: "Bernard, a Chairman is the guarantor of the interests of all the parties, it is proper that the OPA plan should be matured with the help of an external independent adviser" … an OPA was thereafter brought into being, and flourished. AHS, under Lord Ezra's direction and with the support of the mother company, CGC, developed strongly through both internal and external growth, with some noteworthy leaps forward: the acquisition of Parkersell, a company specialising in the production of lighting and energy-saving; also, the creation of ALEC, for the management of the sale of electricity coming from the cross-channel cable with a strength of 2,000 Mw; the acquisition of the facility management group, Symonds; and the creation of

SELCHP, a concessionary company for the bringing about and exploitation of the first large incinerator of domestic waste in Great Britain in the suburbs of London. Lord Ezra could never be other than an enterprising partner, for whom age did not count, open to all the possibilities which might present themselves, and very much on the ball about European economic matters.

Sadly, time passes, but I have always been very proud of Lord Ezra's friendship, since I have an infinitely high regard and respect for the man he is, and for the life's course which he has pursued'. Eloquent comments indeed, in Derek Ezra's favoured, committed European context.

A further Gallic tribute comes from Jean Claude Banon, CEO of the UK holding company over a wide range of interests for *Compagnie Générale des Eaux*: describing Derek Ezra as having a "significant and long-standing impact on the UK energy market ... By the mid 1990s, the Group was the largest French investor n the UK. Through his professional experience and his association with policy-making at the House of Lords, Derek Ezra had an unrivalled ability to understand energy economics, and market trends, and to identify business opportunities. Whereas his input was very wide-ranging, including access to top actors in the energy world ... his most precious attribute had to be his clarity of vision and his capacity to relate this vision in concise and convincing terms".

Fig.34: "*Une haute personnalité britannique*": French press cutting underlines Lord Ezra's standing in French business circles, through his bi-lingual participation in many Anglo-French enterprises during the 1980s/ 1990s: no hint of *perfide Albion!*

The National Home Improvement Council

Another area of Derek's activity was the National Home Improvement Council, a body which he had supported as an aspect of his overall marketing vision for the NCB. He retired as President after 18 active years, having become an Honorary Vice-President in 2002. First mooted in 1971, as Derek became NCB Chairman, this Council – it was not a trade federation - had been finally incorporated, in 1975, by George Plucknett, former MD of TI's domestic appliance company, Creda, on behalf of the heads of the three main nationalised consumer fuel industries – coal, gas, and electricity - and by what is now the Builders' Merchants' Federation. Its aim was to promote what was, by the early 1970s, a novel concept at governmental level: that it made more economic sense to try to improve the UK's existing housing stock than to only invest in 'new build'. Their common ulterior purpose was to increase the outlet for one or other of their fuels and associated products, working through an 'open doors' altruistic Council, sponsoring awards and example schemes around the UK. Based on an American model, it was a deliberately transparent pressure group, designed to influence action and legislation, initially more actively in the Commons. It co-operated with related industries in construction: just the kind of longer-term policy activity that was "up Derek's street".

Another former colleague who recorded recollections of Derek's impact, Martin Cruttenden, who became its temporary Director in 1993, after moving on from the NCB, has emphasised its importance as a part of the Board's broad marketing strategy.

The "Ezra-factors"

Ernest Cantle, its DG from 1980 onwards, got to know the Ezras well, through their involvement, and worked with Derek as a member of its Board for many years: "taking the period of the 1980s onwards, Derek could now bring three main factors to our activity. First, now that he had been elevated to the peerage, he could extend our access to policy-making from the Lib.Dem. benches": (*further examples of this have been covered in Chapter 9, dealing with Derek's work in the House of Lords*). Second, Ernest witnessed yet another aspect of Derek's innate leadership qualities, explored earlier in this Memoir, and vital to the kind of voluntary, pan-industry work of the NHIC: "people trusted him. He had a knack of being able to bridge gaps. I guess people thought, 'Well, if someone cool-headed and objective like Lord Ezra is behind this idea, it must be worth following'.

"Third, and to some extent flowing from that second point, he was reliable; he was always fastidious in the materials he used publicly; you knew that he would do things rightly, and thoroughly. If I was putting a paper up to him with some future 'starred debate' (a private member's motion in the Lords) or speech in mind, he would initially press me, with that historian's rigorously trained mind of his, to quote chapter and verse for every fact or statistic. 'You say this, but where did you get it from?' In due course, when I hope he must have concluded that I could be trusted, this very proper inquisition was put aside, I had passed through a kind of 'barrier', and he took me and my counsel on their merits".

Ernest, like other witnesses to this Memoir, found Derek to be a very private person, whose inner warmth only came out once you had been accepted by him as worth his confidence, and 'past the barrier". He did not think Derek was subjectively ambitious for himself, as much as objectively ambitious for whatever goal – or organisation – he had set his sights on as being necessary or worthwhile. Ernest recalled another aspect of the Ezra "presence" – his concern for – and loyal support by – Julie herself; Ernest and his wife admired her greatly and the two couples enjoyed many such occasions socially. Although Derek had by now become enured to the process of attending public functions where he might not know everybody personally, Julie would be understandably more diffident, and he would not unthinkingly involve her in attending with him unless her concerns could be met. Ernest was often able to reassure her that she would be with people who would be looking after her, and then her mind would be put at ease, and her lovely personality would come shining through. For Ernest, as for so many, the experience of being with – and working with – the Ezras was wholly positive, memorable and enjoyable.

John Demont, first (Domestic) Sales Director for NHIC's Founder-Member, British Gas, represented them on the Board and as a revolving Chairman from 1983 to 1984. 'Derek always kept his finger on the pulse, and even when the Council temporarily ceased to operate in 1992-4 and was run by the NHIC Educational Trust' (under John's Chairmanship) he still maintained his confidence in the Council's ability to survive. Derek had a healthy regard for his competitors on the Board – there was excellent multi-fuel co-operation. In the course of my NHIC career, I was in the company of Lord Ezra, and his wife many times and I always admired his ability to pick up the threads of how the NHIC was performing at any one time, what was going on, what was the latest project, platforms, etc … He was masterful at AGMs, which he always took, and as a figure-head he was extremely helpful … if we needed ministerial support, he was often able to 'arrange' it.

'If we needed a new President or Vice-President, he knew who to get on board. I believe that my boss, British Gas Chairman Sir Denis Rooke, found Derek a formidable opponent, and, for a marketing man, surprisingly difficult! Denis was an engineer through and through – a "superior race"… Before oil gasification, we were at the mercy of the Coal Board; we couldn't survive without coal and Derek used the fact to advantage – no surprise there! During this time the NHIC undertook many campaigns and initiatives, probably the most significant being the Neighbourhood Revitalisation Scheme (NRS) … The NHIC actually had a property portfolio of nearly 300 properties at one time – value £800,000 plus! First and foremost, however, Derek was concerned about the efficient use of fuel – all fuels; innovative techniques e.g. micro-technologies; fuel conservation and fuel poverty; and how important it is to conserve energy … I regarded him very highly – even though a "coal man"!'

The Major Energy Users' Council

A final example of Derek's enthusiasms for all the diverse activities and causes in which he became involved after the NCB is provided by Andrew Bainbridge, a Past Master of The Fuellers, and current Chairman of the Major Energy Users' Council. This is still an ongoing, self-styled 'utility consumer network and lobby', conceived by Derek in 1987 to meet a new perceived need in the market-place: that many fuel users, even major companies with full purchasing staffs, suddenly found that they were having to purchase fuel from a widely varying range of suppliers, private as well as still public. Their fuel-buying arms were not yet geared for this complexity. This concept bears one of the classic Ezra hallmarks: 'inclusivity'.

It was set up as a 'Council' on his advice by Andrew Bainbridge, after the gas industry was privatised. Andrew's work in the energy sector under the umbrella of Grafton Consultants had been brought to Derek's attention. It included public relations campaigns for Satchwell; a world-first book on Employee Participation in Energy-Saving Programmes; and a train-driver motivation campaign which saved British Rail's SE Region £4 million. Andrew seemed the right man to head up this Council. Its aim was to ensure that the large customers of the UK utilities had a forum through which to work together to buy, in the new market opening up under privatisation. It is funded by subscription and was and still is widely welcomed.

Andrew has written: "Derek was the inspiration behind our [Council] … He was our first President, from January 1987 to June 1988, and has always been a staunch supporter of a unique organisation which enjoys excellent relationships with Government, suppliers, trade associations and industry specialists. The initial MEUC meetings in the Penthouse Suite in the old Café Royal, and at the Lords, attracted scores of private and public sector buyers.'

These five instances – Morgan Grenfell, AHS and Symonds, and the Councils for Micropower, National Home Improvement, and The Major Energy Users - must suffice in the framework of this Memoir to highlight not only the contribution that Derek Ezra has made to an enormous number of causes both within and way beyond any narrower connexion with coal and energy, but above all the high esteem in which he has been held in his involvement with them.

They form an insight into a more indirect aspect of his charismatic leadership – here sometimes purely advisory, more often executive – but always disciplined and relevant to the task in hand.

Contributors: Lord Quentin Davies; Rod Castle, Ralph Cohen, Jean Claude Banon, Norman Biddle; Bernard Forterre, Bernard St André; Martin Cruttenden, Ernest Cantle, John Demont, Andrew and Marianne Bainbridge

Chapter 11: The First Fuellers' Energy Lecture – 11 May 2005

Although at the time, it may to some have seemed like a voice in the energy wilderness, it is astonishing how much of Derek Ezra's Energy Lecture of 2005 is still prophetically relevant today, even if some of its scope has been overtaken by events. Excerpts from the lecture are included as a tribute to his foresight and powers of analysis. Several of its themes have already been touched on earlier in this Memoir; self-evidently, many of those problems have yet to be solved …

"The coal industry was nationalised in 1947 and I joined it quite by chance. I was in the wartime army, having been called up in 1939. Shortly before my demobilisation in early 1947, I was walking along Regent Street and happened to meet Val Duncan, whom I had known when he was a Brigadier in 21 Army Group. He asked what I intended to do when I left the Army. I said I was unsure – possibly try to join a large industrial organisation. He suggested I try the Coal Board, which was being set up, and they were looking for people in their Marketing Department. He was its Transport Director – and later was to move to Rio Tinto, which he built up into one of the world's largest mining concerns. I was duly offered a fairly modest post in marketing. Things were a bit disorganised in those early days at the Coal Board. I remember my first office was the pantry of a flat in Berkeley Square. There was plenty of shelf space, but little else. I had nothing to put on the shelves, and nowhere to put myself. I was somewhat disenchanted. I thought I might stay for a few months and look around for another occupation! …

Public Ownership in Concept and Practice

"I would like at this stage to say a few words about the concept of public ownership and how it turned out in practice. The concept, developed by Herbert Morrison [Home Secretary in the post-war Labour Government] was that various basic sectors of the economy would be put under the control of independent boards who would operate them in the public interest. Government intervention would be limited to matters of national interest and would take the form of directives prepared after consultation with the board in question.

"In practice it worked out quite differently. I am not aware of any formal directive on a matter of national interest ever having been issued to the Coal Board. But there was constant detailed intervention of an informal nature. The fact is that the nationalised industries represented an important part of the economy and the temptation for successive governments to intervene in their affairs to support their various policies was too great to be resisted. This had particularly harmful effects for the Coal Board in two respects – in prices and in wages …

"When the collieries were nationalised in 1947 it was received with great joy by the mineworkers as the achievement of a long-cherished ambition. The NUM committed themselves to the settlement of all future wage negotiations by peaceful means, and by arbitration if necessary. But this was soon terminated when they suspected that the government was exerting influence over the arbitrators. Annual wage negotiations became increasingly difficult, culminating in the strikes of 1971 and 1974 (the strike of 1985, which happened after my time, was more politically motivated).

"The strike of 1974 could, in my opinion, have been settled by dealing with the mineworkers as a special case, which both the TUC and the CBI would have supported. The trouble was that the government effectively took over wage negotiations. When we were about to engage in our wages round in 1976, and Jim Callaghan was Prime Minister, I asked him to refuse to see the NUM if they approached him. He agreed and we satisfactorily negotiated.

"We used to take great pains in preparing for wage negotiations. We carefully rehearsed all the arguments, and made sure the negotiations lasted a long time, which is what the NUM expected. I did not attend the negotiations myself, but held a small amount in reserve. In due course they grew wise to this, and Joe Gormley, the President of the NUM, after heated debate, would ask to see the chairman. On one occasion we settled quite quickly and I assumed he would return to tell the troops. But he said he had to be away at least half an hour to give the impression of a tough struggle. 'Bring out the brandy', he said 'and let us chat'. Brandy was his favourite tipple, but not mine, especially in the afternoon – but it was a price worth paying.

Labour Relations

"Developing good labour relations was an essential part of our task as management in order to achieve the best business results … There were two ways in which we worked particularly closely with the Unions – one was safety and the other was research. Safety was paramount, and everyone in the industry was totally committed to it, both management and unions. We achieved the best standards of any coal industry in the world. Inevitably we had accidents but the scale was nothing like what it had been in the past.

"Whenever there was an accident of a serious nature I would drop everything and fly directly to the site. I was always impressed with the quiet and determined way in which the situation was dealt with jointly by management and unions. Apart from these emergency visits I tried to go underground at least twice a month. I learnt a great deal this way – which was of help to me in the boardroom, as I could speak with recent coalface knowledge.

"Research was the other area where we kept closely in touch with the unions. There was never any 'Luddite' spirit against the introduction of new mining methods. On the contrary they were welcomed as contributing to safety and productivity. We used to go through our annual research programme with the union representatives and we discussed with them all the new ideas that had come our way. One of these was biological mining, whereby a particular breed of bugs would convert the coal into a liquid which would then be pumped to the surface. The union people listened to this with interest and then one of them intervened. He asked – 'There is only one question. Which union would they belong to?' Based on our success in creating a partnership with the unions on safety and research I felt that we should widen our discussions with them to cover the full range of our policies. We set up accordingly a Joint Policy Advisory Committee at which we revealed all the details of our costs, proceeds and investments, right down to individual mines. We also discussed our pricing intentions. Some thought we were running a commercial risk in so doing, but there was never any leak – and imparting such information helped in our wage negotiations. In taking this initiative I believe we were in advance of our time.

Luxembourg

"In 1950 six West European countries, including in particular France and Germany, signed the Treaty of Paris, setting up the European Coal and Steel Community, the precursor of the present European Union. Britain had been invited to join but refused. However it asked to be

Fig.35: Lord Ezra delivers the first Fuellers' Energy Lecture, at the Haberdashers Hall, City of London, 11 May 2005

kept in touch with developments and a UK delegation was established in Luxembourg, which was the seat of the High Authority of the new Community. I was appointed by the NCB to be their representative on the delegation, and my wife and I spent four years there from 1952 to 1956.

"The Grand Duchy of Luxembourg, with its population of only 350,000, then retained much of its old charm … There were still steam trams, powered by coal, running through the capital city, and no traffic lights. The American Minister was the redoubtable Washington hostess, Perle Mesta, who was the inspiration of the musical, "Call Me Madam". She entertained frequently. On one occasion she invited all the mayors of Luxembourg to a reception, about 100 of them. They wore their best clothes for the occasion, including a *chapeau melon* or bowler hat. On arrival their hats were taken by an attendant without issuing any tickets. For weeks afterwards the cafés of Luxembourg were filled with mayors exchanging bowler hats to try to find their own.

"The President of the High Authority was Jean Monnet, one of the most remarkable men of the 20th century. He was convinced that in order to avoid future wars and promote stability and prosperity, European countries would have to co-operate on a more integrated basis than ever before. He devised an institutional framework consisting of a council of ministers, an executive, a parliament and a court of justice which has survived to this day over half a century later. Britain remained a reluctant participant – in my opinion much to our disadvantage.

The Problem of Energy Efficiency

"One of the most important aspects of energy policy has been that of energy efficiency. In this, Britain has been at a disadvantage because our abundant indigenous resources, first of coal and then of oil and natural gas, encourage profligate use. It requires strong motivation for people to use energy efficiently. This has only occurred twice in my experience in the past half century – immediately after the war, when coal, the principal energy source, was desperately short – and in the'70s when the Middle East oil crisis pushed up the price of oil, which had then become the dominant fuel, to unheard-of heights. Because of the climate change threat the government is keen at the present time to promote energy efficiency, but it has had relatively little success.

Current Energy Policy

"There are three overriding aspects of current energy policy: climate change, energy dependence and fuel poverty. All three involve making better use of energy and increasing the range of energy sources, while keeping down emissions. But emissions, especially of carbon dioxide, are beginning to rise again and the government is concentrating unduly on renewables, especially wind energy, to solve the problem. I believe the solution goes wider than that. Other options need to be urgently considered, among them the nuclear option. Difficult as it may be, the future of nuclear power will soon have to be settled one way or the other. As energy spokesman for the Liberal Democrats in the House of Lords I have been making proposals for three courses of action. First, I believe that coal, of which we still have abundant reserves, can once again play a major role both in limiting energy import dependence and in reducing emissions by applying clean coal technology. This has been developed and is already being applied in the United States and Canada, and I see no reason why we should not set up some of these plants here. The application of this technology could open up a substantial export market, particularly in China and India, where the consumption of coal is rising very fast. Secondly, there should be a much more determined campaign for the insulation of the poorly constructed 20% of our homes, thus helping to reduce fuel poverty … Thirdly, we should increase the efficiency with which electricity is generated. I attach particular importance to this last issue. Large-scale conventional power stations lose about half the value of their input fuel through waste heat. Up to another 10% is lost in transmission and distribution. If these large losses can be avoided it would make a massive contribution to energy efficiency and correspondingly reduce emissions and costs.

"There is a way of doing this by taking generation as near to the consumer as possible. This is known as microgeneration or micropower. Five years ago, suiting action to words, I set up a company under the name of Micropower to promote the concept of small-scale electricity generation, making use of waste heat and avoiding transmission and distribution losses, thus achieving efficiencies of nearly 90% or double that of the existing power station. Small-scale appliances providing both electricity and heat would be suitable for domestic and commercial use.

Conclusion

"What are the lessons to be learnt? Perhaps there are two. The first is the continuing uncertainty of the energy scene, moving from feast to famine at short notice with corresponding price fluctuations. Predictions almost invariably turn out to be wrong. But the second is that, if there are clearly defined imperatives, such as dealing with climate change, reducing import dependence and eliminating fuel poverty, then, in spite of the uncertainty, firm and vigorous action has to be taken. These problems cannot be solved by themselves."

Derek Ezra

Chapter 12: Ezra on Energy – Communicating with the Public

Although the name Ezra carries with it revered historical antecedents, it is arguable that the writings of this secular 21st-century bearer of that name may well prove in the long run to have been even more beneficial for man. The Old Testament's 'Book of Ezra' prophesied 'the good life'; 'Ezra the Scribe', the monk thought to have transcribed it, is commemorated on lonely Holy Island in Northumberland, heralding the dawn of Britain's Christianity. Yet these distant messengers did not immediately reach beyond the souls – or the soils – of their respective homelands. It is scarcely an exaggeration to say that in contrast the environmental prophesies of Derek Ezra have vital long-term messages across the globe for humanity as a whole, focussing on the planet's capacity to sustain life at all, economic or spiritual.

Derek Ezra's campaign to bring the need for an 'Energy Policy' before government and opinion-formers has been a constant theme throughout his later working life, as well as in the minds of many of those who worked with him. In this concluding section, we bring together excerpts from two key chapters in the books he employed to convey that message to an even wider audience: **Coal and Energy** (the second edition, published in 1978); and **The Energy Debate**, which he conceived and edited. This finally came out in 1983, a year after his retirement from the NCB, albeit at the outset of the equally busy 'second half' of his career on the Boards and managements of many enterprises. (These books would pave the way for the speech which he made later to the Fuellers' Company as the inaugural Energy Lecture, after the Livery's refounding, on 11 May 2005, reproduced above as Chapter 11). The 'Time-Lines' section on p.xxviii records the details.

In all this output he was of course able to draw upon the inputs of many other colleagues and fellow-authorities. The final imprint is, however, unmistakably his. The excerpts chosen illustrate Derek's alpha mind and his breadth of vision, and his ability to organise both a body of work and a body of experts, coupled with a mastery of argument – made all the more readable by virtue of a lucid and often witty style. Apart from a few inevitably anachronistic ironies arising from intervening events, they come across to a 21st-century eye as relevantly and forcefully as when they first appeared. They could still be an excellent blueprint for government action today.

Coal and Energy: The need to exploit the world's most abundant fossil fuel

Chapter 1: The Problem of Energy

'It has been remarked more than once that the pronouncements of politicians, leaders of both sides of industry, spokesmen of the media and others who seek to influence public opinion are full of references to turning points in history which, subsequently, stubbornly refuse to turn. By contrast, however, those who see the events of 1973 as a turning point in the world energy situation can surely expect to be justified by events. For 1973 was the year when the world's leading oil exporters, members of the Organisation of Oil Exporting Countries (OPEC) grasped their opportunity to push up oil prices to hitherto totally unprecedented levels. Importing countries had no choice but to accept the new inflated prices. Cheap energy, it was clear, had gone perhaps for ever, to which was added the recognition that a regular and adequate supply from these sources could no longer be assumed in the future.

'Although oil is only one of the various forms of energy available to mankind, it has assumed such a dominant role that a major interruption in availability inevitably affects the entire world economy. For this very reason, the sudden jolt to the general complacency, nurtured on ideas of super-abundant energy, may yet prove to be a blessing in disguise. It has brought home to everyone the realisation – known already to many of those who have been more closely concerned with energy problems – that the world's supplies of energy, in their present forms, are not nearly as plentiful as has been previously supposed.

'Moreover, what reserves remain will become increasingly expensive to exploit. One of the forms of energy which will have a major role in the future is coal, because it has by far and away the largest reserves of any fossil fuel. On the other hand it suffers, compared with oil and gas, from generally greater problems of production, handling and usage. The challenge for coal in the future is how to overcome these problems. The need for adequate investment and research is vital. Although my immediate concern must necessarily be with the place of coal in the United Kingdom, I fully recognise that the energy problem is essentially a world problem. What we do in the UK will have effects beyond our borders and, still more so, what happens in the rest of the world will affect the lives of all of us in this country. Now that the UK is a full member of the European Community, we have to consider our situation as a part of the wider European scene – a scene, however, in which we can expect to play a powerful part with our very large reserves of fossil fuels – coal, oil and natural gas. It would be comforting to think that the enlarged Community, by pooling its energy resources, could look towards self-sufficiency, but this is not so. A considerable proportion of the energy needs of the area will continue to be obtained from outside and, for this reason in particular, I shall keep international considerations prominently in mind throughout the book.

'Limits to Energy'

'There are limits to potential energy exports around the world. It is necessary therefore to take a global view and consider how demand from other energy-hungry parts of the world will affect Britain's and Europe's prospects for importing their future energy requirements. It is also particularly important to consider how these international supply problems will affect the price at which supplies can be obtained, remembering that changes in the price of one form of energy can influence the prospects and availability of others.

'There are very few parts of the world which are exempt from these influences, though some have a bigger impact than others. Thus the oil producers of the Middle East and Africa, in particular, are exporters of huge quantities of energy, while Japan exerts a big influence as a major importer of energy. The United States is one of the main energy producing areas of the world, but its use of energy has grown to such an extent that it is now a major importer, with the prospect of becoming possibly even more import-dependent in the future. At the moment the USSR [sic] and Eastern Europe are largely self-sufficient in energy and do not compete with the rest of the world for OPEC's oil supplies, nor does it seem likely that they will do so to a major extent in the foreseeable future. On the other hand, the USSR is already an exporter of oil and gas and has the reserves "in the ground" to increase its exports quite considerably, and should it do so this would prove to be significant factor in the world situation. China has started small exports of oil to Japan and it is possible that it could become a sizeable exporter of energy. There are also the vast areas of the world – the Indian sub-continent, Africa and Latin America – where huge, growing populations could eventually exert a big call on world energy reserves, reduced, maybe, by new energy discoveries in their own unexplored regions ...

'World resources of coal, oil and natural gas – the fossil fuels – were built up over millions of years in the remote past and are not being renewed, at least to a measurable extent. It follows therefore that the available world reserves are finite, while consumption has risen at a great rate as people all over the world have grown accustomed to a way of life which demands more and more energy. Oil has illustrated this trend more clearly than any other fuel …

'Everyone assumed that these conditions would continue and that the comforting thought, often expressed a few years ago, that more oil is discovered each year than is consumed, would remain true indefinitely. In recent years, however, not only have major discoveries tended to be in relatively costly areas, such as Alaska and our own North Sea, but the consensus of expert opinion, even before 1973, was that the quantities of oil which could be extracted at costs covered by the then world prices would not be capable of meeting the rising demand for very much longer.

'Possible substitutes for oil (for example, from oil shales and tar sands) did exist but would be much more expensive than oil had been at that time and, in any case, the time-scale for their exploitation was so long that they would not be available in substantial quantity for many years ahead. As matters stood, therefore, given the uneven distribution of oil reserves throughout the world and the high cost of substitutes, oil prices would inevitably have risen over the years. Had not the OPEC countries exploited their monopoly situation as they did, however, the rise in prices would have been more gradual, encouraging the introduction of substitutes, as part of a natural progression which made them economic as oil prices rose.

'End of an Era'

'This possibility ended in October 1973; the public, which had assumed that adequate supplies of fuel at reasonable prices would always be available, apart from temporary local difficulties due to strikes and other emergencies, found that a large proportion of the energy supplies of the UK and many other industrialised countries was dependent on suppliers – whose interests and policies could run counter to those of their customers, resulting in steep price rises and even a cessation of supplies.

'Thus, to put the world's energy problems in true perspective, I believe that we should look both backwards and forwards to encompass the fifty years of the second half of this century. I see ourselves standing at the mid-point of this fifty-year span from which we can look back over twenty-five years to the start of the post Second World War period and forward to the end of the present century.

'This is not just a neat way of dividing up an arbitrarily selected period. On the contrary, it offers an opportunity to examine the trends of the comparatively recent past, to absorb the lessons they teach and apply them to the future. Moreover the past twenty-five years illustrate with particular clarity the trends in the coal industries of Britain and the world, with which this book is principally, though not exclusively, concerned …

'Looking more closely at our fifty year period, I further sub-divide it into a series of shorter periods. The first, running from the end of World War Two till the second half of the nineteen fifties, was a time of energy shortage, occasioned by the war and its aftermath. This was followed by a period of surplus energy which lasted until the early 1970s when a tight supply situation began to emerge, marked by oil price rises in 1970 and 1971 which, however, were modest compared with what was to come.

'With the Middle East War of 1973 came the start of the third of the four periods, confronting the world with an energy crisis, the like of which it had not experienced before …

'Nevertheless, in spite of an apparent air of alarm, this can be described as a "contrived" crisis, brought about by political and other pressures rather than by the logic of the present world energy situation. In other words, the world is not short of energy at the present time but is suffering from one of the symptoms of shortage, in the form of high energy prices, because of man-made policies. What I am saying is that sooner or later the crunch will come and the world will enter the fourth, and final period of the fifty-year span with which this book is concerned. This I describe as the "real" crisis, when energy shortages will become acute, even if there is no artificial stimulation, unless drastic and far-reaching steps are taken sufficiently in advance.

"Real" Crisis and the 21st century

'As the story unfolds, it will be seen that the "real" crisis will become apparent probably in the late 1980s or 1990s and certainly by the opening of the next century … I believe that the timing will be such that decisions necessary to meet the crisis should be at least under active consideration now, while some of the longer term decisions should be taken as soon as possible.

'I am thinking in world terms and, obviously, the onset of the "real" crisis will vary from one individual country to another. It is likely, for example, that Britain's own crisis may be delayed, relative to the rest of Europe, because we shall be self-sufficient in oil and gas, as long as North Sea supplies last, and, of course, in coal for very much longer. On the other hand, oil and gas (but not coal) are likely to be on the decline by the end of the century, so that we may find ourselves having to resume imports just at the time when the world's energy situation is becoming acute.

'Coal, on this showing, will have a continuing key role as the world's largest single fossil fuel resource and many of the decisions which must now be taken relate to the world's coal industries. Although the decisions cover a very wide field, from policies for conserving present forms of energy to the exploitation of completely new types, some of the most urgent are concerned with an expansion in the output of existing fuels, particularly coal, and having secured the increased output, making certain that the fuels are put to optimum use …

'Research along these lines has been carried out for many years and has been stepped up to a certain extent, nevertheless important decisions in this regard should be taken now. Further research is also needed on the many problems surrounding the future development of nuclear power, and, although so-called benign and renewable sources, such as solar power and wind and wave power, seem unlikely to make a major contribution to the overall supplies before the end of the century, research into these sources is to be encouraged.

'Many of the decisions which the world will have to take in order to meet its future energy needs will affect the environment, at a time when people everywhere are becoming increasingly conscious of the damage which can be done to natural surroundings in the search for and exploitation of the different forms of energy, whether an opencast site, electricity pylons, a natural gas pipeline compressor or a nuclear power station. There is no way of providing the increased energy supplies necessary without some effects on the environment but, as I shall aim to show, the fuel industries believe that it is possible to strike a reasonable balance between mankind's need for adequate energy supplies and its justifiable concern for the environment in which we all live …

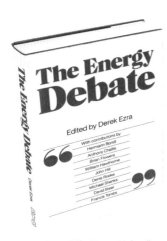

Fig.36: "The Energy Debate",
Derek Ezra's timely compilation of
prophecies about the future UK
energy market, published in 1982

'Environmental protection is only one of the many facets of the world's energy problems which will demand the combined efforts of government, the energy industries and consumers, acting on both national and international levels, if satisfactory solutions are to be found ...

'I believe that the problems can and will be solved, provided they are considered as dispassionately as possible in full knowledge of the facts and that a rational long term strategy is evolved. It is with the aim of making a contribution to public discussion of the world's present and future energy problems that this book has been written ... The broad picture given by the book, with its central theme of the need to press on with the greater production of coal and other indigenous fuels in the main energy consuming countries and to keep down demands on the world's dwindling stocks of oil and natural gas, should however, remain valid for years to come.'

THE ENERGY DEBATE

The second book was conceived and edited by Derek Ezra, with contributions by a galaxy of leading authorities in the field of energy, all known to him personally. (*Brief biographies are included in the section on* **Contributors** *at the end of this chapter*). Excerpts from his final chapter must suffice to give a flavour of the scope of the work, notwithstanding some anachronisms due to the passage of the intervening 30 years.

Summary and Conclusions

'This book has included chapters on the main sources of primary energy (oil, coal, natural gas, and nuclear power), on the main source of secondary energy (electricity), and on the wider aspects of energy (research, conservation, the environment and the consumer's viewpoint). On one issue there is little doubt. The events of October 1973 and subsequently, when the price of OPEC-traded oil was massively increased, started an entirely new post-war energy phase. This followed on the first post-war phase, which lasted from 1945 until about 1957. During this period energy supplies (still largely based on coal) were insufficient to meet all the requirements of post-war construction, and had to be allocated according to agreed priorities. The second phase, from 1957 until 1973, was dominated by the emergence of oil as an abundant, convenient and low-priced energy source. This was soon buttressed by natural gas and nuclear power. Coal, with its generally higher cost and lesser convenience, progressively lost ground. It seemed to many (but not all) that a new energy age had opened with economic growth surging forward on the basis of apparently unlimited supplies of the newer and more economic energy sources. This illusion was rudely shattered at the end of 1973, when the pivotal position of oil was suddenly threatened. The low cost energy era was, it appeared, being succeeded by a high cost era. New priorities and new dispositions appeared essential. But if the broad conclusion must be that a new energy phase started in 1973, it is not yet clear, nearly a decade after, [1983] exactly what form it is likely to take. This is due to the paradox that the oil crisis itself, instead of leading, as might have been expected, to a deficiency in supplies, has led (so far) to a situation of over-abundance. Demand in fact has been substantially reduced because of the economic crisis directly attributable to the oil crisis

'Let us see if some light can be shed on this complexity by identifying the main conclusions reached by the various contributors to this book. It is right to start with *oil*. David Steel, former Chairman of BP, is very clear in his conclusions. "Looking to the future, investment in alternative supplies and in more energy-efficient plant and buildings is seen as the key to avoiding recurrences of (the) cycle of oil price increases followed by recession ... The UK now faces the same challenge as its industrial competitors. It must learn how to use energy more efficiently."

'In the chapter on *coal*, I contend that "increased use of coal will be an essential part of an overall policy to reduce UK dependence on oil", bearing in mind, especially, the temporary nature of North Sea resources. I then propose a six-point policy to bring this about. A fundamental aspect of coal policy is the long lead time between exploring for reserves and bringing new mining prospects into operation.

'Denis Rooke, Chairman of the British Gas Corporation, describes the enormous transformation in the *gas industry* during the post-war period, from an outmoded base to one of Britain's most advanced and successful enterprises ... The most important current problem facing the industry, however, is that of depletion in view of the limited nature of North Sea reserves. "The aim of depletion policy," he writes, "is to husband reserves in order to supply the premium market as long as possible" ... Coal as a source of SNG [Substitute Natural Gas] has been the subject of successful research carried out by the Gas Corporation.

'"*Nuclear power* is now a well-established technology throughout the industrial world", writes John Hill, former Chairman of the UK Nuclear Energy Authority ... he contends that "the nuclear reactor ... is manifestly [!] one of the safest industrial undertakings yet devised", and describes the progress made in dealing with industrial waste ... He supports the view that the UK's long-term energy policy will depend upon a combination of conservation, coal and nuclear power.

'Francis Toombs, former Chairman of the Electricity Council, does not see *electricity* as "just another fuel. It is a unique form of energy which affects every facet of human activity" ... It can be generated from all existing forms of primary energy and from most future sources at present contemplated ... It will be necessary to maintain and even increase coal output and nuclear power production as extensions of present technologies" ... there is a major role for nuclear power, "to secure Britain's future competitive position in an energy-hungry world".

'Hermann Bondi and Anthony Challis see *energy research* being developed against a background "in which major investments will be required to open up replacements for oil and natural gas" ... Energy research has a major role to play in widening the future range of choices.

'William Hawthorne, who was for five years Chairman of the Advisory Council for Energy Conservation, considers the role of *energy conservation* in the present context ... he analyses the factors determining energy demand, considers the various studies made of future energy trends, and concludes that, in spite of intermittent periods of recession, the medium term is likely to be characterized by energy supply difficulties" ... His broad conclusion is that "the UK has made a useful start to the process of adapting our economy to a future in which energy will be scarce and very much more expensive". However, "a great deal more can – and needs to be – done, even to achieve the less than optimistic assumptions of the Department of Energy".

'Brian Flowers, the Rector of Imperial College [now University], deals with the problems of *energy and the environment* ... He emphasizes the need for the environmental consequences of alternative energy strategies to be comprehensively reviewed, explored and assessed ...

He proceeds to analyse the environmental aspects of the various forms of energy. He chaired the inquiry (completed in 1981) into coal and the environment undertaken by the Commission on Energy and the Environment. Apart from three important provisos (on spoil, opencast mining and subsidence), "the Commission came generally to the view that there were no major constrictions on environmental grounds in exploiting coal to fill the energy gap at the end of the century" … He considers that, "the hazards of the nuclear industry (save in one respect) are normal for industries of this scale – that is to say they can be recognized and controlled by normal arrangements which already exist and are at present being improved" … He concludes with a review of planning as it affects the environment and considers that there is a need "to devise procedures which can combine public acceptance and an ability to get things done".

'Michael Shanks, Chairman of the National Consumer Council, in dealing with *energy and the consumer*, states that delegates at the Annual Consumer Congress in 1980, "identified their most urgent priority as being the establishment of a stronger consumer voice in energy policy … He considers that there is a case for examining whether today's consumer should be asked, to the extent applied at present, "to pay for the cost of investment which will benefit tomorrow's consumer … On a more general note he concludes that "there is a need for the formulation of long-term energy policy" …

'It is now time to draw the final conclusions from the wide range of views expressed. I believe that six major issues emerge. *First*, there is the dominating impact of the oil price revolution. The massive price increases in 1973/74 and then again in 1979 have fundamentally changed the energy scene, and this is recognized, and indeed, emphasized by all those who have contributed to this book. Underlying these developments is the combined political strength, complicated by unpredictable crises, of the OPEC countries; and the uncertainty surrounding the economic reserves of oil.

'The conclusion to be drawn … is inescapable: the crucial importance of reducing dependence on imported oil. However, the recurrent oil crises themselves have blurred the simplicity of this conclusion by engendering conditions of major economic recession, which is the *second* issue to emerge. In recent times this has weakened the price of oil, led to over-supply rather than under-supply, and cast doubts on the level of future energy requirements. In consequence, measures have already been taken by certain governments and enterprises to defer, or even cancel, actions previously taken to develop alternative energy sources. Organizations such as the International Energy Agency, have drawn attention to the risks such changes of policy could entail, bearing in mind the fundamental uncertainty of oil supplies.

'This leads to the *third* major issue to emerge, which is that of the implications of energy policy. Any policy which aims on a wide scale to replace a major existing form of energy and to provide practical alternative options, must involve substantial expenditure. In a period of long-lasting recession, with energy readily available and financial resources scarce, there are bound to be questions about major expenditure to guard against some uncertain future difficulty. There are those who consider that the problem can best be dealt with by leaving it to market forces. In the case of energy, however, this simple approach suffers from the defect that effective options to meet differing circumstances can only be provided as a result of long-term investment strategies. Otherwise the market solution could lead to recessions even deeper than those we are suffering from at present (in 1982).

'The *fourth* major issue, which has emerged from the last three chapters in the book, is the social dimension. Conservation, the environment and the consumer all introduce social aspects in different ways. As the purpose of energy is to meet a human need, it follows that the satisfaction of that need should as far as possible be consistent with other human requirements, in which efficiency, the environment, reliability, convenience and cost all play their part. But the essential requirement is to make sure that the energy is there when required. Overriding all other requirements is the need for a degree of insurance. So, all these things have to be balanced. A high degree of skill is required to achieve the proper degree of equilibrium between strategy (or insurance), convenience (including the environment) and economy. These considerations tend to compete, but, whatever the difficulties, a policy of positive action (as opposed to inaction) has to be devised.

'The *fifth* issue relates to technology. We live in an age of rapidly advancing technological growth – and energy is one of the fields in which this has taken place. In each of the forms of energy discussed in this book, enormous technological strides have taken place in the post-war period. The ways in which oil, coal, gas, nuclear power and electricity are now produced, distributed and used bear no relation to the situation existing in the aftermath of war. The last two decades in particular have witnessed a virtual revolution in energy technology. There is great scope for still further improvements. But for these to be realized there has to be the will on the part of governments and enterprises to allocate the necessary resources and skills. Energy research is an activity which needs to be pursued with vigour and continuity. A major reduction of effort could set back achievements by several years. The temptation to cut back such efforts in periods of recession must be strongly resisted.

'The *sixth* issue that emerges from this book, and especially from the chapters dealing with particular forms of energy and research, is the long time-scale required to create valid energy options. The term "keeping options open" is sometimes used synonymously with putting off decisions; but if an option is not available, it is not "open". For energy choices to be available in any given situation, decisions have to be made many years before, and substantial resources and effort allocated. It takes about ten years for a major mining complex, a large-scale power station, a large oil refinery or a gas gathering and distribution system to be planned, constructed and brought into operation. This is a fundamental and determining factor of any energy strategy.

'The main thrust of this book, therefore, is that while the energy debate may ebb and flow, major long-term decisions must continuously be made. And at the present stage this must mean that, while substantial expenditure will be required to bring into production further reserves from more difficult environments, we must at the same time ensure that all energy is used wisely, and that the main available long-term alternatives to oil – namely, coal, with its substantial and widely dispersed reserves, and nuclear power, with its highly developed technology – must be expanded in concert. Research effort must also be devoted to longer-term renewable energy sources, and the social requirements need to be reconciled with the energy requirements. Without such a strategy the energy debates of future generations could be concerned with a series of deepening and recurrent crises'.

Derek Ezra's selection of Contributors to 'The Energy Debate'

Prof. Sir Hermann Bondi, KCB, FRS, FRAS
Former appointments include: Fellow of
Trinity College, Cambridge; Chairman of the
Environment Research Council; Prof. of
Mathematics, King's College, London; Chief
Scientist, Department of Energy.

Dr Anthony Challis, CBE
Former appointments include: Senior Vice-
President, ICI Americas Incorporated;
Director, Polymer Engineering, Science
Research Council; succeeded Sir Hermann
Bondi as Chief Scientist, Dept. of Energy.

Lord Flowers, FRS
Former appointments include: Rector,
Imperial College, London [now University];
Chairman, The Computer Board, & the
Science Research Council; Board of
Governors of the Weizmann Institute and of
the Energy Commission.

Prof. Sir William Hawthorne,
CBE, ScD, FRS, FEng., FIMechE.
Former appointments include: Master of
Churchill College, Cambridge; Hopkinson
and ICI Prof. of Applied Thermodynamics,
and Head of Dept. of Engineering,
Cambridge University.

Sir John Hill, FRS
Former appointments include: Chairman,
UKAEA; Chairman, British Nuclear Fuels Ltd,
and the Radiochemical Centre Ltd; Fellow of
the Institute of Chemical Engineers, the
Institute of Energy and the Institute of
Physics.

Sir Denis Rooke, CBE, FRS, FEng.
Former appointments include: Chairman,
British Gas Corporation. From the coal-tar
works of the South Eastern Gas Board, he was
seconded to the Gas Council's teams on gas
pipelines and natural gas distribution; part-
time member, British National Oil
Corporation; President, Institute of Gas
Engineers; Hon. Fellow, Institute of Energy.

Michael Shanks
Former appointments include: Chairman,
National Consumer Council; Chief Industrial
Advisor, Dept. of Economic Affairs; Director-
General, Employment and Social Affairs,
European Commission; visiting Professor,
Brunel University.

Sir David Steel, DSO, MC, TD
Former appointments include: Managing
Director, Kuwait Oil Co; Chairman, BP;
member, Court of Governors, Bank of
England.

Sir Francis Tombs
Former appointments include: Chairman,
The Electricity Council; President, the
Institution of Electrical Engineers; Vice-
President, the Fellowship of Engineering;
Hon. Member, British Nuclear Energy Society.

The theme of this Memoir has been that of leadership – not only corporate and
industrial, but even more importantly, intellectual – the leadership of ideas.
If this Memoir had been composed in 1981, with a flourishing coal industry
there for all to see, a suitable concluding note might well have been that often
quoted in relation to Christopher Wren and St Paul's, and thus familiar to the
classically-educated Derek Ezra – *si monumentum requiris, circumspice*
[if you seek a memorial, look around you]; However, in an era when one of the
UK's five remaining deep mines, at Daw Mill, in Warwickshire, has at last closed,
a more lasting, conceptual, future-challenging judgment might well be:
Behold the works of Ezra – a prophet with honour.

Postscript by Derek Ezra: 18 August 2013

"When I was first approached by the Fuellers about a Memoir to be prepared about my work, I demurred. I had not written publicly about my experiences and had not intended to do so. However they persisted and said that they wanted it to coincide with the tenth Fuellers' Energy lecture due in September 2014 – an annual lecture by a leading personality in the energy sector which I inaugurated and which has become a well attended fixture in their calendar. I finally agreed to the proposal put to me by the Fuellers which I regard as an honour. The Memoir has been master-minded by Paul Glover, and expertly put together by Roderick Braithwaite, who wrote the admirable "Fueller's Tale", the history of the Livery Company. Many have contributed to the Memoir and their names are listed. I am grateful to them all.

"As the book describes, I have spent the bulk of my life since the war in two organisations, the National Coal Board (35 years) and the House of Lords (30 years to date). I became fully committed to both. My activities in my various roles in the Coal Board are recounted in this book. My commitment to the House of Lords began as soon as I became familiar with its self-regulatory workings and the wide range of its expertise. I was also involved in a number of other activities some of which are referred to in the text.

"I have been asked what was my main objective while I was chairman of the NCB. It was simply this: to change the industry from being largely production oriented to being more market oriented. A start in this had been made by my eminent predecessor Lord Robens. By the very nature of the industry it was dominated by production. The bulk of those employed – the mineworkers, the supervisors and the mining engineers, were concerned with production. And in the early post-war period, when the industry was nationalised, coal was the main fuel and in short supply. But by the mid-fifties the situation began to change and progressively other fuels – oil, gas and nuclear – began to compete for business. That is why I concentrated on the market in the formulation of our policies, in my many speeches and in my talks to mineworkers and management during my visits to pits. That is why I arranged for the main customers of coal to visit pits so that they could see for themselves the efforts being made to produce the quality of coal they wanted and the mineworkers in turn could understand the customer's needs. And that is why we developed close relations with the coal trade and supported them in their endeavours. In all this I was much helped by Malcolm Edwards, Martin Cruttenden and the rest of the marketing team.

"Of course there were other objectives as well – to increase productivity, improve safety, intensify research in mining technology and coal usage and, like any other business, seek to achieve our financial targets. But our overriding objective was to expand and satisfy the market. That way, as I saw it, there would be greater security for those employed in the industry and benefit for the nation.

"In retirement, I continue to keep a close eye on energy developments, and I occasionally ask an energy question in the House of Lords, to which I always get a courteous reply!"

Contributors to the Memoir

Colin Ambler, frmr Staff Officer, Chairman's Office, NCB

Geoff Ashmore, frmr Director, Export Sales, NCB

Andrew Bainbridge, Chairman and founder, MEUC, PM The Fuellers' Company

John Bainbridge, PM The Fuellers' Company, frmr Group Company Secretary, Schroders plc

Jean Claude Banon, frmr CEO, UK Holding Coy. for *Compagnie Générale des Eaux*

Norman Biddle, frmr Director, Symonds/ AHS [Associated Heat Services] Ltd

Michael Bryer Ash, PM The Fuellers' Company, frmr Chairman of National Fireplace Council

Ernest Cantle, frmr DG, NHIC

Rod Castle, frmr Director, AHS Ltd

Thérèse Clarke, wdw of Charles Clarke, Chairman, Stephenson Clarke

Jill Clements, Assistant to Lib.Dem. Peers incl. Lord Ezra, House of Lords

Ralph Cohen, frmr Director, AHS Ltd

Martin Cruttenden, frmr Director of Domestic & Industrial Sales, NCB

Baron Davies of Stamford, Labour Peer, House of Lords

John Demont, frmr DG, NHIC, frmr Commercial Director, British Gas

Malcolm Edwards, frmr Commercial Director, British Coal

Viscount Falkland, hereditary member, cross-bencher, House of Lords

M. Bernard Forterre, frmr Director AHS Ltd

Dr Paul Glover, PM The Fuellers' Company, frmr DG of Staff, NCB

Baroness Harris of Richmond, Lib.Dem.Whip, House of Lords

Brian Harrison, PM The Fuellers' Company, frmr Finance Board Member, NCB

Andrew Horsler, frmr Staff Officer, Chairman's Office, NCB

Peter Jones, frmr Staff Officer, Chairman's Office, NCB

John Josling, frmr MD of Interlink; frmr Chairman, Lords Taverners

Simon Kermode, frmr Staff Officer, Chairman's Office, NCB

Michael Parker, frmr Director of Economics, British Coal

Dr Mark Pegg, frmr Director, Ashridge Business School;
  CE of The Leadership Foundation for Higher Education

Christopher Pennell, frmr Staff Officer, Chairman's Office, NCB

John Price, frmr Chief Mining Engineer, NCB

Baron Prior of Brampton, frmr Secretary of State for Employment

Rex Rose, frmr Archivist, The Fuellers' Company

M. Bernard St André, frmr Director, AHS Ltd

Baron Shutt of Greetland, Lib.Dem. Peer

Baron Steel of Aikwood, frmr Leader, Liberal Party

Baroness Thomas of Winchester, Lib.Dem. Peer

Brig Edward Wilkinson, PM The Fuellers' Company, frmr General Manager, AHS Ltd

Edgar Wille, Consultant, Ashridge Business School

Baroness Williams of Crosby, Lib.Dem. Peer, co-founder SDP

Sources for Notes

Introduction

Evolution …
1. Terence Blacker, *"The I"*, 16 Nov 2012,
   'Where have all the leaders gone?'

   The Tectonic Plates …
2. Andy Beckett, **When the Lights Went Out** p.299;
   Alan Plater, **"Close the Coalhouse Door"**: the revised 1968
   production ran to packed houses across the country during its
   updated revival in 2012. It is widely seen as Alan's finest play,
   bringing the dour, dangerous world of the miner back into
   public consciousness.
3. Derek Ezra, **Coal and Energy**, Ch.1; Ch.10.

   The Formative Years …
4. Elizabeth Sieff, **John Mills' Book of Famous Firsts**, p.61
5. Discussions with Lord Ezra, P.Glover, R.Braithwaite: 15/v/12;
   (subsequent discussions form the basis for relevant parts of
   the editorial commentary)
6. "Solly" Zuckerman, **From Apes to Warlords**,
   pp.300-5, 314-17
7. *Ibid,* Apps. 5, 6
8. BIOS (British Intelligence Objectives Sub-Committee); this
   highly secret and politically sensitive unit evolved from Ian
   Fleming's "James Bond" work in the 1943/4 Italian campaign
   and then in 1944 in France, and most particularly through 'T-
   Force' in Germany, in the spring of 1945. Its purpose was to
   gather German military scientific data and technology – the
   "spoils of war" – initially to hasten the defeat of the Nazis, but
   also to assist the ongoing war with Japan (party to many of
   their ally's technical secrets). It quickly became a race to get
   those secrets, above all the nuclear rocket technology, before
   the illicitly advancing Russians, who were believed to have no
   intention of abiding by the Four-Power "stand-still"
   Agreement of May 5 1945. With the advent of the Labour
   government in July 1945, ex-Trade Union leader now Foreign
   Secretary, Ernie Bevin , was well aware of the communist
   mentality, through their pre-war infiltration in the UK and he
   was prepared in his Foreign Office activities, including BIOS, to
   counter this hitherto unknown opening stage of what turned
   out to become the "Cold War". *See* Sean Longden, **T-Force,
   The Race for Nazi War Secrets, 1945** (London, 2009)
   Chs 9-11, pp.265-304, 322-3

   Coal, Steel … Europe
9. John Gillingham, **Coal, Steel and the Rebirth of Europe**,
   1945-1955, p.321
10. *Ibid,* p.347
11. Norman Moss, **Picking up the Reins**, p.105
12. *Ibid,* p.371-2
13. *Ibid, passim*

    The Politics of Coal …
14. Tom Ellis. **After the Dust has Settled**, p.125
15. Francis Beckett, & David Hencke,
    Marching to the Faultline, *passim*
16. William Ashworth & Mark Pegg, **History of the British Coal
    Industry**, pp.353, 637, 640, 661
17. Andy Beckett, *op cit*, pp.64-5
18. **Whitaker's 1981**, p.424
19. Edward Pearce, **Looking Down on Mrs Thatcher**,
    p.18; Andy Beckett, *op cit*, p.276
20. Anthony Sampson, **Changing Anatomy of Britain**, p.403
21. Beckett/ Hencke, *op cit*, p.17, q. Peter Hennessy,
    Never Again: Britain.
22. Dieter Helm, **Energy, The State**…, pp.21-2, 51, 106
23. Ashworth/ Pegg, *op cit*, p.646 *et seq*
24. Roderick Braithwaite, **The Fueller's Tale:
    The History of the Worshipful Company of Fuellers**
25. Robert Haslam, **An Industrial Cocktail**, pp.116 *et seq*
26. Chauncey Starr, **Current Issues in Energy**, p.iv
27. Helm, *op cit*, p.55 and *passim*
28. Michael Parker, **Thatcherism and the Fall of Coal**, *passim*

    The Man in Context
29. Nigel Lawson, **The View from No.11**, p.155 *et seq*
30. Helm, *op cit*, p.65
31. Lawson, *op cit*, p.155
32. Hugo Young, **One of Us**, p.361, q. Ian MacGregor,
    The Enemies Within, p.111
33. A.N.Wilson, **Our Times**, p.290
34. Beckett/Hencke, *op cit*, p.144
35. *Ibid,* p.32

    Maintaining the balance
36. Sid Kessler & Fred Bayliss, **Contemporary Industrial
    Relations**, pp. 227-9
37. "Jim" Prior, discussions with Paul Glover and editor, Aug 30
    2012, and **A Balance of Power**, *passim*
38. **Oxford Dictionary of Political Quotations**,
    ed. Andrew Jay: 'Harold Macmillan'
39. Ashworth/Pegg, *op cit*, *passim*
40. Tom Hickman, **Called Up**…, *passim*
41. Starr, *op cit*, p.ix
42. *"The Times"*, 21/xii/2012, p.44:
    Report by Dept of Energy & Climate Change, 20/xii/2012
43. Hugh Bicheno, **Razor's Edge**, pp. 85/6

Ch. 1: The Leadership Theme

44. Dr Paul Glover, former Principal, NCB Staff College, Chalfont
    St Giles, and former DG of Staff, NCB:
    Dr Mark Pegg, former NCB Staff Officer, former Director,
    Ashridge Business School, and now Chief Executive,
    The Leadership Foundation for Higher Education.
45. 'Structure is not Organisation', Waterman, Peters & Phillips:
    McKinsey Quarterly, summer 1980
46. Philip Ziegler, **Edward Heath**, p.414 & *passim*
47. **Plan for Coal** (1950)
48. John Garnett, **The Work Challenge**, *passim*
49. Business Schools were not founded in the UK until
    after WW2 – Ashridge 1959, Henley 1945,
    London 1964, (Harvard Business School 1908)
50. John Adair, **Action-Centred Leadership**, *passim*
51. Robert Heller & Lord Weinstock,
    The Making of Managers, *passim*
52. R.H.N.Hardy, **Beeching: Champion of the Railway?**, *passim*
53. R.Goffee, & G.Jones, 'Why should anyone be
    led by YOU?', Harvard
54. Sir Richard Livingstone, Vice-Chancellor, Oxford University,
    to Matriculation students,1944

Ch. 3: The NCB Career …

55. "Jim" Prior, *op cit*, p.275

Ch. 4: How did he do it? …

56. Michael Parker, *op cit*, *passim*

[*End of annotated section of Memoir*]

Abbreviations & Glossary

AA Administrative Assistant (NCB graduate entry: scheme open to all staff)

ADC Amateur Dramatic Club, (Cambridge)

AEA Atomic Energy Agency

AGR Advanced Gas-Cooled Reactor

APEX (clerical workers union)

BACM British Association of Colliery Management

BBSU British Bombing Survey Unit

'Bevin Boys': under draconian Emergency Powers Act (1940), young men conscripted by ballot, or volunteered, to work 'in / around a coal mine', 1940-1948, alternative to serving in armed forces

BIM British Institute of Management (later Chartered Management Institute)

BIOS British Intelligence Objectives Sub-Committee

BOTB British Overseas Trade Board

BSC British Steel Corporation

'Cadbury' Standard Guidance Notes for companies appointing Non-executive Directors (20th C.)

Caprolactam coal-based chemical product

CBI Confederation of British Industries

CE Chief Executive

CEGB Central Electricity Generating Board

C.E.P.C.E.O. Comité d'Etude des Producteurs de Charbon d'Europe Occidentale, ECSC

CGC Compagnie Générale de Chauffe

CiC Commander-in-Chief

CINCC Coal Industry National Consultative Council

CIS Coal Industry Society

contract cover: the amount of coal business secured under period contracts

COSSAC Chief of Staff, Supreme Allied Commander (codename for Gen. Morgan)

CTBA Coal Trade Benevolent Association

DG Director General (NCB)

DTI Department of Trade and Industry

economic rent: the benefit of major investment which by raising efficiency should reduce costs

ECSC European Coal and Steel Community

EEC European Economic Community

ETC European Trade Committee

EU European Union

'face' productivity: measure of O.M.S. at the coal-face

flocculation: process of coal preparation in a washery

GDP Gross Domestic Product

ICI Imperial Chemical Industries Ltd

JNNC Joint National Negotiating Committee

m.t.c.e. million tons/ coal equivalent

MMC Monopolies and Mergers Commission

MD Managing Director

NACODS National Association of Colliery Overmen, Deputies and Shotfirers

NCB National Coal Board

NEC of NUM: National Executive Committee

NED Non-executive Director

NICG Nationalised Industries Chairmen's Group

NIOG Nationalised Industries Overseas Group

NS National Service

NUM National Union of Mineworkers

OCE Office of the Chief Executive [NCB: MacGregor]

OCTU Officer Cadet Training Unit

O.M.S. (coal) output per man shift: Productivity measure including all operations underground and on the surface

OPA offre publique d'achat

OPEC Organisation of Petroleum Exporting Countries

PM (i) Prime Minister; (ii) Past Master (Livery Company)

PPS Principal Private Secretary, the senior 'SO' in the NCB Chairman's Office

PSBR Public Sector Borrowing Requirement

PUS Permanent Under-Secretary

R&D Research & Development

RA Royal Artillery

'road-heading' productivity: (measured by tonnage or lateral progress) per manshift

Section 1 Instructions: Standard escalating definitions of responsibility for safety in the coal industry as defined in the Mines & Quarries Acts

SCM Society of Coal Merchants

SHAEF Supreme HQ, Allied Expeditionary Force

'Social Contract' The 1960s Labour Government's purported philosophy for resolving IR issues

SO Staff Officer (NCB)

SOE Special Operations Executive, WW2

Therm: standard unit of calorific value (heat)

Tons: British unit of measure (coal) [20 cwt=2210 lbs;]

Tonnes: EU/International unit of measure [1,000 kg=2204 lbs]

UDM Union of Democratic Mineworkers

'value in use': value as measured in coal price structures

WAAF Women's Auxiliary Air Force

Select Bibliography

Adair, John, **Action-Centred Leadership** (1979)

Ashworth, William & Pegg, Mark,
The History of the British Coal Industry,
v.5, 1946-1982: **The Nationalised Industry**
(British Coal: 1986, Oxford).

Beckett, Andy,
When the Lights Went Out:
Britain in the Seventies (2009)

Beckett, Francis, & Hencke, David, **Marching to the**
Fault Line: the Miners' Strike and the Battle for
Industrial Britain (2009)

Bicheno, Hugh, Razor's Edge: **The Unofficial History**
of the Falklands War, (2007) pp.85/6

Braithwaite, Roderick, **The Fueller's Tale:**
The History of the Worshipful Company
of Fuellers (2010)

Ellis, Tom, **After the Dust has Settled** (2004)

Ezra, Derek, **Coal and Energy: The Need to Exploit**
the World's Most Abundant Fossil Fuel (1980)

The Energy Debate (ed. 1983) (with David Oates)

Advice from the Top: Business Strategies of
Britain's Corporate Leaders (1989)

(**Below the Surface,**
unpubl. autobiographical sketch) *

"Flixborough NYPRO UK Explosion,
1st June 1974: Accident Summary"
(Health and Safety Executive, 1974)

Garnett, John, **The Work Challenge** (1988)

Gillingham, John,
Coal, Steel & the Rebirth of Europe 1945-1955:
The Germans and French: from Ruhr Conflict to
Economic Community (Cambridge, 1991)

Goffee, R., & Jones, G., **'Why Should Anyone be**
Led by YOU?': (Harvard, 2006)

Gormley, Joe, **Battered Cherub** (1982)

Hardy, R.H.N., **Beeching: Champion of the Railway?**
(1989)

Haslam, Robert, **An Industrial Cocktail** (2003)

Heller, Robert, & Lord Weinstock,
The Making of Managers (1990)

Helm, Dieter, **Energy, The State and the Market:**
British Energy Policy since 1979 (Oxford, 2003)

Hennessy, Peter,
Never Again: Britain 1945-51 (1993)

Hickman, Tom, **Called up, Sent Down:**
The Bevin Boys' War (Stroud, 2010)

Howard, Michael & Louis, Wm Roger, (eds)
The Oxford History of the Twentieth Century
(Oxford, 2002), Ch.16, 'The Remaking of Europe',
pp. 190/1 et seq

Journal of General Management, (Henley), v.3,
no.1, Autumn 1975, pp 3-10

Kessler, Sid & Bayliss, Fred,
Contemporary Industrial Relations (1992)

Lawson, Nigel, **The View from No.11** (1985)

Moss, Norman, **Picking up the Reins; America,**
Britain and the Post-War World (NY: 2009)

NCB Reports & Accounts 1971/2 to 1981/2 (NCB)

Parker, Michael,
Thatcherism and the Fall of Coal (Oxford, 2000)

Pearce, Edward,
Looking Down on Mrs Thatcher (1987)

Plan for Coal (NCB 1974)

Plan 2000 (NCB 1981)

Prior, James, **A Balance of Power** (1986)

Plater, Alan,
"Close the Coalhouse Door" (play: 1968)

Robens, Alfred, **Human Engineering,** (1970)
Ten Year Stint (1972)

Sampson, Anthony, **The Changing Anatomy of**
Britain: The Handbook for the '80s (1983);
The Essential Anatomy of Britain;
Democracy in Crisis (1992)

Sieff, Elizabeth, ed.,
John Mills' Book of Famous Firsts (1984)

Starr, Chauncey, **Current Issues in Energy**
(Oxford, 1979)

Wilson, A.N., **Our Times: 1953-2008** (2008)

Wilson, Harold, **The Governance of Britain** (1976)

Young, Hugo, **One of Us: A Biography of**
Margaret Thatcher (1991)

Ziegler, Philip, **Edward Heath** (2010)

Zuckerman, Solly, **From Apes to Warlords** (1978)

1955: **Report of the Advisory Committee on**
Organisation (The Fleck Report): NCB

1958: **Report of Select Committee on Nationalised**
Industries: (HMSO)

1961: Cmnd 1337: **"The Financial and Economic**
Obligations of the Nationalised Industries": (HMSO)

1967: Cmnd 3437: **"Nationalised Industries – Review**
of Economic and Financial Objectives": (HMSO)

* **"Below the Surface"**: drafts for this earlier
autobiographical essay by Lord Ezra, with
accompanying notes and correspondence, are part of
the Ezra archive at The Fuellers' London Offices. It was
conceived as a joint project in 1982 with John Josling,
and Peter Young, a corporate historian.
It never reached finality, due to various pressures.
Quotations from its text have been incorporated in this
Memoir, which covers all the historical ground that it
set out to describe. Arguably, this present format is
more appropriate for the subject in its widest political
sense, rather than the inevitable 'chairman's viewpoint'
which it embodied. However, future management
students of the detail of Lord Ezra's work might still
benefit from a study of its pages, and first-hand
comments and recollections. It deserves mention in
this Bibliography.

Index

112